CHILTON'S REPAIR & TUNE-UP GUIDE
BMW
1970 to 1979

1600 ● 2002 ● 2002Tii ● 3.OS ● 3.OSi ● Bavaria ● 320i ● 528i
530i ● 630i ● 630CSi ● 633i ● 633CSi ● 733i

Managing Editor KERRY A. FREEMAN, S.A.E.
Senior Editor RICHARD J. RIVELE
Editor JOHN M. BAXTER

President WILLIAM A. BARBOUR
Executive Vice President RICHARD H. GROVES
Vice President and General Manager JOHN P. KUSHNERICK

CHILTON BOOK COMPANY
Radnor, Pennsylvania
19089

1234567890   9876543210

Chilton's Repair & Tune-Up Guide: BMW 1970–79
ISBN 0-8019-6844-5 pbk.

Library of Congress Catalog Card No. 78-20256

Chilton Book Company expresses its appreciation to BMW of North America, Inc.; Bayerische Motoren Werke AG Munich, the Arnolt Corporation; AB Volvo Göteborg; and the Ford Motor Company for the technical information and illustrations contained within this manual. Also, the editor wishes to give a special thanks to Otto K. Mayer of Auto House Continental BMW Inc., Bill Cooney of West German Motor Imports, Larry Baranzano of Speedcraft Enterprises Inc., Armin Rhauda of Rhauda Racing, Conshohoken, Pa., Alfonso and Salvatore Rosati of Foreign Car Service of Willow Grove, Pa., Lukas Foreign Car Service of Wayne, Pa., and the BMW Car Club of America Inc., for their extra efforts in contributing to the technical accuracy and clarity of the information herein.

Although the information in this guide is based on industry sources and is as complete as possible at the time of publication, the possibility exists that the manufacturer made later changes which could not be included here. While striving for total accuracy, Chilton Book Company cannot assume responsibility for any errors, changes, or omissions that may occur in the compilation of this data.

Part numbers in this book are not recommendations by Chilton for any product by brand name. They are references that can be used with interchange manuals and aftermarket supplier catalogs to locate each brand supplier's discrete part number.

SAFETY NOTICE

Proper service and repair procedures are vital to the safe, reliable operation of all motor vehicles, as well as the personal safety of those performing repairs. This book outlines procedures for servicing and repairing vehicles using safe, effective methods. The procedures contain many NOTES, CAUTIONS and WARNINGS which should be followed along with standard safety procedures to eliminate the possibility of personal injury or improper service which could damage the vehicle or compromise its safety.

It is important to note that repair procedures and techniques, tools and parts for servicing motor vehicles, as well as the skill and experience of the individual performing the work vary widely. It is not possible to anticipate all of the conceivable ways or conditions under which vehicles may be serviced, or to provide cautions as to all of the possible hazards that may result. Standard and accepted safety precautions and equipment should be used when handling toxic or flammable fluids, and safety goggles or other protection should be used during cutting, grinding, chiseling, prying, or any other process that can cause material removal or projectiles.

Some procedures require the use of tools specially designed for a specific purpose. Before substituting another tool or procedure, you must be completely satisfied that neither your personal safety, nor the performance of the vehicle will be endangered.

Contents

Quick Reference Specifications

For quick and easy reference, complete this page with the most commonly used specifications for your vehicle. The specifications can be found in Chapters 1 through 3 or on the tune-up decal under the hood of the vehicle.

TUNE-UP

Firing Order _____

Spark Plugs:

    Type _____

    Gap (in.) _____

Point Gap (in.) _____

Dwell Angle (°) _____

Ignition Timing (°) _____

    Vacuum (Connected/Disconnected) _____

Valve Clearance (in.)

    Intake _____   **Exhaust** _____

CAPACITIES

Engine Oil (qts)

    With Filter Change _____

    Without Filter Change _____

Cooling System (qts) _____

Manual Transmission (pts) _____

    Type _____

Automatic Transmission (pts) _____

    Type _____

Differential (pts) _____

    Type _____

COMMONLY FORGOTTEN PART NUMBERS

Use these spaces to record the part numbers of frequently replaced parts.

PCV VALVE	**OIL FILTER**	**AIR FILTER**
Manufacturer _____	Manufacturer _____	Manufacturer _____
Part No. _____	Part No. _____	Part No. _____

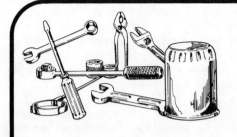

General Information and Maintenance

HOW TO USE THIS BOOK

Chilton's Repair & Tune-Up Guide for the BMW is intended to teach you more about the inner workings of your automobile and save you money on its upkeep. The first two chapters will be used the most, since they contain maintenance and tune-up information and procedures. The following chapters concern themselves with the more complex systems of your car. Operating systems from engine through brakes are covered to the extent that we feel the average do-it-yourselfer should get involved. This book will not explain such things as rebuilding the differential for the simple reason that the expertise required and the investment in special tools make this task uneconomical. We will tell you how to change your own brake pads and shoes, replace points and plugs, and many more jobs that will save you money, give you personal satisfaction, and help you avoid problems.

A secondary purpose of this book is as a reference for owners who want to understand their car and/or their mechanics better. In this case, no tools at all are required.

Before removing any bolts, read through the entire procedure. This will give you the overall view of what tools and supplies will be required. There is nothing more frustrating than having to walk to the bus stop on Monday morning because you were short one bolt on Sunday afternoon. So read ahead and plan ahead.

The sections begin with a brief discussion of the system and what it involves, followed by adjustments, maintenance, removal and installation procedures, and repair or overhaul procedures. When repair is not considered feasible, we tell you how to remove the part and then how to install the new or rebuilt replacement. In this way, you at least save the labor costs. Backyard repair of such components as the alternator is just not practical.

Two basic mechanic's rules should be mentioned here. One, whenever the left side of the car or engine is referred to, it is meant to specify the driver's side of the car. Conversely, the right side of the car means the passenger's side. Secondly, most screws and bolts are removed by turning counterclockwise, and tightened by turning clockwise. Safety is always the most important rule. Constantly be aware of the dangers involved in working on an automobile and take the proper precautions. Use jackstands when working under a raised vehicle. Don't smoke or allow an exposed flame to come near the battery or any part of the fuel system. Always use the proper tool and use it correctly;

bruised knuckles and skinned fingers aren't a mechanic's standard equipment. Always take your time and have patience; once you have some experience, working on your car will become an enjoyable hobby.

BMW model designations are various suffixes which add to the basic number of the car further information. Where a number of different models employ the same repair procedure, the heading for the procedure may generalize. For example, "2002" may refer to the 2002, 2002A, 2002Ti and 2002Tii.

TOOLS AND EQUIPMENT

It would be impossible to catalog each and every tool that you may need to perform all the operations included in this book. It would also not be wise for the amateur to rush out and buy an expensive set of tools on the theory that he may need one of them at some time. The best approach is to proceed slowly, gathering together a good quality set of those tools that are used most frequently. Don't be misled by the low cost of bargain tools. It is far better to spend a little more for quality, name brand tools. Forged wrenches, 10 or 12 point sockets and fine-tooth ratchets are by far preferable to their less expensive counterparts. As any good mechanic can tell you, there are few worse experiences than trying to work on a car or truck with bad tools. Your monetary savings will be far outweighed by frustration and mangled knuckles.

Begin accumulating those tools that are used most frequently; those associated with routine maintenance and tune-up. In addition to the normal assortment of screwdrivers and pliers, you should have the following tools for routine maintenance jobs:

1. Metric wrenches, sockets and combination open end/box end wrenches.
2. Jackstands—for support;
3. Oil filter wrench
4. Oil filler spout or funnel
5. Grease gun—for chassis lubrication
6. Hydrometer—for checking the battery
7. A low flat pan for draining oil
8. Lots of rags for wiping up the inevitable mess.

In addition to the above items, there are several others that are not absolutely necessary, but are handy to have around. These include oil drying compound, a transmission funnel, and the usual supply of lubricants, antifreeze and fluids, although these can be purchased as needed. This is a basic list for routine maintenance, but only your personal needs can accurately determine your list of tools.

The second list of tools is for tune-ups. While the tools involved here are slightly more sophisticated, they need not be outrageously expensive. There are several inexpensive tach/dwell meters on the market that are every bit as good for the average mechanic as a $100.00 professional model. Just be sure that it goes to at least 1200–1500 rpm on the tach scale, and that it works on 4, 6, and 8 cylinder engines. A basic list of tune-up equipment could include:

1. Tach/dwell meter
2. Spark plug wrench
3. Timing light (preferably a DC light that works from the car's battery).
4. A set of flat feeler gauges
5. A set of round wire spark plug gauges.

In addition to these basic tools, there are several other tools and gauges you may find useful. These include:

1. A compression gauge. The screw-in type is slower to use, but eliminates the possibility of a faulty reading due to escaping pressure.
2. A manifold vacuum gauge.
3. A test light.
4. An induction meter. This is used for determining whether or not there is current in a wire. These are handy for use if a wire is broken somewhere in a wiring harness. As a final note, you will probably find a torque wrench necessary for all but the most basic work. The beam type models are perfectly adequate, although the newer click type are more precise.

Special Tools

Normally, the use of special factory tools is avoided for repair procedures, since these are not readily available for the do-it-yourself mechanic. When it is possible to perform the job with more commonly available tools, it will be pointed out, but occasionally, a special tool was designed to perform a specific function and should be used. Before substituting another tool, you should be convinced that neither your safety nor the performance of the vehicle will be compromised.

Some special tools are available commercially from major tool manufacturers. Others can be purchased from your dealer.

The special tools required for work on your BMW are confined primarily to rebuilding the cylinder head. A compression frame permits all the valves to be opened fully at once for easy camshaft removal. There are also guide pins used for removal of the rocker shaft assembly, and various punches used in removing and installing valve guides. These tools will be described and pictured in the procedures to which they apply.

No special tools are required for routine maintenance or minor work except the valve adjusting rod, which is included in the BMW tool kit supplied with the car.

SERVICING YOUR VEHICLE SAFELY

It is virtually impossible to anticipate all of the hazards involved with automotive maintenance and service but care and common sense will prevent most accidents.

The rules of safety for mechanics range from "don't smoke around gasoline," to "use the proper tool for the job." The trick to avoiding injuries is to develop safe work habits and take every possible precaution.

Do's

• Do keep a fire extinguisher and first aid kit within easy reach.

• Do wear safety glasses or goggles when cutting, drilling, grinding or prying. If you wear glasses for the sake of vision, then they should be made of hardened glass that can serve also as safety glasses, or wear safety goggles over your regular glasses.

• Do shield your eyes whenever you work around the battery. Batteries contain sulphuric acid; in case of contact with the eyes or skin, flush the area with water or a mixture of water and baking soda and get medical attention immediately.

• Do use safety stands for any undercar service. Jacks are for raising vehicles; safety stands are for making sure the vehicle stays raised until you want it to come down. Whenever the vehicle is raised, block the wheels remaining on the ground and set the parking brake.

• Do use adequate ventilation when working with any chemicals. Asbestos dust resulting from brake lining wear can cause cancer.

• Do disconnect the negative battery cable when working on the electrical system. The primary ignition system can contain up to 40,000 volts.

• Do follow manufacturer's directions whenever working with potentially hazardous materials. Both brake fluid and antifreeze are poisonous if taken internally.

• Do properly maintain your tools. Loose hammerheads, mushroomed punches and chisels, frayed or poorly grounded electrical cords, excessively worn screwdrivers, spread wrenches (open end), cracked sockets, slipping ratchets, or faulty droplight sockets can cause accidents.

• Do use the proper size and type of tool for the job being done.

• Do when possible, pull on a wrench handle rather than push on it, and adjust your stance to prevent a fall.

• Do be sure that adjustable wrenches are tightly adjusted on the nut or bolt and pulled so that the face is on the side of the fixed jaw.

• Do select a wrench or socket that fits the nut or bolt. The wrench or socket should sit straight, not cocked.

• Do strike squarely with a hammer— avoid glancing blows.

• Do set the parking brake and block the drive wheels if the work requires that the engine be running.

Don't's

• DON'T run an engine in a garage or anywhere else without proper ventilation— EVER! Carbon monoxide is poisonous; it is absorbed by the body 400 times faster than oxygen; it takes a long time to leave the human body and you can build up a deadly supply of it in your system by simply breathing in a little every day. You may not realize you are slowly poisioning yourself. Always use power vents, windows, fans or open the garage doors.

• Don't work around moving parts while wearing a necktie or other loose clothing. Short sleeves are much safer than long, loose sleeves. Hard-toed shoes with neoprene soles protect your toes and give a better grip on slippery surfaces. Jewelry such as watches, fancy belt buckles, beads or body adornment of any kind is not safe working around a car. Long hair should be hidden under a hat or cap.

• Don't use pockets for toolboxes. A fall or bump can drive a screwdriver deep into your body. Even a wiping cloth hanging from the back pocket can wrap around a spinning shaft or fan.

• Don't smoke when working around gasoline, cleaning solvent or other flammable material.

• Don't smoke when working around the battery. When the battery is being charged, it gives off explosive hydrogen gas.

• Don't use gasoline to wash your hands; there are excellent soaps available. Gasoline may contain lead, and lead can enter the body through a cut, accumulating in the body until you are very ill. Gasoline also removes all the natural oils from the skin so that bone dry hands will suck up oil and grease.

• Don't service the air conditioning system unless you are equipped with the necessary tools and training. The refrigerant, R-12, is extremely cold and when exposed to the air, will instantly freeze any surface it comes in contact with, including your eyes. Although the refrigerant is normally non-toxic, R-12 becomes a deadly poisonous gas in the presence of an open flame. One good whiff of the vapors from burning refrigerant can be fatal.

HISTORY

BMW (Bavarian Motor Works) began its life in 1916 as a builder of aircraft engines (called the "Bavarian Aircraft Works"), although the name was changed to the present one only a year later. The company logo which still appears several places on each car represents a propeller spinning against a blue sky. Thus, the high performance associated with BMW engines has its origin in the necessity to minimize weight in an aircraft. BMW's first car was a vehicle produced by the Dixi automobile works which BMW purchased in 1928.

In 1933, BMW produced its first in-house design, the BMW 303. This model series began two BMW traditions which are well known—the six cylinder engine and twin kidney grills. By the end of the 30s, BMW was making the 328, which featured an engine using a light alloy head, with V-type overhead valves and hemi-head combustion chambers.

BMW's history as a major manufacturer of performance cars was eclipsed by the destruction of the Munich plant in World War II. The 50s were dominated by the extremes—the too-large 501, and the Isetta with a BMW motorcycle engine propelling it. Neither brought much profit to the company.

In 1959 Dr. Herbert Quant invested heavily in the company to save it from a sale of assets. In 1961, the 1500 was introduced, in the

Model Identification

1970–71 1600-2

1969–71 2002 Series

1972 2002Tii

1972 2002 Series

1973 and later 2002 Series

2800

528i

2002

630CSi, 633CSi

320i

528i

3.0

530i

tradition of the later models. This "new wave" of four cylinder sports-sedans has become recognized for its high output, low displacement and fuel efficient engine and light and compact chassis-body, which offers excellent road holding and braking. With the introduction of the 530i in 1975, BMW began to be associated with luxury-performance cars as well as sports-sedans.

With sales forced continually upward by increasing fuel prices and spot shortages, BMW continues to grow rapidly; thus, sales for 1979 are projected to be between 15% and 20% over those of 1978.

Wheel arch location of the serial number—typical

SERIAL NUMBER IDENTIFICATION

Vehicle

On 1970–74 models, this number is stamped on a plate attached to the upper steering column and on a Certification Label located on the edge of the driver's door. On most 1975 and later models, the number is located both at the end of the dashboard on the driver's

Firewall location of the serial number—3.0 and 3.0Si

Engine compartment location of the serial number

Removing the filter element—1600-2, 2002

side and on the support plate of the right hand wheel arch, accessible by opening the hood. On 3.0 models, the engine compartment number is located, instead, on the firewall.

Engine

The vehicle number is also stamped on the engine on a plate attached to the rear left-hand side of the crankcase, above the starter.

Removing the air filter element—2002Tii

Use of Serial Numbers

The serial number should be quoted whenever requesting parts for any part of the car. BMW makes changes many times during a model year; without the serial number for the car, there would be no way to ensure getting a part which would be completely compatible with the car.

ROUTINE MAINTENANCE

Air Cleaner

On carbureted engines, simply unsnap the over-center catches, remove the top from the air cleaner, and remove the filter elements. On the 2002Tii, after unsnapping the over-center catches, lower the base of the unit away from it, and then pull the element off.

On the 320i, first loosen the clamp connecting the vacuum limiting valve to the air intake duct. Then, remove the two bolts fastening this valve and its companion valve, the cold start air valve, to the bracket near the injection pump. Unsnap the overcenter catches and, while holding the two valves out of the way, pull the filter element vertically upward out of the air cleaner.

On the 320i, first loosen the clamp attaching the hose from the vacuum limiting valve to the air intake duct

Remove the two bolts fastening this valve and its companion to the bracket near the injection pump—320i

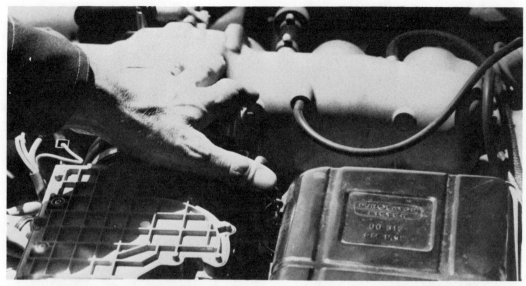

Unsnapping overcenter catches—typical six cylinder, fuel injected air cleaner

On all fuel injected six cylinder models, unsnap the over-center catches, split the two halves of the housing, pull the element upward to separate it from the lower half, and pull the filter out on the engine side of the unit. When replacing the square type element used on later models, make sure to position the element so the arrow indicating airflow points toward the engine (or into the manifold).

On some 1970–74 models, cleaning in the middle of the element's useful life is recommended. To do this, rap it lightly against a hard surface to loosen heavier dirt particles, and then blow compressed air through the element from inside to outside.

Fuel Filters

1600-2, 2002, 2002Tii, 2800

On all carbureted models, the fine mesh filter screen in the fuel pump is removed at 8,000 mile intervals for cleaning. On 1600-2 models, this is accomplished by removing the 8mm cover plate bolt. On 2002, 2002A and 2800 models, this is accomplished by removing the filter sieve retaining bolt (13 mm). Discard the old sealing ring and wash out the filter sieve in clean gasoline or kerosene. On 1600-2 models, clean the cover plate also. The replace the filter sieve using a new sealing ring, and tighten the retaining bolt. At this time, check that the six cheese headed screws on the fuel pump are evenly tightened with a screwdriver.

Removing the fuel pump cover plate—1600-2

On all fuel-injected models, a total of four fuel filters must be cleaned or replaced at 40,000 mile intervals. They consist of a fine mesh filter in the fuel tank pick-up screen, a

Removing fuel pump filter sieve retaining bolt— 2002

Fuel tank pick-up screen—2002Tii

Main fuel filter—2002Tii

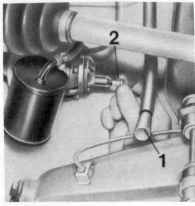

Removing the mesh filter for the electric fuel pump—2002Tii

Removing the mesh filter for the injection pump—2002Tii

fine mesh filter in the electric fuel pump, an inline main fuel filter in the engine compartment and another fine mesh filter in the mechanical fuel injection pump.

To clean the fuel tank pick-up screen, the following procedure is used:

1. Remove the right-hand trunk floor panel which covers the fuel tank.

2. Loosen the hose clamps and disconnect the fuel lines from the pick-up unit.

3. Using two screwdrivers, turn the pick-up unit counterclockwise in its bayonet mount until it releases. Lift out the pick-up unit.

4. Clean the fine mesh pick-up screen.

5. Reverse the above procedure to install, taking care to install a new sealing ring on the pick-up unit.

To clean the fine mesh filter in the electric fuel pump, the following procedure is used:

1. Locate the fuel pump underneath the car near the differential housing.

2. Loosen the hose clamp on the fuel feed

pipe. Disconnect and plug the end of the feed pipe with a golf tee or other suitable object.

3. Pull out the thimble-sized, bag-type fine mesh filter from the pump and clean it in clean gasoline or kerosene.

4. Reverse the above procedure to install.

To replace the inline main fuel filter, the following procedure is used:

1. Loosen both hose clamps and the filter retaining clamp. Mark the fuel lines for reassembly.

2. Disconnect and plug both fuel lines, remove and discard the old filter.

3. Install a new filter, taking care to note the prescribed direction of flow shown on the filter label.

To clean the fine mesh filter in the fuel injection pump, the following procedure is used:

1. Remove the 17 mm hollow screw in the fuel inlet pipe.

2. Clean the thimble-sized fine mesh filter

located in the hollow screw using clean gasoline or kerosene.

3. Reverse the above procedure to install.

320i, 528i, 3.0si 530i, 630i, 633i, 633CSi, 733i

Mesh Strainer in Fuel Tank

On the 320i, remove the rear seat to gain access to this unit. On the 528i and 733i, remove the left luggage compartment floor panel. On the 3.0 Si, 530, 630 and 633 models, remove the right side luggage compartment floor panel. On all models, first disconnect the electrical connector. Then, on 320i and 3.0Si models, remove bolts or nuts, detach hoses, and pull the pump/sensor unit out of the tank. On the remaining models, unplug hoses, and turn the unit counter clockwise using screwdrivers as levers.

The strainer should then be cleaned in fresh gasoline. Be careful about the fire hazard related to using gasoline as a solvent. Install the unit in reverse order, using a new gasket and making sure to plug in hoses securely and check for leaks before replacing the luggage compartment cover or seat. See the Maintenance Intervals Chart below for the service interval.

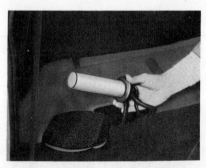

Removing the mesh strainer in the fuel tank—320i

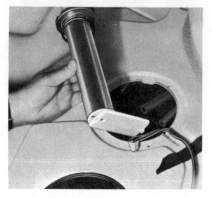

Removing the mesh strainer in the fuel tank—530i

Full Flow Filter

These filters are located as follows:

320i—near the electric fuel pump on the left side of the rear axle.

528i, 530i, 630SCi, 633CSi—above the rear suspension, left/rear

3.0Si—left wheel well, under the fusebox

733i—above and slightly to the left of the rear axle

To replace this unit, loosen the hose clamps, remove the unit, and then replace it

Removing the full flow fuel filter—530i

Removing the full flow filter—3.0Si

with a new one, making sure the arrow indicating direction of flow is facing the same direction as with the old unit (away from the tank). See the Maintenance Intervals Chart below for frequency of service.

Fuel Pump Strainer (3.0Si only)

Loosen the intake clamp hose (1) on the fuel pump, which is located above the right/rear halfshaft. Remove the fine mesh, basket type filter located inside the hose connection, and clean it in fresh fuel. This should be performed when the full flow filter is replaced.

PCV Valve and Fuel Canister Service

The BMW employs crankcase ventilation and fuel canister systems which do not require fresh air for their operation. This eliminates the need for periodic replacement of the

PCV valves and canister filters used on other types of systems.

Battery

CAUTION: *The gases formed inside the battery cells are highly explosive. Never check the level of electrolyte with a match or lighter.*

Batteries should be checked periodically for adequate electrolyte level, proper output and good connections. Add nothing but distilled water, and fill when necessary to about $3/16''$ above the plates.

Inspect the battery case for cracks and weakness. A leaky battery should be replaced. Check the specific gravity of the battery electrolyte with a hydrometer. Readings from a fully charged battery will depend on the make but will be in the range of 1.260 to 1.310 times as heavy as pure water at 80° F.

NOTE: *All cells should produce nearly equal readings.*

If one or two cell readings are sharply lower, the cells are defective, and if they continue to be low after charging, the battery must be replaced.

As a battery releases its charge, sulphate ions in the electrolyte become attached to the plates—reducing the density of the fluid. The specific gravity of the electrolyte varies not only with the percentage of acid in the liquid, but also with the temperature. As temperature increases, the electrolyte expands so that specific gravity is reduced. As temperature drops, the elctrolyte contracts and specific gravity increases. To correct readings for temperature variation, add .004 to the hydrometer reading for every 10° F that the electrolyte is above 80° F, and subtract .004 for every 10° F that the electrolyte is below 80° F. The drawing shows the total correction to make for any temperature above or below 80° F.

The state of charge of the battery can be determined roughly from the following specific gravity readings:

Hydrometer Readings	Condition
1.260–1.310	Fully charged
1.230–1.250	¾ charged
1.200–1.220	½ charged
1.170–1.190	¼ charged
1.140–1.160	Almost discharged
1.110–1.130	Fully discharged

Checking the battery electrolyte level

Make a light-load voltage test to detect weak cells. First draw off the transient surface charge by operating the starter for three seconds and then turning on the low beam lights. After one minute, test each cell (with lights still on) with the voltmeter. A fully charged battery will have no cell voltage below 1.95 volts and no cell will vary more than .05 volts from the others. A greater variation at full charge indicates a defective cell.

Another battery check requires connecting a charger for three minutes under 40 amperes for a 12-volt battery. Read the battery voltage with the charger still operating. Voltage over 15.5 volts indicates a defective battery. If battery voltage is under this limit and individual cell readings are within 0.1 volt, the battery is usable.

Charging a weak battery is best done by a slow-charge method. If quick charging is attempted, check the cell voltages and the color of the electrolyte a few minutes after charge is started. If cell voltages are not uniform or if electrolyte is discolored with brown sediment, quick charging should be stopped in favor of a slow charge. In either case, do not let electrolyte temperature exceed 120° F.

If high electrical circuit voltage is suspected, the voltage regulator might be cutting in abnormally due to corroded or loose battery connections. The symptoms are hard starting, full ammeter charge and lights flaring brightly. After cleaning, coat battery terminals with petroleum jelly (vaseline) to prevent recurrence of problem.

Overcharging is a common cause of battery failure. A symptom of overcharging is a frequent need for addition of water to the battery. The generating system should be corrected immediately to prevent internal battery damage.

Air Intake Preheat Flap

Every 8,000 miles on 1970–74 models check the function of the air intake flap as follows:

1. With the engine cold, remove the fresh air intake line at the air cleaner. The outside temperature should be cool, preferably 70 degrees F. or below. Start the engine and immediately observe the flap. It should close tightly. Shut the engine off and verify that the valve opens all the way.

Belts

INSPECTION

Belts should be inspected for both tension and condition at intervals of 12,500 miles and shortly after replacement. Belt tension is checked by applying pressure (about 10–15 lbs) with your thumb midway between two pulleys. The belt should deflect (stretch) about ½–¾ in. for each 10 in. of distance between pulley centers. The belt should be spring tight—not sagging or having "play," but not so tight that it requires tremendous effort to get a slight deflection. Excessive belt tension may wear the bearings of the accessory being driven, or may stretch and crack the belt, while insufficient tension will cause slippage and glazing.

Inspect the belt for separation between the outer surface and the Vee, and for radial cracks, which usually begin at the inner surface. Check also for glazing—a perfectly smooth (almost melted) driving surface. The

Checking belt tension

driving surfaces should be rough—slightly cross-hatched because they are fabric covered. If the surface is perfectly smooth, the belt has slipped, and this has caused overheating. A glazed belt cannot offer a sufficient amount of friction to carry the load without excessive tension. Belts which show cracks or glazing should be replaced.

REPLACEMENT

First, a few rules:

1. Replace belts with the proper part. A belt of the wrong length will have to be pried on if too short, a procedure that will seriously damage the belt even before it turns around once, or which may prevent sufficient tightening to compensate for wear long before the belt has really worn out. If you must use a belt that is just a little too short, you might be able to avoid stretching it during installation by completely dismounting the driven accessory, working the belt around the pulleys, and then remounting the accessory.

2. Replace multiple belts in sets only, as worn belts stretch and mixing stretched belts with new ones will prevent even division of the load.

3. Do not attempt to change belt tension or rotate an accessory for belt replacement without loosening *both* the adjustment bolt (the bolt which runs in a slotted bracket) *and* the pivot bolt. Do not pry belts on to avoid rotating the driven accessory.

4. Do not pry the driven accessory with a heavy metal bar if you can get sufficient belt tension by hand. This applies especially to aluminum castings or air/fluid pumps, where distortion of the housing can be a critical problem. If you must pry, pry on a substantial steel bracket *only* or, failing that, on the part of the casting the adjusting bolt screws into. Some accessory mounting brackets are designed with a slot or square hole into which you can insert a socket drive for tensioning purposes.

To replace a belt, first locate the pivot bolt. This holds the unit to the engine block or to a short bracket which has only a hole—no slot. If the pivot bolt does not use a nut welded onto the back of the accessory or a bracket, you will have to apply wrenches at both ends—to both the bolt *and* nut to loosen this bolt. Loosen the bolt slightly—don't release all tension, as you will want the accessory to stay securely mounted to get an accurate tension adjustment later.

Then, loosen the adjusting bolt. This

On the 530i, to adjust the tension of the fan belt ("1"), slide the alternator back and forth after loosening the arrowed bolts; to adjust the air pump belt ("2"), loosen the two arrowed air pump bolts and slide that back and forth

Disconnecting the lower radiator hose

passes through a long slot in a bracket and usually runs right into threads cut into the main body of the accessory. Now, all belt tension will be gone.

Next, move the accessory all the way toward the engine, and pull off the belt. Position the new belt around all the pulleys. Make sure it tracks in all the pulley grooves and, if there are multiple pulleys or pulleys and belts involved, make sure the belt runs in pulleys which are directly in line with one another.

Be ready to tighten the adjusting bolt, pull or pry the accessory away from the engine until the tension is correct (see above), and then tighten the adjusting bolt, finally, tighten the pivot bolt.

NOTE: *When installing a new belt (one run less than 10 minutes) put a little extra tension on it to allow for stretch and seating in the pulley Vees during break-in. About 30–40 percent extra tension will do. Instead of deflecting as much as ¾ in., the belt should deflect a little less than ½ in. for each 10 inches of distance between the pulley centers. Recheck tension of new belts several days after installation in case of stretch.*

Hoses

SPOTTING WORN HOSES

Worn hoses will feel brittle, the lower hose may be permanently narrowed at one point from suction, or may appear frayed or cracked. New hoses will be springy and pliable yet firm, the rubber surface will be solid

and smooth, and there will be no evidence of string reinforcements showing through.

HOSE REPLACEMENT

1. Put a bucket of about 2 gallons capacity under the radiator drain (some models are so equipped) or the radiator end of the lower hose (if there's no drain plug). Remove the drain plug or loosen the hose clamp and pull the bottom of the hose off the radiator connection. Remove the radiator cap.

2. If a heater hose is being replaced, turn the rotary heater control to "Warm", and allow any water contained in the heater core and hoses to drain.

3. Loosen the clamps at both ends of the hoses. Work the hose ends off the radiator or heater core and engine block connections.

4. Install the new hose in reverse order. If the hose has certain bends molded into it, make sure to position the hose so that it does not become crimped at these points. Also, install *new* hose clamps onto the hose from both ends *before* sliding hose ends onto connections. Make sure hoses slide all the way onto the connectors. Make sure you then slide the clamps over the lips on the connectors but not all the way at the ends of the hoses.

5. Tighten the clamps securely, and then refill the cooling system as described below.

Cooling System

DRAIN AND REFILL

1. Remove the radiator cap.
CAUTION: *Make sure the system is well below operating temperature before removing the cap!*

2. Turn the heater control to "Warm."

3. Loosen the radiator end clamp on the

Loosen the bleeder screw on top of the thermostat housing—six cylinder engines

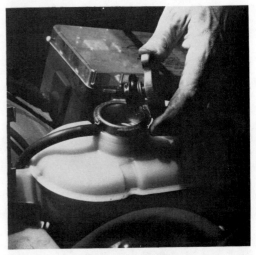

Radiator cap located on top of the expansion tank—six cylinder engines

lower radiator hose, and pull the hose off the radiator connector.

4. Remove the 19 mm plug from the right/rear of the engine block.

5. To refill the system, first replace the drain plug and reconnect the radiator hose and clamp it.

6. On six cylinder engines, loosen the bleeder screw on the thermostat housing. On all engines, make sure the heater control is still in the "Warm" position.

7. Fill the system with at least a 35% mix of antifreeze and water and then replace the filler cap, turning it to the second stop. Start the engine and run it at 2,500 rpm until normal operating temperature is reached, and then stop it. Watch for water to come out at the bleed point and close the bleeder screw as soon as this happens.

8. Start the engine after a wait of at least 1 minute and then run it a 4,000 rpm for 30 seconds. Release the throttle and make sure heat comes from the heater at idle speed. Then, shut off the engine again.

Radiator cap located on top of the radiator header tank—four cylinder engines

9. If necessary, allow the engine to cool until the temperature gauge needle is in the center of the white zone; then, refill the radiator of four cylinder engines to a point within ¾ in. of the cap, or refill the overflow tank of six cylinder engines to a point within 18 in. of the filler cap.

Air Conditioner

SAFETY WARNINGS

The air conditioner is filled with refrigerant R-12, which produces very high pressure even when the system is not operating. Not only can a component broken by mishandling crack or break explosively, but the escaping refrigerant will immediately drop to -27 degrees F., causing severe frostbite to any part of the body exposed nearby. The problem is worsened by the fact that refrigerant systems employ thin sections of light alloys to transfer heat efficiently—thus, components are readily damaged by inexperienced mechanics.

Thus, we recommend that you make no attempt whatever to repair any component on the air conditioning system. If a refrigerant component must be moved to gain access to another part, we recommend you leave at least the part of the job involving the refrigerant component to someone with the specialized training, tools, and experience to handle the job safely.

CHECKING THE SYSTEM

Once a year, before hot weather sets in, it is advisable to check the refrigerant charge in

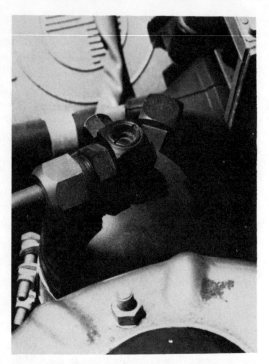

Air conditioner sight glass location—528i

charged, bubbles will appear in the sight glass a few seconds after the unit is turned off and disappear when it is turned on although they may linger awhile in extremely hot weather. If no bubbles appear when the unit is in the "OFF" position, then the system should be serviced by an authorized dealer and checked for leaks. Do *not* operate the unit if you suspect that the refrigerant has leaked out.

Windshield Wipers
WIPER BLADE REPLACEMENT

BMW wiper blade units are replaced by pulling outward on a small tang, located on the windshield side of the arm where a pin on the blade assembly engages with it. Pull out on the arm until it points straight outward, disengage the tang, and then pull the blade assembly pin out of the arm. To replace the unit, simply push the arm pin in until the tang snaps into the groove in the pin to lock it.

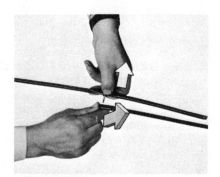

Wiper blade removal

WIPER ARM REPLACEMENT

Lift upward on the cover at the inner end of the arm. Remove the nut located under the cover with a wrench, and pull the arm off the driveshaft. These arms are best removed with the system in parked position—that is, with the wipers brought to rest with the wiper switch off and ignition turned on. Install the arm in reverse order, positioning it so that the blade is parallel to the chrome moulding below the windshield before installing the nut.

Fluid Level Checks
ENGINE OIL

The oil level of the engine should be checked at regular intervals (i.e. at fuel stops). The

the air conditioner system. This may be accomplished by looking at the sight glass located in the engine compartment on the right fender well. First, wipe the sight glass clean with a cloth wrapped around the eraser end of a pencil. Connect a tachometer to the engine with the positive line connected to the distributor side of the ignition coil and the negative line connected to a good ground, such as the steering box. Have a friend operate the air conditioner controls while you look at the sight glass. Have your friend set the dash panel control to maximum cooling. Start the engine and idle at 1,500 rpm. While looking at the sight glass, signal your friend to turn the blower switch to the High position. If a few bubbles appear immediately after the blower is turned on and then disappear, the system is sufficiently charged with refrigerant. If, on the other hand, a large amount of bubbles, foam or froth continue after the blower has operated for a few seconds, then the system is in need of additional refrigerant. If no bubbles appear at all, then there is either sufficient refrigerant in the system, or it is bone dry. The way to clear this question up is to have your friend turn the unit off and on (engine running at 1,500 rpm) about every 10 seconds or so while you look at the sight glass. This will cycle the magnetic clutch. If the system is properly

Wiper arm removal

check should be made with the engine warm and switched off for a period of about one minute to allow the oil time to drain back down to the crankcase. The car must be standing on level ground to obtain an accurate reading. The dipstick is located on the driver's side of the engine, next to the air cleaner. Pull out the dipstick, wipe it clean

Dipstick removal

and reinsert it. The oil level must be maintained between the upper and lower marks (representing 3.2 pints) on the dipstick. If the oil level rises above the upper mark, heavy oil consumption and excessive crankcase pressure may result, possibly blowing out the front and rear crankcase seals or causing other oil leaks. If the oil level remains below the lower mark, the engine will lose oil pressure, possibly resulting in severe bearing damage.

When adding oil, make sure that the new oil is of the same type and viscosity as that already in the crankcase.

MANUAL TRANSMISSION OIL

At intervals specified in the Maintenance Intervals Chart below, the oil of the manual transmission should be checked. Make the check with the transmission warm (driven a few miles) and the car standing on level ground. Using a 14 mm wrench, unscrew the oil filler plug from the side of the transmission (not the drain plug underneath the transmission). Make sure that the oil level is maintained at the bottom of the filler plug hole. Top up as necessary with SAE 80 gearbox oil (not hypoid gear oil), or SAE 30 HD motor oil if no gearbox oil is available.

AUTOMATIC TRANSMISSION FLUID

The fluid level in the automatic transmission should be checked at least every 12,500 miles. This must be done after the car has been driven about 5 miles or more to get the transmission hot and with the car on a perfectly level surface. Put the gear selector in Neutral or Park and leave the engine idling. Using a clean, lint free rag, remove the dipstick, wipe it off, and reinsert it fully. Then, pull it out and read the level. If it is between the two marks on the dipstick it is ok. If at the lower level, you should add just under 1 pint of Dexron ATF. If the fluid level is too high for any reason, fluid should be drained until the level is within limits. See the Transmission section.

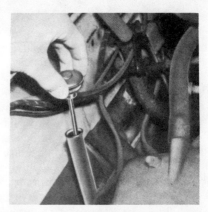

Filler tube and dipstick location—automatic transmission

BRAKE OR BRAKE/CLUTCH MASTER CYLINDER FLUID LEVEL

On all but the 1600 models, the fluid reservoir services both the brake and clutch master cylinder. On the 1600, no fluid is involved in clutch operation. The fluid level should be checked at every oil change.

Master cylinder reservoir location—1600, 2002

Rear axle fluid filler plug (side) and drain plug (bottom) locations

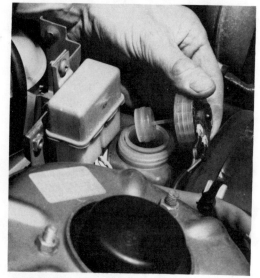

Combination brake/clutch master cylinder location (528i)

Wipe the reservoir cap and surrounding area clean. Make sure the level is up to the full mark (the reservoir is translucent). If necessary, add DOT 4 specification fluid that is *brand new* (do not attempt to reuse fluid). Be careful not to drop any dirt into the fluid, and avoid spilling fluid on the paint work, or wipe it up immediately if it spills. Make sure the vent hole used in earlier type reservoirs is clean by blowing through it.

REAR AXLE (DIFFERENTIAL) OIL

Every 8,000 miles on 1970–74 cars, and every 12,500 miles on 1975 and later cars, remove the filler plug on the side of the differential with the vehicle standing on a level surface, using a 10 mm allen wrench. If the fluid level does not reach the lower edge of the filler hole, add SAE 90 hypoid gear oil.

Special syringes are available for this purpose, if you're doing the work yourself.

STEERING FLUID

On 1970–74 models, at 8,000 mile intervals, check the level of oil in the steering box. Pry up the plastic plug on the steering gear top cover and check to see that the oil level reaches the lower edge of the filler aperture. Top up as necessary with SAE 90 hypoid gear oil.

On four cylinder models built in 1975 and

Remove the wing nut on top of the power steering fluid reservoir (late model cars with six cylinder engines)

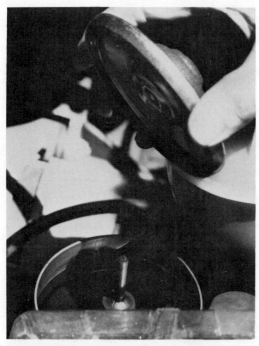

Pull the cap off and watch the fluid level

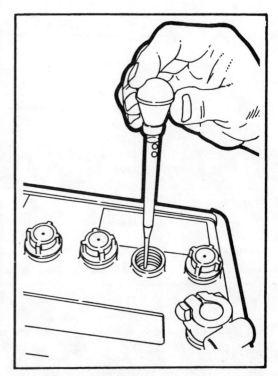

Checking battery with a hydrometer

later years, the vehicle is equipped with a rack and pinion unit which requires only greasing. On 1975 and later six cylinder cars, check the power steering fluid as follows at every oil change:

1. With the engine off, remove the wing nut located at the top of the reservoir. The oil level should be just above the mark on the reservoir. If necessary, refill with a Dexron type automatic transmission fluid.

2. Start the engine and watch the fluid level. If it drops to below the level of the line, add fluid until the level just reaches the line. Then, shut the engine off and observe that the fluid level rises to slightly above the line.

3. Reinstall the reservoir cover, making sure the seal seats properly. Check for any leaks in the steering box.

BATTERY CARE

Every six months or 6,000 miles, the battery's state of charge should be checked with a hydrometer. A fully-charged battery should have a hydrometer reading of 1.260–1.310 specific gravity of 80° F electrolyte temperature. To correct readings for temperature variations, add 0.004 to the hydrometer reading for every 10° F that the electrolyte is above 80° F; subtract 0.004 for every 10° F below 80° F electrolyte temperature. The readings obtained in all six cells should be

nearly equal. If any cell is markedly lower, it is defective. If this low reading is not improved by charging, the battery should be replaced, particularly before cold weather sets in. When charging a weak or sulphated (brownish color of electrolyte) battery, the slow charging method must be used. Never allow electrolyte temperature to exceed 120° F during charging.

Inspect the battery terminals for a tight fit on the poles and check for corrosion. Remove any deposits with a wire brush and coat the terminals, after placing them on the poles, with petroleum jelly to prevent further corrosion. Check the battery case for cracks or leakage.

Tires

The tread wear of the tires should be checked about twice a year. Tread wear should be even across the tire. Excessive wear in the center of the tread indicates overinflation. Excessive wear on the outer corners of the tread indicates underinflation. An irregular wear pattern is usually an indication of improper front wheel alignment or incorrect wheel balance. On a vehicle with improper front wheel alignment, the car will tend to pull to one side of a flat road if the steering

Capacities

| Year | Model | Engine Displacement Cu In. (cc) | Engine Crankcase (qts) | | Transmission (pts) | | | Drive Axle (pts) | Gasoline Tank (gals) | Cooling System (qts) | |
			With Filter	Without Filter	Manual 4-spd	5-spd	Automatic			W/ AC	W/O AC
1970–72	1600-2, 2002, 2002Tii	95.99 (1573) 121.44 (1990)	4.5	4.25	2.1	—	3.6	1.7①	12.1	—	7.0
1973–74	2002, 2002Tii	121.44 (1990)	4.5	4.25	2.1	—	3.6	1.9	13.5	—	7.0
1970–72	2800	170.14 (2788)	6.1	5.3	2.5	—	3.2	2.6	19.8	—	25.4
1975–76	2002 2002Tii	121.44 (1990)	4.5	4.25	2.8	—	3.6	1.9	13.5	—	7.0
1977–79	320i	121.44 (1990)	4.25	4.0	2.2	—	4.2	2.0	15.9	7.4	7.4
1973–76	3.0s, 3.05i	182 (2985)	5.3	5.0	2.5	—	3.8	3.4	16.5	12.7	12.7
1977–78	530i, 630CSi	182 (2985)	5.3	5.0	2.3	—	4.2	3.4	16.4	12.7	12.7
1979	528i	170.1 (2788)									
1978–79	633CSi	195.9 (3210)	5.3	6.1	2.4	—	4.2	3.4	16.4	12.7	12.7
1978–79	733i	195.9 (3210)	5.3	6.1	2.4	—	4.2	4.0	22.5	12.7	12.7

① This figure refers to the capacity of the short neck differential. The long neck differential was used in the 1600-2 up to chassis No. 1567845 and in the 2002 up to chassis No. 1664750, and has a capacity of 2.1 pts.

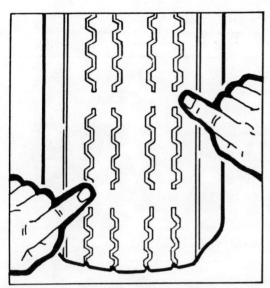

Tread wear indicators leave a bare strip across the tread—it's time to replace the tire

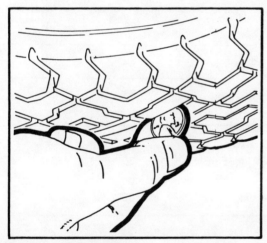

Checking tread depth

wheel is released while driving the car. Incorrect wheel balance will usually produce vibrations at high speeds. When the front wheels are out of balance, they will produce vibration in the steering wheel, while rear wheels out of balance will produce vibration in the floor pan of the car.

TIRE PRESSURE

One way to prolong tire life is to maintain proper pressure in the tires. This should be checked at least once a month and should be done with the tires cold (not driven for one hour). If you check the tire pressure when the tires are warm, you will obtain a falsely high reading. Refer to the accompanying tire inflation chart, or to the sticker attached to the right-hand door lock pillar. Sustained high speed driving (over 75 m.p.h.) requires adjustment of tire pressure levels to 4 psi over the normal rating, front and rear, as long as this does not cause the pressure to exceed the maximum rating stamped on the tire. Snow tires require a 4 psi cold increase in the rear tire pressure above that listed in the chart. For example, a B78 × 13 snow tire will require 30 psi to be properly inflated. Under no circumstances must the maximum inflation pressure, which is stamped on the sidewall of the tire, be exceeded. If you plan to do any trailer towing, it is recommended that tire pressure (cold), be increased by 6 psi on the rear wheels, again being careful not to exceed the maximum inflation pressure.

TIRE ROTATION

Another way to prolong tire life is to rotate the tires at regular intervals. These intervals depend on the type of tire and on the type of driving you do, but generally they should be about 6,000 miles or twice a year, or sooner if

Tire Inflation Chart

Application		Load	Front (psi)	Rear (psi)
1969–71	1600-2①	Up to 3 persons	24	24
		4 persons + luggage	24	27
1969–72	2002/①	Up to 3 persons	26	26
	2002A①	4 persons + luggage	26	29

Tire Inflation Chart (cont.)

Application		Load	Front (psi)	Rear (psi)
1973–74	2002/①	Up to 3 persons	28	26
	2002A①	4 persons + luggage	28	30
1972	2002Tii①	Up to 3 persons	27	27
		4 persons + luggage	27	30
1973–76	2002Tii①	Up to 3 persons	31	29
		4 persons + luggage	32	33
1970–72	2800	Up to 4 persons	28	27
		5 persons + luggage	30	32
1977–79	320i	Up to 4 persons	27	27
		5 persons + luggage	28	30
1973–76	3.0S	Up to 4 persons	32	30
	3.0Si	5 persons + luggage	33	34
1977–78	530i	Up to 4 persons	29	26
		5 persons + luggage	30	32
1979	528i	Up to 4 persons	33	33
		5 persons + luggage	35	36
1977–78	630CSi	Up to 4 persons	33	30
		5 persons + luggage	35	35
1978–79	633CSi	Up to 4 persons	33	33
		5 persons + luggage	35	36
1978–79	733i	Up to 4 persons	32	32
		5 persons + luggage	33	36

① Add 3 psi for snow tires

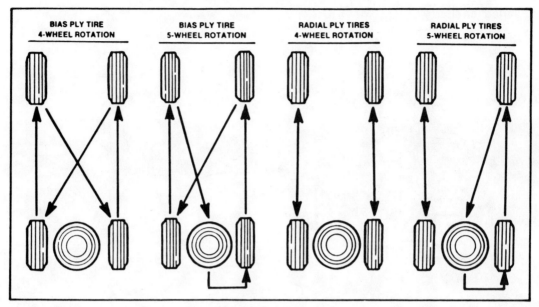

| BIAS PLY TIRE 4-WHEEL ROTATION | BIAS PLY TIRE 5-WHEEL ROTATION | RADIAL PLY TIRES 4-WHEEL ROTATION | RADIAL PLY TIRES 5-WHEEL ROTATION |

Tire rotation patterns

abnormal wear due to front end misalignment is apparent. See the "Maintenance Intervals Chart" below. Follow the accompanying tire rotation diagram for the type of tires your car is equipped with; conventional (bias-ply or bias-belted) or radial-ply. Because of the design of radial-ply tires, it is imperative that they remain on the same side of the car and travel in the same direction. Therefore, in a 4-tire rotational sequence, the front and rear radial tires of the same side are merely swapped. Studded snow tires, radial or conventional, are just as choosy about the direction they travel in. If you equip your car with studded snow tires, mark them "LR" or "RR" prior to removal so that next year they may be installed on the same side of the car. If a studded snow tire that was used on the left rear wheel one year is installed on the right rear wheel the next year, the result will be a dangerous condition where the studs pull out of the tire and are flung to the rear. Remember, never mix radial, belted, and/or conventional type tires on your car. Always make sure that all tires and wheels are of the same size, type and load-carrying capacity.

LUBRICATION

Oil and Fuel Recommendations

The latest recommendations by BMW are for the use of brand name HD (Heavy Duty) oil of "SE" (Severe) grade, made for use in spark ignition engines. The chart below gives the latest recommendations at the weight of the oil you should use for each range of outside temperature you expect to pertain during the time the oil will be in service.

For the years 1970–74, premium grade fuel is recommended. The actual octane required varies with the year and model. Follow these recommendations which refer to the "Research" (higher) octane number:

    1600, 2002—95
    2002Tii—98
    2800—99

For the years 1975–79, octane requirements are standardized at 87 AKI (which means "Anti-Knock Index"), which is an average of "Motor" and "Research" octane ratings. All BMWs made in the 1975–79 model years, except the 528i, use regular, leaded fuel, as afterburning of the exhaust occurs in an ordinary manifold or thermal reactor. In the 528i, however, a catalytic converter is used to convert unburnt fuel and nitrogen oxides into nitrogen and completely burned fuel. Lead coats the active parts of the converter, making them useless in control of emissions, and requiring expensive replacement of the noble metals which make the emissions system work. So, it is to your advantage to make sure *only* unleaded fuel is ever used.

Lubrication chart

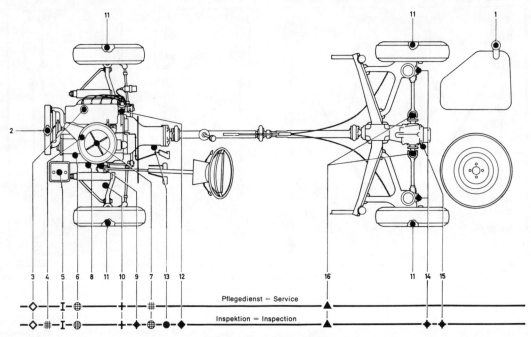

Lubrication chart—2002

Maintenance Interval Chart

**4 Cylinder Models
1970–74**

1,000 miles or 1 month	1
4,000 miles or 4 months	4
6,000 miles or twice yearly	6
8,000 miles or 8 months	8
12,000 miles or 12 months	12
16,000 miles or 16 months	16
22,000 miles or 22 months	22
24,000 miles or 24 months	24
40,000 miles or 40 months	40
56,000 miles or 56 months	56

CHASSIS

Brake drum and lining check—adjust rear brakes	8
Brake hydraulic system draining and flushing—inspect for leakage	12
Brake master cylinder fluid level check	4
Brake pad and rotor check	8
Clutch disc wear check—2002 models	40
Clutch free play adjustment—1600-2 models	8
Differential fluid level check	8
Front wheel bearing adjustment	8
Front wheel bearing cleaning, inspection, and repacking	40

Maintenance Interval Chart (cont.)

Parking brake adjustment	8
Rear axle and half-shaft rubber coupling check (models so equipped)	8
Steering box fluid level check	8
Steering and track rod joint play check	8
Tire pressure check	4
Tire rotation	8
Toe-in adjustment check	8
Transmission fluid level check (manual and automatic)	8
Transmission fluid change (manual and automatic)	22
Wheel and tire assembly balance check	8

ENGINE

Air filter cleaning	4
Air filter replacement	8
Air preheat valve position adustment (carbureted models)	6
Battery electrolyte level check	1
Carburetor idle adjustments check	4
Contact points and condenser replacement—dwell angle adjustment	8
Coolant level check	4
Cooling system draining and flushing	24
Cylinder head bolt torque check	②
Distributor cap and rotor replacement	24

Maintenance Interval Chart (cont.)

Distributor lubrication	8
Drive (fan) belt tension adjustment	8
Emission control air pump drive belt tension check (up to mid-1972①)	8
Emission control air pump hose connections check (up to mid-1972①)	8
Emission control modulation device, hoses and connections check (from mid-1972②)	24
Evaporative control system hose check from 1971)	8
Exhaust gas recirculation system servicing and cleaning (from 1973)	16
Exhaust gas recirculation system cyclone filter and diaphragm valve assembly replacement (from 1973)	56
Exhaust system fixings tightness check	8
Fuel filter screen cleaning (carbureted models)	8
Fuel tank, fuel pump, and injection pump filter screen cleaning—main fuel filter replacement (2002Tii)	40
Fuel injection pump, throttle butterfly joints and bearing points lubrication (2002Tii)	8
Ignition timing adjustment	8
Oil and filter change	4
Spark plug gap check	4
Spark plug replacement	8
Throttle linkage lubrication	8
Valve clearance adjustment check	8

① Air pump emission control systems were used in all late model 1600-2 models and on 2002 and 2002A models until mid-1972. Starting with the following serial numbers, the air pump systems were eliminated; 2002— 2583406, 2002A—2532753.

② After the first 4,000 miles on a new engine, or after 4,000 miles of driving if the cylinder head has been removed and installed.

NOTE: *Consult your dealer as to which maintenance operations are necessary to keep the emission control warranty valid on your car.*

6 Cylinder Models
1970–74

1,000 miles	1
Every 8,000 miles, starting at 4,000	2
Every 8,000 miles, starting at 8,000	3
Every 16,000 miles	4
Every 24,000 miles	5
Change engine oil and filter	1, 2, 3

Maintenance Interval Chart (cont.)

Change gearbox oil	1, 4
Change automatic transmission fluid	5
Change rear axle oil	1
Check oil levels in gearbox or automatic transmission and rear axle and refill if necessary	3
Check coolant level and refill if necessary①	2
Check power steering fluid level and refill if required	1, 2, 3
Check manual steering box for leaks and refill if required	1
Check battery acid level and add distilled water. Clean battery terminals	2, 3
Check brake fluid level and fill reservoir, if necessary. Check brake system lines and connections for leaks	1, 2, 3
Check thickness of brake pads and linings	2
Check rear axle halfshaft bellows for leaks	1, 3
Clean mesh filter in fuel pump and tighten pump mounting bolts	1, 3
Tighten carburetor mounting bolts	1, 3
Check automatic air preheating flap for free operation	1, 3
Check belt tension	1, 3
Lubricate distributor felt pad with 2 drops of engine oil; lubricate base plate guide ball track with ignition grease; lubricate cam follower with ignition grease	3
Clean air cleaner elements with compressed air and inspect; replace if clogged	1, 2
Replace air cleaner elements	3
Oil throttle linkage joints and pivots	3
Replace spark plugs	3
Torque head studs, engine mount bolts, intake and exhaust manifold bolts, oil pan bolts, exhaust pipe flange bolts	1, 3
Check and adjust valve clearances	1, 3
Check steering for excessive play and adjust steering box if required; inspect track rods and steering U-joints	1, 3
Check contact breaker gap and dwell angle, set ignition timing	1
Replace breaker points, set breaker gap and dwell angle, adjust ignition timing	3
Check condition of all driveline U-joints and rubber coupling	1, 3

Maintenance Interval Chart (cont.)

Torque front axle bolts, steering, gearbox, driveshaft, rear axle, and brake component mounting bolts	1, 3
Tighten body and exhaust system mounting bolts	1, 3
Check front wheel bearings for play and adjust if necessary	1, 3
Check tire pressures	1, 2
Check tire pressures, rotate tires and balance wheels	3②
Check for clutch drive plate wear	3
Check headlight aiming and adjust as necessary	1, 3
Oil door and hood hinges and grease strikers and catches; apply silicone to all rubber seals	3
Adjust engine idle speed settings	1, 3
Make a complete safety check (lights, instruments, mirrors, etc.)	1, 2, 3

① At 1,000 miles only, also tighten hose clamps	1
② At 1,000 miles only, also balance wheels, if necessary	2

All Models
1975–79

At 600 miles	1
Every 6,250 miles	2
Every 12,500 miles	3
Every 25,000 miles	4
Every 37,500 miles	5
Change engine oil and filter	1, 2, 3
Replace spark plugs and ignition points. Lubricate breaker cam	3
Check gearbox or automatic transmission oil level and fill as necessary	3
Change oil in gearbox or automatic transmission	1, 4
Check oil level in rear axle and fill as necessary	3
Change oil in rear axle	1, 4
Check halfshafts bellows for leaks	1, 3
Check power steering for leaks; check fluid level and refill as necessary	1, 3
Check radiator coolant level and refill as necessary	1, 3
Check battery electrolyte level and refill as necessary	1, 2
Check fuel tank cap and connections for tightness	2
Refill windshield washer reservoir	2
Check and adjust idle speed and CO	2
Check brake fluid in reservoir and refill as necessary	2

Maintenance Interval Chart (cont.)

Check hose clamps and screws on throttle butterfly manifold, intake pipe, and air container and flow meter and tighten as required	3
Tighten hose and line connections on the auxiliary air valve	1, 3
Check belt tension and adjust as necessary	1, 3
Oil throttle butterfly joints and pivots	3
Check fuel distribution lines and injection valves for tightness	1, 3
Replace main fuel filter	3
Torque engine head bolts, intake and exhaust manifold bolts, and mounting bolts	1
Tighten thermal reactor mounting bolts (if so equipped). Inspect engine mounts	3
Check and adjust valve clearances	1, 3
Replace air cleaner	3
Replace EGR filter	3
Check thickness of disc brake pads and replace if necessary	3
Torque: steering box mounting, brake caliper mountings, wheel nuts. Examine tie rods for wear	3
Check and adjust front wheel bearing play	1, 3
Check for uneven tire wear and set alignment if necessary	3
Check brake lines and connections for leaks, damage or distortion. Check handbrake cable for freedom of operation and adjust handbrake	3
Tighten bolts and nuts on doorlocks and strikers	3
Oil door and hood hinges, and grease all locks. Check operation	3
Clean air filter ring in carbon canister (except 1979 models)	3
Check both EGR valve stages and inspect control valve function. Test air pump and diverter valve. Check all air pump system parts for tightness	3
Unscrew thermal reactor and check for cracks. Reset milage counter	4
Replace distributor cap and rotor. Check all vacuum connections	4
Clean filter in fuel tank. Tighten engine mounts and intake manifold	4
Check clutch plate for wear	4
Adjust headlamps	4
Repack front wheel bearings	4

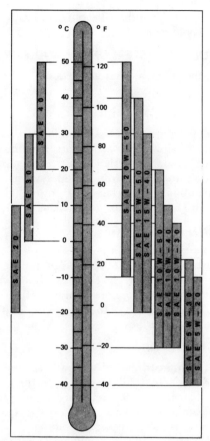

Oil viscosities chart

Engine oil drain plug location—2002

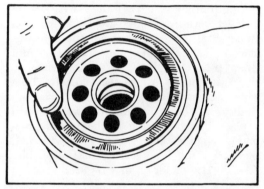

Lubricate the gasket on the new filter with clean engine oil to prevent leakage

Fluid Changes

ENGINE OIL AND FILTER

After the engine reaches operating temperature, shut it off, place a drip pan beneath the sump and remove the 19 mm drain plug. Allow the engine to drain thoroughly before replacing the drain plug. Place the drip pan beneath the oil filter (located on the left-side of the eingine behind and below the battery).

NOTE: *It may be necessary to disconnect and remove the battery to gain access to the filter from the top.*

To remove the filter, turn it counterclockwise using a strap wrench. Wipe the contact surface of the new filter clean of all dirt and coat the rubber gasket with clean engine oil. Also clean the adapter on the block. To install, hand-turn the filter clockwise until the gasket just contacts the cylinder block.

NOTE: *Do not use a strap wrench to install.*

Then hand-turn the filter one additional turn. Unscrew the filler cap on the valve (cam) cover and fill the crankcase to the proper level on the dipstick with the recommended grade of oil. Install the filler cap, start the engine, and operate at fast idle. Check the oil filter contact area and the drain plug for leakage.

NOTE: *Certain operating conditions may*

The oil filler cap is located on the cam cover on all engines

warrant more frequent oil and filter changes. If the vehicle is used for short trips, water condensation and low-temperature deposits may make it necessary to change the oil sooner. If the vehicle is used mostly in stop-and-go city traffic, corrosive acids and high temperature deposits may necessitate shorter changing intervals. The shorter intervals also apply to industrial or rural areas where high concentrations of dust contaminate the oil.

TRANSMISSION OIL

Manual Transmission

First drive the vehicle for 5–7 miles to warm up the transmission. With the car parked on a level surface, firmly apply the parking brake. Place a drip pan beneath the transmission. Remove the filler plug and the 17 mm drain plug and allow the transmission to drain thoroughly. Clean the magnetic drain plug and check for excessive metal particles (indicating abuse or excessive wear). The replace the drain plug in the transmission and fill up to the filler plug (2.1 pts) with SAE 80 gearbox oil. If no gearbox oil is available, SAE 30 HD motor oil may be used.

Automatic Transmission

This must be performed after the engine has reached operating temperature. Park the car on a level surface, firmly apply the parking brake, place the selector lever in Park, and shut off the engine. Place a drip pan under the transmission. Unscrew the 17 mm drain plug from the transmission oil pan and drain the oil. After the oil has stopped draining, install and firmly tighten the drain plug. Consult the "Capacities" Chart for the amount needed to fill the transmission. Oil is added to the transmission slowly and in stages. First, add 2.1 pts to the transmission through the filler tube. Then, start the engine and operate at idle. Continue to add oil until the fluid level reaches the top third of the space between the two marks on the dipstick. After filling, road test the car and check for proper shifting.

CHANGING DIFFERENTIAL OIL

Drive the car 5–7 miles. Remove both the filler and drain plugs (10 mm allen wrench), allowing the warm oil to drain into a pan. Be sure to wipe clean the magnetic drain plug to remove all filings and impurities. Then, install the drain plug and fill the differential up

to the bottom of the filler plug hole with SAE 90 hypoid gear oil.

COOLING SYSTEM DRAIN AND REFILL

See the "Cooling System" section.

Chassis Greasing

The steering rods, suspension joints and ball joints of BMW suspension are maintenance free. The only chassis items that require attention are the distributor on systems with conventional contacts, the throttle linkage, and, on early models, the halfshafts.

THROTTLE LINKAGE

Apply a few drops of engine oil to the joints and bearings of throttle linkage and, on injected models with the distributor type pump (4 cylinder engines only), oil the joints and bearing points of the injection pump and throttle butterflies.

DISTRIBUTOR

At the intervals listed in the "Maintenance Intervals" chart: fill the oil cup on the side of the distributor with light engine oil; grease the cam lobes and fiber heel on the contacts with distributor grease; and lubricate the advance mechanism by applying 2–3 drops of light oil to the felt wick in the end of the distributor shaft.

NOTE: *Take care not to allow oil or grease to contaminate the breaker points. Contamination may result in misfiring or accelerated contact point erosion.*

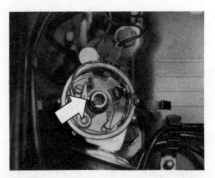

Location of the felt wick in the end of the distributor shaft

PUSHING, TOWING, AND JUMP STARTING

Pushing is not recommended for your BMW. The bumpers were not designed for this pur-

Front towing sling

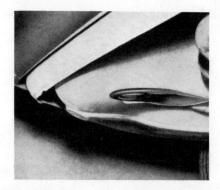

Rear towing sling

pose. Possible mismatching of bumper heights, especially around turns and over undulating road surfaces, may result in rear-end body damage to your car.

BMWs may be towed, however, by attaching a tow rope or chain to the towing loop attached to the chassis/frame near the front crossmember. Never attach a tow chain or rope to the bumper.

If your BMW fails to start, it may be started with jumper cables, or, if equipped with manual transmission, by tow-starting. When tow-starting a car, the towing vehicle should start out smoothly and be driven at an even speed to keep slack out of the tow line. Switch the ignition to the ON position (not the start position) and depress the clutch pedal. On older models, pull out the choke if the engine is cold. Place the transmission in Third gear and, as the towing car picks up speed, gradually release the clutch. Once the engine fires, depress the clutch pedal and feather the gas, so as to not collide with the friend who is towing you.

If the car is in a reasonably decent state of tune but the battery is dead, the car may be started with the use of jumper cables.

CAUTION: *All models are equipped with 12 volt negative ground electrical systems. Make sure that the car (or battery) that is supplying the jump has the same system. Always connect the positive cable of the assist battery to the positive pole of the car battery, and connect the negative cable of the assist battery to a good ground in your car's engine compartment. The idea here is to keep sparks away from your car's battery, as the battery does emit explosive hydrogen and oxygen gases.*

If all else fails, the car will have to be towed to a garage. If the car is equipped with automatic transmission, a few special precautions must be taken to prevent the transmis-

sion from being damaged. The car must be towed with the selector lever in the "O" or "Neutral" position. The car may be towed a maximum distance of 30 miles at a maximum towing speed of 25–30 mph. If the car must be towed a greater distance or at a greater speed than stated above, either the driveshaft must be disconnected or an additional 2.1 pts of DEXRON must be added to the transmission (to be drained immediately after towing). Cars with automatic transmissions may *not* be started by towing.

JACKING AND HOISTING

Always use the jack supplied with the car according to the safety warnings, remembering especially to block the wheel opposite the jack with the chock provided.

If the car is to be lifted or supported by axle stands below the outer body seam, place them immediately adjacent to the reinforcement points used for the jack which is supplied with the car.

If the car is to be supported via the front axle beam or final drive, use a suitable fixture such as a thick, durable block of wood to spread weight and avoid damaging these assemblies.

Jackstand correctly positioned under front support area

2

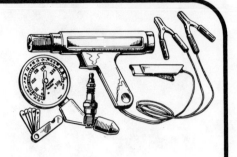

Tune-Up and Troubleshooting

TUNE-UP PROCEDURES

The following specific procedures are designed to supplement the more general tune-up procedures given in the "Tune-Up and Troubleshooting" Section at the end of this Chapter. The ignition, valve lash, and carburetor tuning procedures should be performed at the intervals stated in the "Maintenance Interval" chart.

CAUTION: *When working on a running engine, make sure that there is sufficient ventilation. Also make sure that the transmission is in Neutral and the parking brake is firmly applied. Always keep hands, clothing, tools, and hair well clear of the radiator fan and drive pulleys.*

Spark Plugs

It is recommended that the spark plugs be removed for inspection and regapped every 4,000 miles, and replaced at 8,000 mi. intervals on models built until 1974. Later models require only periodic replacement—see the "Maintenance Intervals" chart. All BMWs are equipped with aluminum alloy cylinder heads, so that the spark plugs should be removed and threaded with extreme care.

The best tool you can use to break the initial torque when removing them is a "T-bar" handle with a long extension and a spark plug ($^{13}/_{16}$ in.) socket. Be sure you get "square" on the plug. Once the plug is loose, remove the T-bar and twist the long extension by hand. This will lessen the chances of botching up those aluminum spark plug threads. The same care must be exercised when installing the plugs. First clean and lightly oil the plug threads. Then slowly thread the plugs into the cylinder head, turning them by hand (using the long extension and socket) until they become tight. Final torque figure for spark plugs is 18.1–21.7 ft lbs which should be achieved with a torque wrench of known accuracy, preferably a preset click type. Better to be on the low side than to end up stripping the threads. All that is necessary is that the metal gasket seats against the cylinder head, forming a good compression seal.

REMOVAL AND INSTALLATION

Prior to removal, number each spark plug with a piece of masking tape bearing the cylinder number. Remove each spark plug wire by grasping its rubber boot on the end and twisting slightly to free the wire from the plug. Using a $^{13}/_{16}$ in. spark plug socket, turn the plugs counterclockwise to remove them. Do not allow any foreign matter to enter the cylinders through the spark plug holes.

Consult the spark plug inspection chart in

Tune-Up Specifications

When analyzing compression test results, look for uniformity among cylinders, rather than specific pressures.

Year	Engine Displacement (Cu In.)	SPARK PLUGS Type	Gap (in.)	DISTRIBUTOR Point Dwell (deg)	Point Gap (in.)	IGNITION TIMING (deg) MT	AT	Intake Valve Opens (deg)	Fuel Pump Pressure (psi)	Idle Speed (rpm)	VALVE CLEAR (in.) In	Ex
1970–71	95.3	①	.024–.028	61–65	.016	②	—	4BTDC	4.12	1000	.0059–.0079	.0059–.0079
1970–72	170	Bosch WG160T30	.024–.028	35–41	.014–.016	22BTDC @ 1700		6BTDC	2.85–3.5	900	.010–.012	.010–.012
1970–76	121.4	Bosch W200T30	.024–.028	59–65	.016	25BTDC @ 1400		4B	3–3.6	800	.006–.008	.006–.008
1972–74③	121.4	Bosch W175T30	.024–.028	59–65	.016	25BTDC @ 2400		4B	22–29	925	.006–.008	.006–.008
1977–79⑦	121.4	Bosch W145T30	.024–.028	59–65	.016	25B @ 2200 (2400)④		4B	67–74	950	.006–.008	.006–.008
1973–74	182	Bosch W145T30	.024–.028	35–41	.015	22BTDC @ 2400		26B	3.3	900	.010–.012	.010–.012
1975–76	182	Bosch W145T30	.024–.028	35–41	.015	22BTDC @ 2400		26B	3.3	900	.010–.012	.010–.012
1977–78⑤	182	Bosch W145T30	.024–.028	35–41	.015	22BTDC @ 1700 (2700)④		26B	35	950	.010–.012	.010–.012

Tune-Up Specifications (cont.)

When analyzing compression test results, look for uniformity among cylinders, rather than specific pressures.

Year	Engine Displacement (Cu In.)	SPARK PLUGS Type	Gap (in.)	DISTRIBUTOR Point Dwell (deg)	Point Gap (in.)	IGNITION TIMING (deg) MT	AT	Intake Valve Opens (deg)	Fuel Pump Pressure (psi)	Idle Speed (rpm)	VALVE CLEAR (in.) In	Ex
1979	170	Bosch W125T30	.024–.028	32–52⑧	—	22BTDC @ 2100		14B	34–38	800	.010–.012	.010–.012
1977–78⑥	182	Bosch W145T30	.024–.028	35–41	.015	22BTDC @ 1700 (2700)④		14B	34–38	950	.010–.012	.010–.012
1978–79	195.9	Bosch W145T30	.024–.028	32–52⑧	—	22BTDC @ 2400 (2750)④		14B	28.5	950	.010–.012	.010–.012

① Bosch W200T30 or WG190T30
② Dynamic timing—Align steel ball pressed into flywheel with pointer in window at flywheel housing as follows:
   1700–2000 rpm on 1969–72 1600-2, 2002, 2002A
   1500–1700 rpm on 1973–74 2002, 2002A
   2500–2700 rpm on 1972–74 2002Tii

③ 2002Tii
④ Figures in parentheses—California
⑤ 530i
⑥ 630CSi
⑦ 320i
⑧ @ 1500 rpm

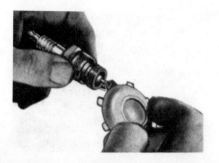

Checking spark plug gap

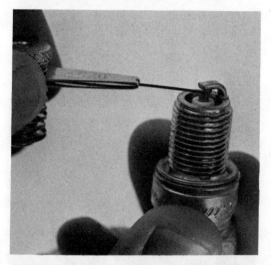

Checking spark plug gap with a wire gauge

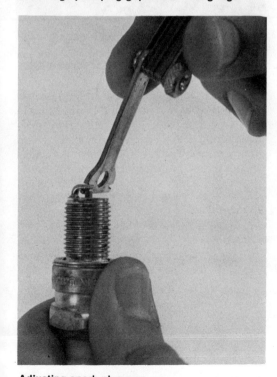

Adjusting spark plug gap

the "Troubleshooting" Section. If the plugs are to be reused, check the porcelain insulator for cracks and the electrodes for excessive wear. Replace the entire set if one plug is damaged. Clean the reusable plugs with a stiff wire brush, or a sandblasting machine. Uneven wear of the center or ground electrode may be corrected by leveling off the unevenly worn section with a file. The gap must be checked with a feeler gauge. With the ground electrode positioned parallel to the center electrode, a 0.024 in. wire gauge must pass through the opening with a slight drag. If the air gap between the two electrodes is not correct, the ground electrode must be bent to bring it to specifications.

After the plugs are gapped correctly, they may be inserted into their holes and hand-tightened. Be careful not to cross-thread the plugs. Torque the plugs to their proper specification. Install each numbered plug wire onto its respective plug.

RETHREADING

Should you encounter uneven or unduly stiff resistance when removing or installing the spark plugs in the head, the threads may be stripped or cross-threaded. This will necessitate either rethreading of the existing threads or the installation of a Heli-Coil®. Consult the "Engine Rebuilding" Section in Chapter 3 for details on these procedures.

Breaker Points and Condenser
REMOVAL AND INSTALLATION

On 1970–74 cars, BMW recommends that the breaker points be inspected and adjusted every six months or 8,000 miles. If, upon inspection, the points prove to be faulty, they must be replaced with the condenser as a unit. On later models, replace the points every 12,500 miles, if the car is so equipped.

CAUTION: *Make sure that the ignition is off.*

Remove the distributor cap and rotor from the top of the distributor, taking note of their placement. Place a screwdriver against the breaker points and examine the condition of the contacts. Replace the points if the contacts are blackened, pitted, or worn excessively, if the breaker arm has lost its tension, or if the fiber rubbing block on the breaker has become worn or loose. Contact points that have become slightly burned (light gray) may be cleaned with a point file.

To replace the points and condenser, dis-

Examining condition of breaker points. Mild pitting (1) is acceptable. Excessive transfer (2) is unacceptable.

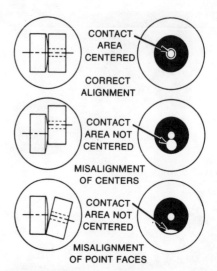

Checking breaker point alignment

connect the electrical leads for both at the primary connection. Remove the lockscrew for the contact breakers and lift them straight up. Loosen the condenser bracket retaining screw and slide out the condenser. While the points are out, lubricate the breaker cam with a very light coating of silicone-based grease. Clean the distributor base plate with alcohol to free it of any oil film that might impede completion of the ground circuit. Also clean the contact point surfaces with the solvent. Install the new points and new condenser and tighten their retaining screws. Connect the electrical leads for both at the primary connection. Make sure that the point contacts are aligned horizontally and vertically. If the points are not aligned properly, bend the stationary arm to suit.

The breaker points must be correctly gapped before proceeding any further. Turn

Here is what the distributor looks like with the rubbing block on the high point of the cam lobe

the engine until the rubbing block on the point assembly is resting on the high point of a breaker cam lobe. Loosen the point hold-down screw slightly and insert a feeler gauge of the proper thickness between the point contacts. Fine adjustment is made by insert-

Breaker point attachment and lubrication points: (1) primary connection, (2) hold-down screw, (3) advance mechanism lubrication wick, (4) breaker arm rubbing block

Checking point gap with a feeler gauge

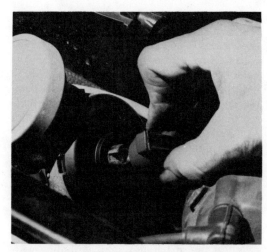

Place the rotor back on top of the distributor shaft with the tab inside aligned with the slot in the shaft

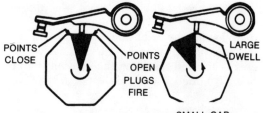

POINTS CLOSE

POINTS OPEN PLUGS FIRE

LARGE DWELL

NORMAL DWELL-NORMAL GAP

SMALL GAP EXCESSIVE DWELL

SMALL DWELL

WIDE GAP INSUFFICIENT DWELL

Dwell angel

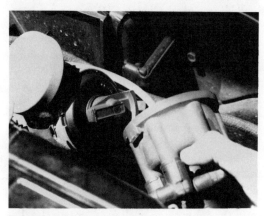

Replacing the rotor

ing a screwdriver into the adjusting recess and turning the screwdriver until the proper size feeler gauge passes between the point contacts with a slight drag. Without disturbing the setting, tighten the breaker point retaining screw.

Replace the rotor on top of the distributor shaft, making sure the tab inside the rotor aligns with the slot in the distributor shaft. Place the cap on top of the distributor and snap the clasps securely into the slots on the cap. If the clasps won't fit, rotate the cap to make sure it is properly seated. When this occurs, the cap will drop down onto the top of the distributor, as it locks into place at only one angle, much as the rotor does. Make sure the plug wires are still attached snugly to the cap. If a dwell meter is available, proceed to "Dwell Angle Adjustment." If not, proceed to, "Ignition Timing Adjustment."

Dwell Angle Adjustment

The dwell angle is the number of degrees of distributor cam rotation through which the breaker points remain fully closed (conducting electricity). Increasing the point gap decreases dwell, while decreasing the point gap increases dwell.

Using a dwell meter of known accuracy, connect the red lead (positive) wire of the meter to the distributor primary wire connection on the positive (+) side of the coil, and the black ground (negative) wire of the meter to a good ground on the engine.

The dwell angle must be checked with the distributor cap and rotor installed and the engine running. The meter gives a constant reading with the engine running. Never attempt to change dwell angle while the ignition is on. Touching the point contacts or primary wire connection with a metal screwdriver may result in a 12 volt shock.

To change the dwell angle, loosen the point retaining screw slightly and make the approximate correction. Increase the point gap to decrease dwell; decrease the point gap to increase dwell. Tighten the retaining screw and test the dwell with the engine cranking. If the dwell appears to be correct, install the breaker point protective cover, if so equipped, the rotor and distributor cap, and test the dwell with the engine running. Take the engine through its entire rpm range and observe the dwell meter. The dwell should remain within specifications at all times. Great fluctuation of dwell at different engine speeds indicates worn distributor parts.

Following the dwell angle adjustment, the ignition timing must be checked. A 1° increase in dwell results in the ignition timing being retarded 2° and vice versa.

Ignition Timing

The ignition timing should be checked or adjusted at the intervals shown in the "Maintenance Intervals" chart, or whenever the distributor contact points have been replaced or adjusted. A dwell angle adjustment must always precede an ignition timing adjustment as dwell angle influences ignition timing. Ignition timing on 1968 and later four-cylinder

Notch on rotor aligning with notch on distributor housing with No. 1 cylinder at top dead center (TDC)

"OT" mark on first notch aligning with raised ridge on timing cover with No. 1 at top dead center (TDC)

BMWs is particularly critical as it is a controlling factor in the emission control system in these cars. In addition, ignition timing, if not within specifications, will lessen the efficiency of your car's cooling system.

If the distributor has been removed for any reason, and the timing has been disturbed, the engine may be timed statically to obtain an initial setting. This will ensure that the dynamic timing adjustment will be an easier operation. Simply crank the engine until the No. 1 cylinder is at the top dead center (TDC) position and that piston is on its compression stroke. At this point both intake and exhaust valves for that cylinder will be closed (clearance at rocker arms), the engraved notch in the distributor rotor will align with the notch in the distributor housing (cap removed), the No. 1 piston will be at the top of its stroke, the notch in the camshaft flange will align with the notch in the cylinder head (valve cover removed), and the "OT" or first notch in the crankshaft pulley will align with the raised ridge in the center of the timing case cover. If necessary, loosen the distributor clamp bolt and rotate the distributor housing so that the two marks coincide. This will at least guarantee that the engine will start so that a dynamic timing adjustment may be performed.

Another method of static timing is the 12 volt test light method. Connect a test light between the distributor primary connection and ground. With the point gap correctly set and the timing marks aligned, rotate the distributor housing counterclockwise slightly until the breaker points just start to open. With the ignition switch turned on, the test light will light the moment the points open. Tighten the distributor hold-down clamp slightly in this position and proceed to dynamic timing adjustment.

In order to set the ignition timing dynamically, the engine must be at operating temperature and running at a specified rpm (see the "Tune-Up Specifications" chart). A stroboscopic timing light and tachometer are needed for this operation. First, disconnect and plug the vacuum line(s) at the distributor. After attaching a timing light and tachometer according to the manufacturer's instructions, raise the idle speed to that listed in the "Tune-Up Specifications" chart under "Ignition Timing." Most timing lights are battery powered. The red and black leads are connected to the positive and negative battery terminals, respectively. Then, the trig-

1. Cold start butterfly
2. Float chamber breather
3. Fuel inlet
4. Idling adjustment screw
5. Vacuum regulator connection

6. Idling jet
7. Idling mixture control screw
8. Accelerator pump
9. Main jet closure plug
10. Cold start connecting link

Solex 38 PDSI, 40 PDSI adjustment locations

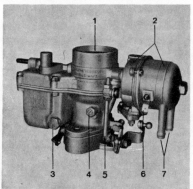

1. Cold start butterfly
2. Automatic choke
3. Main jet cover screw
4. Venturi retaining screw
5. Choke connecting linkage
6. Terminal for electric heating of automatic choke
7. Collant unions for heating of automatic choke
8. Float chamber breather
9. Fuel feed
10. Vacuum diaphragm housing
11. Idling speed adjusting screw
12. Vacuum regulator connection
13. Idling jet
14. Idling mixture adjusting screw
15. Accelerator pump

Solex 40 PDSIT adjustment locations

ger lead is either connected in series between No. 1 spark plug and No. 1 plug wire, or if an induction type trigger is used (this is usually a black, plastic claw) it is simply clamped around No. 1 plug wire without disconnecting it from the plug.

On 1970–72 1600-2 and 2002 models equipped with Solex 38 PDSI, 40 PDSI, and 40 PDSIT carburetors, the idle speed is increased by turning the idle speed adjusting screw clockwise.

On 1973–75 2002 and 2002A models using the Solex 32/32 DIDTA carburetor, the idle speed is increased by rotating the vacuum dashpot located on the right rear of the carburetor. First, disconnect and plug the vacuum line at the bottom of the dashpot. To rotate the dashpot on the 32/32 DIDTA carburetor, loosen the 17 mm locknut underneath the dashpot and rotate it until engine rpm reaches specifications.

On 1972–74 2002Tii models, the idle speed is increased by removing the cap from the top of the butterfly port and turning the idling speed screw until engine rpm reaches specifications.

Solex 32/32 DIDTA carburetor details: dashpot (1), and vacuum hose (2)

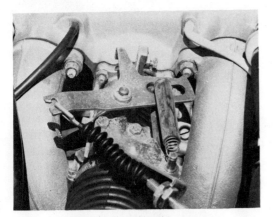

Location of the idle speed screw (320i)

NOTE: *Do not confuse the idling speed screw with the throttle butterfly screw as this will alter the emission control adjustments.*

On 2800 models with Zenith Type 35/40 INAT carburetors, both idle speed screws, the larger screws located at the base of the carburetor on the engine side, must be turned out in small, exactly equal increments, and you must carefully count the turns so they can be returned to exactly the same position.

On all later models with electronic type injection, the idle adjusting screw is located near the throttle on the throttle body, accessible from above. Do not adjust the throttle stop screw (it has a locknut, while the idle screw does not).

With the idle speed adjusted to the proper rpm for purposes of ignition timing, direct the stroboscopic timing light beam straight down through the opening in the flywheel housing flange adjacent to the starter, and align the steel ball pressed into the flywheel with the timing mark on the flywheel housing. Loosen the distributor hold-down bolt and rotate the distributor as necessary. After the adjustment has been made, tighten the hold-down bolt and recheck the timing at the specified rpm to make sure that the setting was not disturbed during tightening.

After the ignition timing is properly set.

1. Cold start butterfly
2. Breather tube
3. Fuel inlet
4. Fuel return valve
5. Vacuum bore for distributor and return valve
6. Accelerator pump
7. Electromagnetic idling shutoff valve
8. Idle air by-pass control screw

9. Idling mixture control screw
10. Throttle valve adjusting screw (do not adjust)
11. Connection for electric choke heater
12. Automatic choke
13. Connection for coolant heating of the automatic choke
14. Vacuum diaphragm housing
15. Electromagnetic starter valve

Solex 32/32 DIDTA adjustment locations

Kugelfischer fuel injection adjustment locations: (1) idling speed screw, (2) air adjustment screw

Aiming stroboscopic timing light at window in the flywheel housing

return the idle speed to its normal setting. On 16002-2 and 2002 models using the Solex 38 PDSI, 40 PDSI, and 40 PDSIT carburetors, this is accomplished by reconnecting the vacuum hose at the distributor and turning the idle speed adjusting screw counter-clockwise until the idle is returned to the 900–1000 rpm range. On 2002Tii models, this is accomplished by reconnecting the vacuum hose at the distributor (1974 models) and turning back the idling speed screw until the idle reaches the 900 rpm range, then installing the throttle butterfly cap. On 2002 and 2002A models equipped with the Solex 32/32 DIDTA carburetor, this is accomplished by connecting the vacuum retard hose at the distributor and rotating the carburetor dashpot until a 1600 rpm figure is reached. Then, without disturbing the dashpot, tighten the 17 mm locknut and unplug and reconnect the vacuum hose to the carburetor dashpot. Idle speed should now be in the 900 rpm range.

On the 2800, reconnect distributor vacuum connections and return both idle speed screws exactly the number of turns counted while raising the idle speed earlier. If idle speed is not according to the figure in the "Tune-Up Specifications" chart, see the procedure below describing carburetor synchornization.

On 1975 and later models with electronic injection, reconnect vacuum hoses to the distributor and turn the idle speed screw counter-clockwise until the idle speed is correct.

Valve Lash Adjustment

Valve lash should be adjusted at 8,000 mile or 12,500 mile intervals, depending on the year of the car. See the "Maintenance Intervals" chart. It is important to adjust the lash to make up for wear in the valve train, which will cause noisy valve operation and reduced power, or, in some cases, excessive tightness in the train, which can cause the valves to burn and may even reduce compression. The BMW features a unique adjuster design that makes it easy to hold the required dimension while tightening the locknut; thus, valve adjustment is unusually easy.

1. Make sure the engine is as cold as possible. It need not actually sit overnight, but must be cool to the touch (under 95 degrees F.) Several hours should be allowed for cooling if the engine started out at operating temperature.

2. Remove the valve cover. This will require, in some cases, removal of the air cleaner or main air intake hose, and disconnecting the PCV line or other vacuum lines. Note that the cam cover is retained to the cylinder head by cap nuts, while bolts attach it to the timing cover on the front of the engine. Make sure you remove all the fasteners. Then, lift the cover straight off.

Removing the cam cover-to-timing cover bolts

3. The engine must be rotated to a position that will ensure that there will be no closing effect from the camshaft when the valves are adjusted. This requires a different position for the adjustment of each cylinder. The charts below list the cylinder to be adjusted in the first (left hand) column, and the cylinder whose valves must be watched while positioning the engine in the right hand column. Cylinders are numbered from front to rear, 1 through 4 or 1 through 6. The engine may be rotated by rolling the car in third gear (if it is equipped with a manual transmission) or by installing a socket wrench on the bolt which attaches the front pulley and rotating the engine with the wrench. The valves of the cylinder to be adjusted (left hand column) will be in the fully closed position, so that you can wiggle the rockers up and down slightly due to clearance in the valve train, when the engine is in the proper position. The valves in the cylinder to be watched while rotating the engine (right hand column) must be in the overlap position. At this position, both valves will be just slightly open. For example, to position the engine for adjustment of the valves on No. 1 cylinder, watch cylinder No. 4 on four cylinder engines, and cylinder No. 6 on six cylinder engines. As you rotate the engine in the di-

rection of normal rotation, you'll note a point at which the valve on the right side of the engine (the exhaust valve) begins closing (moving upward). If you crank very slowly, you'll note that, just before the exhaust valve has closed, the intake begins opening. You want to stop rotating the engine when the valves are both open about the same amount (see the illustration). Now, you are ready to adjust cylinder No. 1., as described in the next two steps.

4. Check the clearances on one of the valves with a feeler gauge that falls within the limits given in the "Tune-Up Specifications" chart. For example, if the dimension is .010–.012", use a .011 in. gauge. The gauge should pass through between the valve and the *outer* end of the rocker with a slight resistance (don't check between the camshaft and rocker, at the center of the engine). If there is any doubt about the clearance, check with the gauges equivalent to the minimum and maximum specifications. If the specification is, for example, .010–.012", and the .010" gauge passes through, but the .012" gauge will not, the valve meets specification and will not need adjustment. If the clearance is not right, insert the bent wire tool supplied with the car into the small hole in the adjusting cam, which is located in the outer end of

The valves on the cylinder at the left are both open the same amount. Note cams above and below the crossbar at the center

Checking valve clearance with a *flat* feeler gauge

Tightening the cam cover capnuts. Don't forget the bolts, located at the front of the cover and going into the engine timing cover

the rocker lever. Then, use a 10 mm wrench to loosen the adjusting locknut, also located on the end of the rocker. Rotate the adjusting cam with the wire as you slide the gauge between the cam and valve. When the gauge will go in between the valve and adjusting cam and can be slid back and forth with just a slight resistance, hold the position of the cam with the adjusting wire and then tighten the locknut.

5. Recheck the clearance to make sure it has not changed—if the minimum and maximum dimension gauges behave as described in the step above, the adjustment is correct.

6. Repeat the adjustment for the other valve on cylinder No. 1, located directly across from the one you've already adjusted.

7. Then, rotate the engine to the next cylinder listed in the left hand column of the ap-

propriate chart below, watching the valves of the cylinder listed in the right hand column. When the engine is positioned for this cylinder, adjust the valves for it as described in Steps 4, 5, and 6. Then, proceed with the next cylinder in the left hand column in the same way, until all four or six cylinders have had their valves adjusted.

8. Replace the cam cover, using a new

Engine Position Chart— 4 Cylinder Engines

To Adjust Cylinder:	Put This Cylinder at Overlap Position
1	4
3	2
4	1
2	3

Engine Position Chart— 6 Cylinder Engines

To Adjust Cylinder:	Put This Cylinder at Overlap Position
1	6
5	2
3	4
6	1
2	5
4	3

Adjusting valves with bent rod. Secure the adjustment with the locknut (1)

gasket. Tighten the cover cap nuts or bolts a very little at a time and alternately in order to bring the cam cover down onto the gasket evenly in all areas. Be careful not to over-tighten the cover cap nuts/bolts.

9. Reconnect all disconnected hoses and, if necessary, replace the air cleaner.

Idle Speed and Mixture Adjustment

NOTE: *With the advent of emission control legislation on the Federal level as well as emission equipment state inspection legislation, it has become increasingly important that carburetor adjustments do not violate the letter of the law. The only way to make sure that the idle mixture setting remains at a legal level is to have it checked with an exhaust analyzer of known accuracy. This is an extremely expensive electronic device which your BMW dealer or a reputable independent garage is required to have on hand to make these adjustments. Therefore, it is recommended that the mixture adjustment be referred to them.*

SOLEX 38 PDSI, 40 PDSI, AND 40 PDSIT

1. Run the engine until it reaches operating temperature. Disconnect the air pump outlet hose (leading from the air pump to the exhaust manifold) at the air pump.

2. Adjust the idle speed to 1000 rpm with the idle speed screw.

3. With a CO meter attached to the exhaust pipe of the car, turn the idle mixture adjustment screw to obtain a reading of "0.7% CO", plus or minus 1% CO. This should compute to a 75.5% combustion efficiency reading.

4. Reset idle to 1000 rpm, as necessary, and reconnect the air pump outlet hose.

SOLEX 32/32 DIDTA

1. Run the engine until it reaches operating temperature.

2. Adjust the idle speed by turning the idle air by-pass control screw until the reading is 850–950 rpm.

3. With a CO meter attached to the exhaust pipe of the car, turn the idle mixture control screw to obtain a reading of 0.8–1.2% CO.

4. Return the idle speed to that rpm listed on the engine compartment sticker.

KUGELFISCHER MECHANICAL FUEL INJECTION

1. Run the engine until it reaches operating temperature. Remove the cap from the top of the throttle butterfly port.

2. Adjust the idle speed by turning the idling speed screw to obtain an 850–950 rpm reading.

3. With a CO meter attached to the exhaust pipe of the car, turn the throttle stop (throttle butterfly air adjustment screw) to obtain a reading of 2.0–3.0% CO. Turning the screw in clockwise will lean the mixture and turning counter-clockwise will richen the mixture.

4. Grabbing hold of the throttle linkage, take the engine through its rpm range a few times and see if it returns to idle properly. If necessary, readjust each screw (Steps 2 and 3) until the CO reading and idle speed remain constant.

5. Return the idle speed to that rpm listed on the engine compartment sticker.

ZENITH 35/40 INAT TWIN CARBURETORS (2800 AND 3.0)

NOTE: *Making this adjustment requires a carburetor synchronizing meter with caps which replace the effect of the air cleaner on each carburetor, and a CO meter with taps designed to connect with the BMW exhaust manifolds.*

1. Run the engine until it reaches operating temperature. Remove the plugs from the exhaust manifolds and insert the test probes.

2. Remove the air cleaner (note that engine rpm will drop about 100 rpm).

3. Disconnect the throttle linkage rod at the ball stud (2) near the rear carburetor.

4. Install the two caps over the carburetor tops, and connect them to the synchronizer. Now, adjust the two idle screws (3 and up) (the larger screws near the base of each carburetor) to get an idle rpm of 900–1000 *and* a reading of "O" on the synchronizing meter. If the meter shows greater vacuum on one side than the other, adjust the screws in opposite directions in equal amounts, adjusting the screw of the carburetor with the higher vacuum in the clockwise direction.

5. Adjust the idle mixture screws 5 and 6 (the smaller screws near the idle screws) in or out to bring the CO content in the exhaust under each carburetor to 1.95–2.05%.

6. If this changes the idle speed, reset the idle screws as described above. Then, reread the CO meter and, if necessary, readjust the

Adjusting idle speed and mixture on the 2800 and 3.0. Stop screws (7) are *not* to be disturbed. See test for identification of remaining adjusting screws and linkage parts

mixture screws as necessary. Continue in this manner until both idle speed (including balance) and mixture are within speficiation.

7. Finally, stop the engine, reinstall the air cleaner, disconnect exhaust probes and reinstall the pipe plugs, and reconnect the throttle linkage. When reconnecting the throttle linkage, adjust the length of the connecting rod with the knurled nut so that the rod can be connected without changing idle speed.

530i

1. Run engine to normal operating temperature.

2. Disconnect the hose from the collector to the charcoal filter. Do not plug the line.

NOTE: *The hose is located between the first and second air induction tubes.*

Removal of hoses before adjustment of CO level—530i

CO level adjusting screw location—530i

3. Disconnect the air pump hose at the air pump and plug the line.

4. Adjust the idle speed by turning the screw on the side of the throttle housing.

5. The CO level should be between 1.5–3.0% at idle speed.

6. If necessary, adjust the CO to specifications with the idle air screw located on the air volume control, by turning the screw to the left or right.

7. Reconnect the hoses.

320i

1. Run the engine to normal operating temperature.

2. Adjust the engine idle speed with the screw located near the throttle valve linkage.

3. Detach the exhaust check valve and plug the hose.

4. To adjust the CO, remove the plug

Adjusting CO level with special tool. Hole plug shown—320i

Remove plus (3) and use special tool 13-1-060 or equivalent to adjust the CO level with the screw in the bottom of the air intake sensor—530i, 630CSi, 633CSi, and 733i

from the fuel distributor and with a special wrench, adjust the CO level to a maximum of 2.0% for the 49 state vehicles or 3.5% for the California cars.

5. Reconnect the exhaust check valve hose and check the idle speed.

733i, 630i, AND 633i

1. Run the engine to normal operating temperature.

2. Disconnect the throttle housing-to-activated carbon filter hose. Disconnect and plug the air hose at the air pump.

3. Adjust the idle speed to specifications with the idle adjusting screw, located in the side of the throttle housing.

4. Adjust the CO to 1.5–3.0% at idle. Remove the cap from the air flow sensor and with the aid of a special tool, or short screwdriver, turn the bypass air screw located in the air flow sensor, until the CO level is as specified.

5. Reconnect the 2 hoses.

528i

1. Remove the CO test plug at the rear of the exhaust manifold and connect a CO meter. Start the engine and run it until operating temperature is reached. Measure the CO reading. CO must be .2–.8% (by volume).

2. Disconnect the connector for the oxygen sensor from the wiring harness. The connector is on the right side of the firewall in the engine compartment. The CO value should not change.

3. If CO is not to specification, adjust the mixture by turning the adjusting screw, located low on the airflow meter. Adjust for .5% CO.

4. Reconnect the oxygen sensor and check CO again. If CO does not meet specification, have the car checked by someone professionally trained to troubleshoot the injection system.

5. Disconnect the test probe and reinstall the test plug into the exhaust manifold.

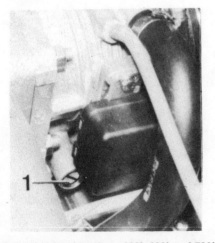

Idle speed screw location—630i, 633i and 733i

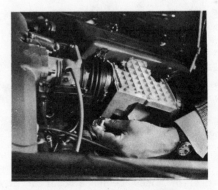

Location of CO adjusting screw—528i

Troubleshooting

The following section is designed to aid in the rapid diagnosis of engine problems. The systematic format is used to diagnose problems ranging from engine starting difficulties to the need for engine overhaul. It is assumed that the user is equipped with basic hand tools and test equipment (tach-

dwell meter, timing light, voltmeter, and ohmmeter).

Troubleshooting is divided into two sections. The first, *General Diagnosis*, is used to locate the problem area. In the second, *Specific Diagnosis*, the problem is systematically evaluated.

General Diagnosis

Problem: Symptom	Begin at Specific Diagnosis, Number _____
Engine Won't Start:	
Starter doesn't turn	1.1, 2.1
Starter turns, engine doesn't	2.1
Starter turns engine very slowly	1.1, 2.4
Starter turns engine normally	3.1, 4.1
Starter turns engine very quickly	6.1
Engine fires intermittently	4.1
Engine fires consistently	5.1, 6.1
Engine Runs Poorly:	
Hard starting	3.1, 4.1, 5.1, 8.1
Rough idle	4.1, 5.1, 8.1
Stalling	3.1, 4.1, 5.1, 8.1
Engine dies at high speeds	4.1, 5.1
Hesitation (on acceleration from standing stop)	5.1, 8.1
Poor pickup	4.1, 5.1, 8.1
Lack of power	3.1, 4.1, 5.1, 8.1
Backfire through the carburetor	4.1, 8.1, 9.1
Backfire through the exhaust	4.1, 8.1, 9.1
Blue exhaust gases	6.1, 7.1
Black exhaust gases	5.1
Running on (after the ignition is shut off)	3.1, 8.1
Susceptible to moisture	4.1
Engine misfires under load	4.1, 7.1, 8.4, 9.1
Engine misfires at speed	4.1, 8.4
Engine misfires at idle	3.1, 4.1, 5.1, 7.1, 8.4

Engine Noise Diagnosis

Problem: Symptom	Probable Cause
Engine Noises:①	
Metallic grind while starting	Starter drive not engaging completely
Constant grind or rumble	* Starter drive not releasing, worn main bearings
Constant knock	Worn connecting rod bearings
Knock under load	Fuel octane too low, worn connecting rod bearings
Double knock	Loose piston pin
Metallic tap	* Collapsed or sticky valve lifter, excessive valve clearance, excessive end play in a rotating shaft
Scrape	* Fan belt contacting a stationary surface
Tick while starting	S.U. electric fuel pump (normal), starter brushes
Constant tick	* Generator brushes, shreaded fan belt
Squeal	* Improperly tensioned fan belt
Hiss or roar	* Steam escaping through a leak in the cooling system or the radiator overflow vent
Whistle	* Vacuum leak
Wheeze	Loose or cracked spark plug

①—It is extremely difficult to evaluate vehicle noises. While the above are general definitions of engine noises, those starred (*) should be considered as possibly originating elsewhere in the car. To aid diagnosis, the following list considers other potential sources of these sounds.

Metallic grind:
Throwout bearing; transmission gears, bearings, or synchronizers; differential bearings, gears; something metallic in contact with brake drum or disc.

Metallic tap:
U-joints; fan-to-radiator (or shroud) contact.

Scrape:
Brake shoe or pad dragging; tire to body contact; suspension contacting undercarriage or exhaust; something non-metallic contacting brake shoe or drum.

Tick:
Transmission gears; differential gears; lack of radio suppression; resonant vibration of body panels; windshield wiper motor or transmission; heater motor and blower.

Squeal:
Brake shoe or pad not fully releasing; tires (excessive wear, uneven wear, improper inflation); front or rear wheel alignment (most commonly due to improper toe-in).

Hiss or whistle:
Wind leaks (body or window); heater motor and blower fan.

Roar:
Wheel bearings; wind leaks (body and window).

Index

Topic		Group
Battery	*	1
Cranking system	*	2
Primary electrical system	*	3
Secondary electrical system	*	4
Fuel system	*	5
Engine compression	*	6
Engine vaccuum	**	7
Secondary electrical system	**	8
Valve train	**	9
Exhaust system	**	10
Cooling system	**	11
Engine lubrication	**	12

  * The engine need not be running
** The engine must be running

Sample Section

Test and Procedure	Results and Indications	Proceed to
4.1—Check for spark: Hold each spark plug wire approximately ¼″ from ground with gloves or a heavy, dry rag. Crank the engine and observe the spark.	→ If no spark is evident:	→ 4.2
	→ If spark is good in some cases:	→ 4.3
	→ If spark is good in all cases:	→ 4.6

NOTE: *The BMW 528i is equipped with a catalytic converter. Since raw fuel entering the converter can damage it, do not attempt to check for spark by cranking the engine with plug leads disconnected. This model and several others are equipped with electronic ignition. The voltage supplied to the high tension wires with the system is very high, and you should always be careful to avoid electrical shock when checking out the system. For instructions on troubleshooting electronic ignition, see "Troubleshooting Electronic Ignition" at the beginning of Chapter 3.*

Specific Diagnosis

This section is arranged so that following each test, instructions are given to proceed to another, until a problem is diagnosed.

1.1—Inspect the battery visually for case condition (corrosion, cracks) and water level.	If case is cracked, replace battery:	1.4
	If the case is intact, remove corrosion with a solution of baking soda and water (**CAUTION:** *do not get the solution into the battery*), and fill with water:	1.2
1.2—Check the battery cable connections: Insert a screwdriver between the battery post and the cable clamp. Turn the headlights on high beam, and observe them as the screwdriver is gently twisted to ensure good metal to metal contact. **Testing battery cable connections using a screwdriver**	If the lights brighten, remove and clean the clamp and post; coat the post with petroleum jelly, install and tighten the clamp:	1.4
	If no improvement is noted:	1.3

1.3—Test the state of charge of the battery using an individual cell tester or hydrometer.	If indicated, charge the battery. **NOTE:** *If no obvious reason exists for the low state of charge (i.e., battery age, prolonged storage), the charging system should be tested:*	1.4

Spec. Grav. Reading	Charged Condition
1.260–1.280	Fully Charged
1.230–1.250	Three Quarter Charged
1.200–1.220	One Half Charged
1.170–1.190	One Quarter Charged
1.140–1.160	Just About Flat
1.110–1.130	All The Way Down

State of battery charge

Electrolyte temperature (°F)	Specific gravity correction
+ 120	+ 016
+ 100	+ 012
	+ 008 ADD to reading
	+ 004
+ 80	no correction
	− 004
+ 60	− 008
	− 012
+ 40	− 016
	− 020
+ 20	− 024 SUBTRACT from reading
	− 028
0	− 032
	− 036
− 20	− 040

The effect of temperature on the specific gravity of battery electrolyte

1.4—Visually inspect battery cables for cracking, bad connection to ground, or bad connection to starter.	If necessary, tighten connections or replace the cables:	2.1

Test and Procedure	Results and Indications	Proceed to

Tests in Group 2 are performed with coil high tension lead disconnected to prevent accidental starting.

Test and Procedure	Results and Indications	Proceed to
2.1—Test the starter motor and solenoid: Connect a jumper from the battery post of the solenoid (or relay) to the starter post of the solenoid (or relay).	If starter turns the engine normally:	**2.2**
	If the starter buzzes, or turns the engine very slowly:	**2.4**
	If no response, replace the solenoid (or relay).	**3.1**
	If the starter turns, but the engine doesn't, ensure that the flywheel ring gear is intact. If the gear is undamaged, replace the starter drive.	**3.1**
2.2—Determine whether ignition override switches are functioning properly (clutch start switch, neutral safety switch), by connecting a jumper across the switch(es), and turning the ignition switch to "start".	If starter operates, adjust or replace switch:	**3.1**
	If the starter doesn't operate:	**2.3**
2.3—Check the ignition switch "start" position: Connect a 12V test lamp between the starter post of the solenoid (or relay) and ground. Turn the ignition switch to the "start" position, and jiggle the key.	If the lamp doesn't light when the switch is turned, check the ignition switch for loose connections, cracked insulation, or broken wires. Repair or replace as necessary:	**3.1**
	If the lamp flickers when the key is jiggled, replace the ignition switch.	**3.3**

Checking the ignition switch "start" position

Test and Procedure	Results and Indications	Proceed to
2.4— Remove and bench test the starter, according to specifications in Chapter 3.	If the starter does not meet specifications, repair or replace as needed:	**3.1**
	If the starter is operating properly:	**2.5**
2.5—Determine whether the engine can turn freely: Remove the spark plugs, and check for water in the cylinders. Check for water on the dipstick, or oil in the radiator. Attempt to turn the engine using an 18″ flex drive and socket on the crankshaft pulley nut or bolt.	If the engine will turn freely only with the spark plugs out, and hydrostatic lock (water in the cylinders) is ruled out, check valve timing:	**9.2**
	If engine will not turn freely, and it is known that the clutch and transmission are free, the engine must be disassembled for further evaluation:	**Next Chapter**
3.1—Check the ignition switch "on" position: Connect a jumper wire between the distributor side of the coil and ground, and a 12V test lamp between the switch side of the coil and ground. Remove the	If the lamp lights:	**3.2**
	If the lamp flickers when the key is jiggled, replace the ignition switch:	**3.3**
	If the lamp doesn't light, check for loose or open connections. If none are found, remove	

Test and Procedure	Results and Indications	Proceed to
high tension lead from the coil. Turn the ignition switch on and jiggle the key.	the ignition switch and check for continuity. If the switch is faulty, replace it:	3.3

Checking the ignition switch "on" position

3.2—Check the ballast resistor or resistance wire for an open circuit, using an ohmmeter.	On cars with point-type ignition systems, replace the resistor or resistance wire if the resistance is zero.	3.3
3.3—On point-type ignition systems, visually inspect the breaker points for burning, pitting or excessive wear. Gray coloring of the point contact surfaces is normal. Rotate the crankshaft until the contact heel rests on a high point of the distributor cam and adjust the point gap to specifications. On electronic ignition models, remove the distributor cap and visually inspect the armature. Ensure that the armature is on tight and rotates when the engine is cranked. Make sure there are no cracks, chips or rounded edges on the armature.	If the breaker points are intact, clean the contact surfaces with fine emery cloth, and adjust the point gap to specifications. If the points are worn, replace them. On electronic systems, replace any parts which appear defective. Adjust the armature gap if necessary. See Chapter 3. If condition persists:	3.4
3.4—On point-type ignition systems, connect a dwell-meter between the distributor primary lead and ground. Crank the engine and observe the point dwell angle. On electronic ignition systems, see "Troubleshooting the Electronic Ignition System".	On point-type systems, adjust the dwell angle if necessary. **NOTE:** *Increasing the point gap decreases the dwell angle and vice-versa.*	3.6
	If the dwell meter shows little or no reading;	3.5
	On electronic ignition systems, if the stator is bad, replace the stator. If the stator is good, proceed to the other tests in the electronic ignition troubleshooting section.	
3.5—On point-type ignition systems, check the condenser for short: connect an ohmmeter across the condenser body and the pigtail lead.	If any reading other than infinite is noted, replace the condenser:	3.6

Checking the condenser for short   OHMMETER

| **3.6**—Test the coil primary resistance: On point-type ignition systems, connect an ohmmeter across the coil primary terminals, and read the resistance on the low scale. Note whether an external ballast | Coils utilizing ballast resistors or resistance wires should have approximately 1.0 ohms resistance. Coils with internal resistors should have approximately 4.0 ohms resistance. If values far from the above are noted, replace the coil. | 4.1 |

Test and Procedure	Results and Indications	Proceed to
resistor or resistance wire is utilized. On electronic ignition systems, test the coil primary resistance.	Resistance should be 1.7 to 2.1 ohms for electronic ignition systems. If the coil is defective, replace the coil. Otherwise:	4.1
4.1—Check for spark: Hold each spark plug wire approximately ¼" from ground with gloves or a heavy, dry rag. Crank the engine, and observe the spark.	If no spark is evident: If spark is good in some cylinders: If spark is good in all cylinders:	4.2 4.3 4.6
4.2—Check for spark at the coil high tension lead: Remove the coil high tension lead from the distributor and position it approximately ¼" from ground. Crank the engine and observe spark.	If the spark is good and consistent: If the spark is good but intermittent, test the primary electrical system starting at 3.3: If the spark is weak or non-existent, replace the coil high tension lead, clean and tighten all connections and retest. If no improvement is noted:	4.3 3.3 4.4
4.3—Visually inspect the distributor cap and rotor for burned or corroded contacts, cracks, carbon tracks, or moisture. Also check the fit of the rotor on the distributor shaft (where applicable).	If moisture is present, dry thoroughly, and retest per 4.1: If burned or excessively corroded contacts, cracks, or carbon tracks are noted, replace the defective part(s) and retest per 4.1: If the rotor and cap appear intact, or are only slightly corroded, clean the contacts thoroughly (including the cap towers and spark plug wire ends) and retest per 4.1: If the spark is good in all cases: If the spark is poor in all cases:	4.1 4.1 4.6 4.5
4.4—Check the coil secondary resistance: On point-type systems, connect an ohmmeter across the distributor side of the coil and the coil tower. Read the resistance on the high scale of the ohmmeter. On electronic ignition systems, this test is not required.	The resistance of a satisfactory coil should be between 4,000 and 10,000 ohms. If resistance is considerably higher (i.e. 40,000 ohms) replace the coil and retest per 4.1. **NOTE: this does not apply to high performance coils.** 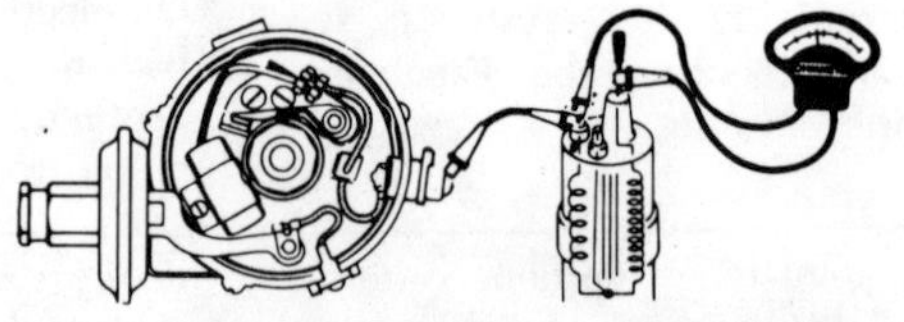 Testing the coil secondary resistance	
4.5—Visually inspect the spark plug wires for cracking or brittleness. Ensure that no two wires are positioned so as to cause induction firing (adjacent and parallel). Remove each wire, one by one, and check resistance with an ohmmeter.	Replace any cracked or brittle wires. If any of the wires are defective, replace the entire set. Replace any wires with excessive resistance (over 8000Ω per foot for suppression wire), and separate any wires that might cause induction firing. On electronic ignition systems, wire resistance should be .4–.6 ohms.	4.6
4.6—Remove the spark plugs, noting the cylinders from which they were removed, and evaluate according to the chart below.	See following.	**See following.**

	Condition	Cause	Remedy	Proceed to
	Electrodes eroded, light brown deposits.	Normal wear. Normal wear is indicated by approximately .001″ wear per 1000 miles.	Clean and regap the spark plug if wear is not excessive: Replace the spark plug if excessively worn:	4.7
	Carbon fouling (black, dry, fluffy deposits).	If present on one or two plugs:		
		Faulty high tension lead(s).	Test the high tension leads:	4.5
		Burnt or sticking valve(s).	Check the valve train: (Clean and regap the plugs in either case.)	9.1
		If present on most or all plugs: Overly rich fuel mixture, due to restricted air filter, improper carburetor adjustment, improper choke or heat riser adjustment or operation.	Check the fuel system:	5.1
	Oil fouling (wet black deposits)	Worn engine components. **NOTE:** *Oil fouling may occur in new or recently rebuilt engines until broken in.*	Check engine vacuum and compression: Replace with new spark plug	6.1
	Lead fouling (gray, black, tan, or yellow deposits, which appear glazed or cinder-like).	Combustion by-products.	Clean and regap the plugs: (Use plugs of a different heat range if the problem recurs.)	4.7
	Gap bridging (deposits lodged between the electrodes).	Incomplete combustion, or transfer of deposits from the combustion chamber.	Replace the spark plugs:	4.7
	Overheating (burnt electrodes, and extremely white insulator with small black spots).	Ignition timing advanced too far.	Adjust timing to specifications:	8.2
		Overly lean fuel mixture.	Check the fuel system:	5.1
		Spark plugs not seated properly.	Clean spark plug seat and install a new gasket washer: (Replace the spark plugs in all cases.)	4.7

	Condition	Cause	Remedy	Proceed to
	Fused spot deposits on the insulator.	Combustion chamber blow-by.	Clean and regap the spark plugs:	**4.7**
	Pre-ignition (melted or severely burned electrodes, blistered or cracked insulators, or metallic deposits on the insulator).	Incorrect spark plug heat range.	Replace with plugs of the proper heat range:	**4.7**
		Ignition timing advanced too far.	Adjust timing to specifications:	**8.2**
		Spark plugs not being cooled efficiently.	Clean the spark plug seat, and check the cooling system:	**11.1**
		Fuel mixture too lean.	Check the fuel system:	**5.1**
		Poor compression.	Check compression:	**6.1**
		Fuel grade too low.	Use higher octane fuel:	**4.7**

Test and Procedure	Results and Indications	Proceed to
4.7—Determine the static ignition timing. Using the crankshaft pulley timing marks as a guide, locate top dead center on the compression stroke of the number one cylinder.	The rotor should be pointing toward the no. 1 tower in the distributor cap, and the armature spoke for that cylinder should be lined up with the stator.	**4.8**
4.8—Check coil polarity: Connect a voltmeter negative lead to the coil high tension lead, and the positive lead to ground (**NOTE: *reverse the hook-up for positive ground cars*).** Crank the engine momentarily. Checking coil polarity	If the voltmeter reads up-scale, the polarity is correct:	**5.1**
	If the voltmeter reads down-scale, reverse the coil polarity (switch the primary leads):	**5.1**
5.1—Determine that the air filter is functioning efficiently: Hold paper elements up to a strong light, and attempt to see light through the filter.	Clean permanent air filters in gasoline (or manufacturer's recommendation), and allow to dry. Replace paper elements through which light cannot be seen:	**5.2**
5.2—Determine whether a flooding condition exists: Flooding is identified by a strong gasoline odor, and excessive gasoline present in the throttle bore(s) of the carburetor.	If flooding is not evident:	**5.3**
	If flooding is evident, permit the gasoline to dry for a few moments and restart. If flooding doesn't recur:	**5.6**
	If flooding is persistent:	**5.5**
5.3—Check that fuel is reaching the carburetor: Detach the fuel line at the carburetor or fuel injection inlet. Hold the end of the line in a cup (not styrofoam), and crank the engine.	If fuel flows smoothly:	**5.6**
	If fuel doesn't flow (**NOTE: *Make sure that there is fuel in the tank*),** or flows erratically:	**5.4**

Test and Procedure	Results and Indications	Proceed to
5.4—Test the fuel pump: Disconnect all fuel lines from the fuel pump. Hold a finger over the input fitting, crank the engine (with electric pump, turn the ignition or pump on); and feel for suction.	If suction is evident, blow out the fuel line to the tank with low pressure compressed air until bubbling is heard from the fuel filler neck. Also blow out the carburetor fuel line (both ends disconnected):	**5.6**
	If no suction is evident, replace or repair the fuel pump:	**5.6**
	NOTE: *Repeated oil fouling of the spark plugs, or a no-start condition, could be the result of a ruptured vacuum booster pump diaphragm, through which oil or gasoline is being drawn into the intake manifold (where applicable).*	
5.5—Check the needle and seat: Tap the carburetor in the area of the needle and seat.	If flooding stops, a gasoline additive (e.g., Gumout) will often cure the problem:	**5.6**
	If flooding continues, check the fuel pump for excessive pressure at the carburetor (according to specifications). If the pressure is normal, the needle and seat must be removed and checked, and/or the float level adjusted:	**5.6**
5.6—Test the accelerator pump by looking into the throttle bores while operating the throttle.	If the accelerator pump appears to be operating normally:	**5.7**
	If the accelerator pump is not operating, the pump must be reconditioned. Where possible, service the pump with the carburetor(s) installed on the engine. If necessary, remove the carburetor. Prior to removal:	**5.7**
5.7—Determine whether the carburetor main fuel system is functioning: Spray a commercial starting fluid into the carburetor while attempting to start the engine.	If the engine starts, runs for a few seconds, and dies:	**5.8**
	If the engine doesn't start:	**6.1**
5.8—Uncommon fuel system malfunctions: See below:	If the problem is solved:	**6.1**
	If the problem remains, remove and recondition the carburetor.	

Condition	Indication	Test	Usual Weather Conditions	Remedy
Vapor lock	Car will not re-start shortly after running.	Cool the components of the fuel system until the engine starts.	Hot to very hot	Ensure that the exhaust manifold heat control valve is operating. Check with the vehicle manufacturer for the recommended solution to vapor lock on the model in question.
Carburetor icing	Car will not idle, stalls at low speeds.	Visually inspect the throttle plate area of the throttle bores for frost.	High humidity, 32–40°F.	Ensure that the exhaust manifold heat control valve is operating, and that the intake manifold heat riser is not blocked.

Condition	Indication	Test	Usual Weather Conditions	Remedy
Water in the fuel	Engine sputters and stalls; may not start.	Pump a small amount of fuel into a glass jar. Allow to stand, and inspect for droplets or a layer of water.	High humidity, extreme temperature changes.	For droplets, use one or two cans of commercial gas dryer For a layer of water, the tank must be drained, and the fuel lines blown out with compressed air.

Test and Procedure	Results and Indications	Proceed to
6.1—Test engine compression: Remove all spark plugs. Insert a compression gauge into a spark plug port, crank the engine to obtain the maximum reading, and record.	If compression is within limits on all cylinders:	**7.1**
	If gauge reading is extremely low on all cylinders:	**6.2**
	If gauge reading is low on one or two cylinders: (If gauge readings are identical and low on two or more adjacent cylinders, the head gasket must be replaced.)	**6.2**

Testing compression
(© Chevrolet Div. G.M. Corp.)

Compression pressure limits
(© Buick Div. G.M. Corp.)

Maxi. Press. Lbs. Sq. In.	Min. Press. Lbs. Sq. In.	Maxi. Press. Lbs. Sq. In.	Min. Press. Lbs. Sq. In.	Max. Press. Lbs. Sq. In.	Min. Press. Lbs. Sq. In.	Max. Press. Lbs. Sq. In.	Min. Press. Lbs. Sq. In.
134	101	162	121	188	141	214	160
136	102	164	123	190	142	216	162
138	104	166	124	192	144	218	163
140	105	168	126	194	145	220	165
142	107	170	127	196	147	222	166
146	110	172	129	198	148	224	168
148	111	174	131	200	150	226	169
150	113	176	132	202	151	228	171
152	114	178	133	204	153	230	172
154	115	180	135	206	154	232	174
156	117	182	136	208	156	234	175
158	118	184	138	210	157	236	177
160	120	186	140	212	158	238	178

Test and Procedure	Results and Indications	Proceed to
6.2—Test engine compression (wet): Squirt approximately 30 cc. of engine oil into each cylinder, and retest per 6.1.	If the readings improve, worn or cracked rings or broken pistons are indicated:	**Next Chapter**
	If the readings do not improve, burned or excessively carboned valves or a jumped timing chain are indicated: **NOTE:** *A jumped timing chain is often indicated by difficult cranking.*	**7.1**
7.1—Perform a vacuum check of the engine: Attach a vacuum gauge to the intake manifold beyond the throttle plate. Start the engine, and observe the action of the needle over the range of engine speeds.	See below.	**See below**

	Reading	Indications	Proceed to
	Steady, from 17–22 in. Hg.	Normal:	**8.1**

	Reading	Indications	Proceed to
	Low and steady.	Late ignition or valve timing, or low compression:	**6.1**
	Very low.	Vacuum leak:	**7.2**
	Needle fluctuates as engine speed increases.	Ignition miss, blown cylinder head gasket, leaking valve or weak valve spring:	**6.1, 8.3**
	Gradual drop in reading at idle.	Excessive back pressure in the exhaust system:	**10.1**
	Intermittent fluctuation at idle.	Ignition miss, sticking valve:	**8.3, 9.1**
	Drifting needle.	Improper idle mixture adjustment, carburetors not synchronized (where applicable), or minor intake leak. Synchronize the carburetors, adjust the idle, and retest. If the condition persists:	**7.2**
	High and steady.	Early ignition timing:	**8.2**

Test and Procedure	Results and Indications	Proceed to
7.2—Attach a vacuum gauge per 7.1, and test for an intake manifold leak. Squirt a small amount of oil around the intake manifold gaskets, carburetor gaskets, plugs and fittings. Observe the action of the vacuum gauge.	If the reading improves, replace the indicated gasket, or seal the indicated fitting or plug:	**8.1**
	If the reading remains low:	**7.3**
7.3—Test all vacuum hoses and accessories for leaks as described in 7.2. Also check the carburetor body (dashpots, automatic choke mechanism, throttle shafts) for leaks in the same manner.	If the reading improves, service or replace the offending part(s):	**8.1**
	If the reading remains low:	**6.1**
8.1—Remove the distributor cap and check to make sure that the armature turns when the engine is cranked. Visually inspect the distributor components.	Clean, tighten or replace any components which appear defective.	**8.2**

Test and Procedure	Results and Indications	Proceed to
8.2—Connect a timing light (per manufacturer's recommendation) and check the dynamic ignition timing. Disconnect and plug the vacuum hose(s) to the distributor if specified, start the engine, and observe the timing marks at the specified engine speed.	If the timing is not correct, adjust to specifications by rotating the distributor in the engine: (Advance timing by rotating distributor opposite normal direction of rotor rotation, retard timing by rotating distributor in same direction as rotor rotation.)	8.3
8.3—Check the operation of the distributor advance mechanism(s): To test the mechanical advance, disconnect all but the mechanical advance, and observe the timing marks with a timing light as the engine speed is increased from idle. If the mark moves smoothly, without hesitation, it may be assumed that the mechanical advance is functioning properly. To test vacuum advance and/or retard systems, alternately crimp and release the vacuum line, and observe the timing mark for movement. If movement is noted, the system is operating.	If the systems are functioning: If the systems are not functioning, remove the distributor, and test on a distributor tester:	8.4 8.4
8.4—Locate an ignition miss: With the engine running, remove each spark plug wire, one by one, until one is found that doesn't cause the engine to roughen and slow down.	When the missing cylinder is identified:	4.1
9.1—Evaluate the valve train: Remove the valve cover, and ensure that the valves are adjusted to specifications. A mechanic's stethoscope may be used to aid in the diagnosis of the valve train. By pushing the probe on or near push rods or rockers, valve noise often can be isolated. A timing light also may be used to diagnose valve problems. Connect the light according to manufacturer's recommendations, and start the engine. Vary the firing moment of the light by increasing the engine speed (and therefore the ignition advance), and moving the trigger from cylinder to cylinder. Observe the movement of each valve.	See below.	See below

Observation	Probable Cause	Remedy	Proceed to
Metallic tap heard through the stethoscope.	Sticking hydraulic lifter or excessive valve clearance.	Adjust valve. If tap persists, remove and replace the lifter:	10.1

Observation	Probable Cause	Remedy	Proceed to
Metallic tap through the stethoscope, able to push the rocker arm (lifter side) down by hand.	Collapsed valve lifter.	Remove and replace the lifter:	**10.1**
Erratic, irregular motion of the valve stem.*	Sticking valve, burned valve.	Recondition the valve and/or valve guide:	**Next Chapter**
Eccentric motion of the pushrod at the rocker arm.*	Bent pushrod.	Replace the pushrod:	**10.1**
Valve retainer bounces as the valve closes.*	Weak valve spring or damper.	Remove and test the spring and damper. Replace if necessary:	**10.1**

*—When observed with a timing light.

Test and Procedure	Results and Indications	Proceed to
9.2—Check the valve timing: Locate top dead center of the No. 1 piston, and install a degree wheel or tape on the crankshaft pulley or damper with zero corresponding to an index mark on the engine. Rotate the crankshaft in its direction of rotation, and observe the opening of the No. 1 cylinder intake valve. The opening should correspond with the correct mark on the degree wheel according to specifications.	If the timing is not correct, the timing cover must be removed for further investigation:	
10.1—Determine whether the exhaust manifold heat control valve is operating: Operate the valve by hand to determine whether it is free to move. If the valve is free, run the engine to operating temperature and observe the action of the valve, to ensure that it is opening.	If the valve sticks, spray it with a suitable solvent, open and close the valve to free it, and retest. If the valve functions properly:	**10.2**
	If the valve does not free, or does not operate, replace the valve:	**10.2**
10.2—Ensure that there are no exhaust restrictions: Visually inspect the exhaust system for kinks, dents, or crushing. Also note that gasses are flowing freely from the tailpipe at all engine speeds, indicating no restriction in the muffler or resonator.	Replace any damaged portion of the system:	**11.1**

Test and Procedure	Results and Indications	Proceed to
11.1—Visually inspect the fan belt for glazing, cracks, and fraying, and replace if necessary. Tighten the belt so that the longest span has approximately ½″ play at its midpoint under thumb pressure. 	Replace or tighten the fan belt as necessary:	**11.2**

Checking the fan belt tension

Test and Procedure	Results and Indications	Proceed to
11.2—Check the fluid level of the cooling system.	If full or slightly low, fill as necessary:	**11.5**
	If extremely low:	**11.3**
11.3—Visually inspect the external portions of the cooling system (radiator, radiator hoses, thermostat elbow, water pump seals, heater hoses, etc.) for leaks. If none are found, pressurize the cooling system to 14–15 psi.	If cooling system holds the pressure:	**11.5**
	If cooling system loses pressure rapidly, reinspect external parts of the system for leaks under pressure. If none are found, check dipstick for coolant in crankcase. If no coolant is present, but pressure loss continues:	**11.4**
	If coolant is evident in crankcase, remove cylinder head(s), and check gasket(s). If gaskets are intact, block and cylinder head(s) should be checked for cracks or holes.	
	If the gasket(s) is blown, replace, and purge the crankcase of coolant:	**12.6**
	NOTE: *Occasionally, due to atmospheric and driving conditions, condensation of water can occur in the crankcase. This causes the oil to appear milky white. To remedy, run the engine until hot, and change the oil and oil - filter.*	
11.4— Check for combustion leaks into the cooling system: Pressurize the cooling system as above. Start the engine, and observe the pressure gauge. If the needle fluctuates, remove each spark plug wire, one by one, noting which cylinder(s) reduce or eliminate the fluctuation. 	Cylinders which reduce or eliminate the fluctuation, when the spark plug wire is removed, are leaking into the cooling system. Replace the head gasket on the affected cylinder bank(s).	

Radiator pressure tester

Test and Procedure	*Results and Indications*	*Proceed to*
11.5—Check the radiator pressure cap: Attach a radiator pressure tester to the radiator cap (wet the seal prior to installation). Quickly pump up the pressure, noting the point at which the cap releases.	If the cap releases within ± 1 psi of the specified rating, it is operating properly:	**11.6**
	If the cap releases at more than ± 1 psi of the specified rating, it should be replaced:	**11.6**

Testing the radiator pressure cap

Test and Procedure	*Results and Indications*	*Proceed to*
11.6—Test the thermostat: Start the engine cold, remove the radiator cap, and insert a thermometer into the radiator. Allow the engine to idle. After a short while, there will be a sudden, rapid increase in coolant temperature. The temperature at which this sharp rise stops is the thermostat opening temperature.	If the thermostat opens at or about the specified temperature:	**11.7**
	If the temperature doesn't increase: (If the temperature increases slowly and gradually, replace the thermostat.)	**11.7**
11.7—Check the water pump: Remove the thermostat elbow and the thermostat, disconnect the coil high tension lead (to prevent starting), and crank the engine momentarily.	If coolant flows, replace the thermostat and re-test per 11.6:	**11.6**
	If coolant doesn't flow, reverse flush the cooling system to alleviate any blockage that might exist. If system is not blocked, and coolant will not flow, recondition the water pump.	—
12.1—Check the oil pressure gauge or warning light: If the gauge shows low pressure, or the light is on, for no obvious reason, remove the oil pressure sender. Install an accurate oil pressure gauge and run the engine momentarily.	If oil pressure builds normally, run engine for a few moments to determine that it is functioning normally, and replace the sender.	—
	If the pressure remains low:	**12.2**
	If the pressure surges:	**12.3**
	If the oil pressure is zero:	**12.3**
12.2—Visually inspect the oil: If the oil is watery or very thin, milky, or foamy, replace the oil and oil filter.	If the oil is normal:	**12.3**
	If after replacing oil the pressure remains low:	**12.3**
	If after replacing oil the pressure becomes normal:	—
12.3—Inspect the oil pressure relief valve and spring, to ensure that it is not sticking or stuck. Remove and thoroughly clean the valve, spring, and the valve body.	If the oil pressure improves:	—
	If no improvement is noted:	**12.4**

Oil pressure relief valve
(© British Leyland Motors)

Test and Procedure	Results and Indications	Proceed to
12.4—Check to ensure that the oil pump is not cavitating (sucking air instead of oil): See that the crankcase is neither over nor underfull, and that the pickup in the sump is in the proper position and free from sludge.	Fill or drain the crankcase to the proper capacity, and clean the pickup screen in solvent if necessary. If no improvement is noted:	**12.5**
12.5—Inspect the oil pump drive and the oil pump:	If the pump drive or the oil pump appear to be defective, service as necessary and retest per 12.1:	**12.1**
	If the pump drive and pump appear to be operating normally, the engine should be disassembled to determine where blockage exists:	**Next Chapter**
12.6—Purge the engine of ethylene glycol coolant: Completely drain the crankcase and the oil filter. Obtain a commercial butyl cellosolve base solvent, designated for this purpose, and follow the instructions precisely. Following this, install a new oil filter and refill the crankcase with the proper weight oil. The next oil and filter change should follow shortly thereafter (1000 miles).		

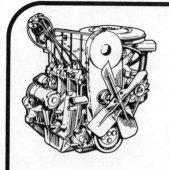

3

Engine and Engine Rebuilding

ENGINE ELECTRICAL

Troubleshooting the Electronic Ignition

1. Pull the high tension wire out of the center of the distributor cap and hold it within about ⅜ in. of a good ground. If there is a spark, proceed to Step 2; otherwise, follow the lettered steps below:

A. Pull the black/red wire off the starter terminal #16 and connect a voltmeter between the connector on the wire and a good ground. Operate the starter and read the voltage on the meter. Then read the voltage across the battery terminals, also with the starter operating. If the voltage read at the end of the black/red wire is significantly below battery voltage, repair the wire or connectors as necessary.

B. Detach transmitter wires at the plugs near the control unit and measure the voltage coming from the transmitter (in the distributor). The voltmeter should be set on the most sensitive scale—the red connector going to connection 7, and the black to 31d. At cranking speed, voltage should be at least .05 volts. If not, check the gap between rotor and stator with engine turned so as to align teeth—it should be .014–.027 in. Replace defective

parts as necessary. Replace the transmitter wiring, if defective, or replace the pulse transmitter, if necessary.

2. Inspect spark plugs, distributor cap, and rotor, and ignition wires, and replace defective parts as necessary.

3. Measure the voltage between the coil primary terminal leading to the control unit (1) and ground. If there is less than 2 volts, go on with the next step. Otherwise:

A. Check for voltage at the plug going into control unit terminal 15. If there is no voltage, repair the ignition switch.

B. Check for voltage at the plug going into control unit terminal 16. If there is no voltage, repair the wire leading from ignition coil terminal 1 to terminal 16.

C. Check to see that the control unit is properly grounded (terminal 31). If not, repair the ground connection.

If none of these checks reveal the problem, or if making the required repairs still results in more than 2 volts as read in Step 3, replace the control unit.

4. Measure the voltage between ignition coil terminal 15 and ground. It should be more than 3 volts. Otherwise, replace a defective resistor or ignition coil.

5. If the above tests are passed, the engine should start. Adjust ignition timing as described in the previous chapter. Then, con-

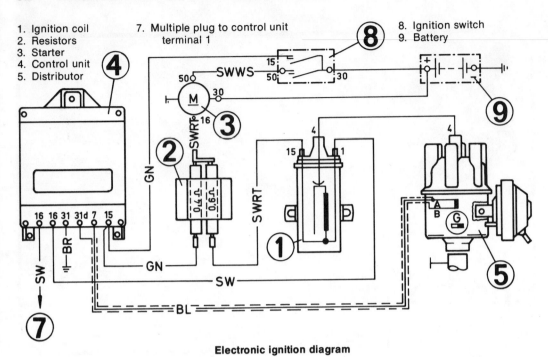

1. Ignition coil
2. Resistors
3. Starter
4. Control unit
5. Distributor

7. Multiple plug to control unit
   terminal 1

8. Ignition switch
9. Battery

Electronic ignition diagram

nect a dwell meter between coil terminal 1 and ground. Check the dwell angle at 1500 rpm and at 6000 rpm. The figures should be 32–53 degrees at 1500 and 43–56 degrees at 6000. If dwell is incorrect, substitute a new or known good pulse transmitter. If dwell is still incorrect, replace the control unit.

Distributor

REMOVAL AND INSTALLATION

4 Cylinder Engines

1. Prior to removal, using paint, chalk or a sharp instrument, scribe alignment marks showing the relative position of the distributor body to its mount on the rear of the cylinder head.

2. Following the accompanying firing order illustration, mark each spark plug wire with a dab of paint or chalk noting its respective cylinder. It will be easier and faster to install the distributor and get the firing order right if you leave the plug wires in the cap.

3. Pull up and disconnect the secondary wire (high tension cable leading from the coil to the center of the distributor cap), and remove the spark plug loom retaining nut(s) from the valve (cam) cover. Disconnect the vacuum line(s) from the vacuum capsule.

4. Disconnect the primary wire (low tension wire running from one of the coil terminals to the side of the distributor) at the distributor.

5. Unsnap the distributor cap retaining clasps and lift off the cap and wire assembly.

6. Now, with the aid of a remote starter switch or a friend, "bump" the starter a few times until the No. 1 piston is at Top Dead Center (TDC) of its compression stroke. At this time, the notch scribed on the metal tip of the distributor rotor must be aligned with a corresponding notch scribed on the distributor case. Before removing the distributor, make sure that these two marks coincide as per the illustration.

7. Loosen the clamp bolt at the base of the distributor (where it slides into its mount) and lift the distributor up and out. You will

Notches on distributor body and rotor aligning with the No. 1 piston TDC

Position of the rotor prior to distributor installation

Distance (A) rotor moves from the housing mark during the removal of the electronic distributor

notice that the rotor turns clockwise as the distributor is removed. This is because the distributor is gear driven and must be compensated for during installation.

8. Reverse the above procedure to install. Remember to rotate the rotor approximately 1.4 in. counterclockwise (see illustration) from the notch scribed in the distributor body. This will ensure that when the distributor is fully seated in its mount, the marks will coincide. Adjust the ignition timing as described in Chapter 2. Tighten the clamp bolt to 8.0 ft lbs.

6 Cylinder Engines

1. Pull vacuum hoses for advance and retard off the distributor, as required.

2. With chalk or paint, mark the relationship between the distributor body and the cylinder head. Then, rotate the engine until the line on the tip of the rotor is directly in line with the notch in the distributor housing (this puts the engine at TDC for No. 1

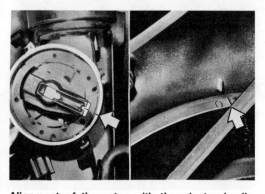

Alignment of the rotor with the electronic distributor housing and alignment of the balancer pulley TDC mark with the timing housing lug, before distributor removal

cylinder). Make sure TDC timing marks on the flywheel or balancer pulley are in line.

3. Loosen the clamp bolt at the bottom of the distributer.

4. Unscrew the mounting bracket screw for the electrical connector on the distributor body, pull the mounting bracket off, and unplug the connector.

5. Pull the distributor out of the cylinder head.

6. To install, first position the rotor about 1½ in. counterclockwise from the notch in the distributor housing. Then, position the distributor body so the alignment marks you made in Step 1 are aligned. Insert the distributor into the head. If necessary, shift the tip of the rotor just very slightly one way or the other to get the distributor and camshaft gears to mesh properly; otherwise, the distributor cannot be inserted into the head.

7. When the distributor is fully seated, reconnect the electrical connector and all vacuum lines and install the cap. Adjust the ignition timing as described in Chapter 2.

Installing the Distributor if Timing has Been Disturbed

Sometimes, the engine is accidentally turned over while the distributor is removed; in this case, it will be necessary to find TDC position for No. 1 cylinder before installing the distributor. First, go to the Valve Lash Adjustment procedure in Chapter 2, remove the cam cover, and set the position of the engine as described there for adjustment of the valves for No. 1 cylinder. Check the exact position of the crankshaft via the timing marks on the flywheel or front pulley, and obtain exact alignment as indicated by them. Then, proceed to install the distributor as described above.

Firing Order

NOTE: *Distributor positions sometimes vary. A notch on the top of the distributor body identifies the location of No. 1 ignition wire.*

NOTE: *To avoid confusion, replace spark plug wires one at a time.*

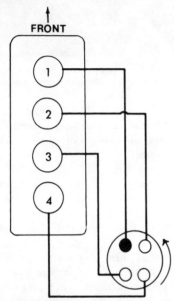

4 cylinder firing order 1-3-4-2

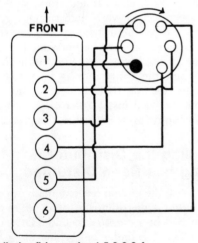

6 cylinder firing order 1-5-3-6-2-4

Alternator

ALTERNATOR PRECAUTIONS

Several precautions must be observed with alternator equipped vehicles to avoid damaging the unit. They are as follows:

1. If the battery is removed for any reason, make sure that it is reconnected with the correct polarity. Reversing the battery connections may result in damage to the one-way rectifiers.

2. When utilizing a booster battery as a starting aid, always connect it as follows: positive to positive, and negative (booster battery) to a good ground on the engine of the car being started.

3. Never use a fast charger as a booster to start cars with alternating-current (AC) circuits.

4. When servicing the battery with a fast charger, always disconnect the car bettery cables.

5. Never attempt to polarize an alternator.

6. Avoid long soldering times when replacing diodes or transistors. Prolonged heat is damaging to alternators.

7. Do not use test lamps of more than 12 volts (V) for checking diode continuity.

8. Do not short across or ground any of the terminals on the alternator.

9. The polarity of the battery, alternator, and regulator must be matched and considered before making any electrical connections within the system.

10. Never operate the alternator on an open circuit. Make sure that all connections within the circuit are clean and tight.

11. Disconnect the battery terminals when performing any service on the electrical system or charging the battery. This will eliminate the possibility of accidental reversal of polarity.

12. Disconnect the battery ground cable if arc welding is to be done on any part of the car.

REMOVAL AND INSTALLATION

1. Disconnect the battery cables at the battery. On some models, it may be necessary to remove the battery for clearance. If so, remove it.

2. Remove the stabilizer bar, if necessary, on 2002Tii models. See Chapter 8.

3. Mark any individual electrical leads that could be installed to the wrong terminal on reinstallation. Then, pull off any multiple connectors. To disconnect individual leads, remove rubber covers, remove attaching nuts, and pull leads off.

4. Remove the bolt which runs in the slotted adjusting bar and loosen the mounting belt. Slide the unit toward the engine, remove the belt, and then remove the main

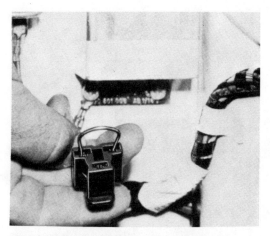

Disconnecting multiple plug from regulator

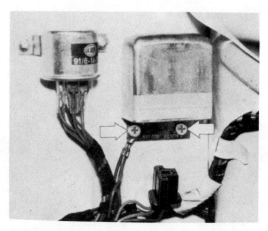

Voltage regulator installation

Alternator electrical connections—2002 series

mounting bolt and remove the alternator from the engine.

5. In installation, first locate the alternator in its normal position and install the main mounting bolt loosely. Then, install the fan belt onto the alternator pulley; position the sliding bracket appropriately and install the mounting bolt for that bracket. Finally, tension the fan belt as described in Chapter 1.

6. Remake all electrical connections. Install the stabilizer bar or battery if necessary; reconnect the battery.

Regulator

REMOVAL AND INSTALLATION

Models with Separate Regulator

1. Disconnect the negative battery cable.
2. Disconnect the multiple connector from the bottom of the regulator.
3. Remove the phillips head holddown screws and ground wires.

4. Lift off the regulator. If you are replacing it with another unit, make sure that the color coding is the same: yellow tape—non-suppressed (radio), white or green tape—suppressed (radio).

5. To install, position the regulator and ground wires, install the retaining screws, connect the multiple connector and lastly, the negative battery cable.

Models with Integral Regulator

1. On these models, the regulator and carbon brushes are an integral assembly, and the regulator cannot be adjusted. Simply remove the two mounting screws, one located at either end of the unit, remove it, and replace it in reverse order. During installation, make sure brushes are located flat on the slip rings and then install mounting screws.

Remove the two screws and remove the carbon brush holder—models with integral regulator

Alternator and Regulator Specifications

| | | ALTERNATOR | | | | REGULATOR | | | | | |
| | | | | | | Field Relay | | | Regulator | | |
Year	Model	Bosch Part No.	Field Current @ 12 v	Output (amps)	Bosch Part No.	Air Gap (in.)	Point Gap (in.)	Volts to Close	Air Gap (in.)	Point Gap (in.)	Volts @ 68° F
1970–71	1600-2	K1/14V/35A20	3	35	AD1/14V		Non-Adjustable				13.5–14.2
	2002, 2002A	K1/14V/35A20	3	35	ADN1/14V①		Non-Adjustable				13.5–14.2
1970–72	2800	K1/14V/45A20	3	45	AD1/14V		Non-Adjustable				13.5–14.2
1972	2002, 2002A	K1/14V/35A20	3	35	AD1/14V		Non-Adjustable				13.5–14.2
	2002Tii	K1/14V/45A20	3	45	AD1/14V		Non-Adjustable				13.5–14.2
1973–76	2002	K1/14V/45/24	3	45	AD1/14V		Non-Adjustable				13.5–14.2
		K1/14V/45/24	3	45	ADN1/14V		Non-Adjustable				13.5–14.2
1973–74	2002Tii	K1/14V/45/22	3	45	AD1/14V		Non-Adjustable				13.5–14.2
		K1/14V/45/22	3	45	ADN1/14V		Non-Adjustable				13.5–14.2
1973–74	3.0S	14V/45A	3	45	ADN1/14V		Non-Adjustable				13.5–14.2
1975–76	3.0Si	14V/55A	3	55	ADN1/14V		Non-Adjustable				13.5–14.2
1977–79	320i	0120489608	4	55	0192052004		Non-Adjustable				14.0–14.2
1977–79	530i, 633CSi	14V/55A	3	55	AD1/14V		Non-Adjustable				13.5–14.2
1977–79	528i, 630CSi, 733i	0120489619	4	65	0192052004		Non-Adjustable				13.5–14.2

① Used when vehicle has a radio-noise suppression type

VOLTAGE ADJUSTMENT

NOTE: *The voltage regulators used on most BMWs are non–adjustable; the procedure below describes the means of adjusting the regulators used on four cylinder models built up until 1975. Tools required include a voltmeter, an ohmmeter, a tachometer, and test equipment which will permit you to isolate the battery and alternator from the rest of the vehicle's electrical system (called a "battery post adapter"), and a load rheostat to permit loading the system a set amount.*

Install the battery post adapter on the positive post of the battery. Connect the voltmeter across the battery. Hook up the tachometer. With all electrical accessories turned off and the battery post adaptor switch closed, start the engine. Open the post adapter switch as soon as the engine is started. Adjust engine speed to 2500 rpm, and load the system with a ¼ ohm resistance. With the voltage reading stabilized, any figure between 13.5 and 14.8 volts is acceptable. If the reading is unacceptable, remove the regulator cover and adjust the armature spring tension until the voltmeter reads 14.0 volts.

Starter

1. Disconnect the battery ground cable. Then, disconnect the starter main power cable at the solenoid by removing the nut and washer, and pulling the connection off the terminal.

2. On injected four cylinder models, remove the intake cowl from the mixture control unit. On six cylinder injected models, remove No. 6 intake tube.

3. Pull off the two solenoid connectors,

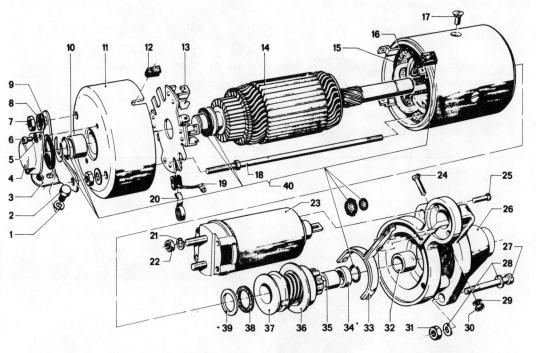

1. Spring ring	12. Rubber bushing	21. Lockwasher	31. Hex nut
2. Screw	13. Brush support plate	22. Nut	32. Bearing shell
3. Support angle	14. Armature	23. Magnetic coupler switch	33. Switch lever
4. Cover cap	15. Insulating strip	24. Cylinder screw	34. Stop face ring
5. Lockwasher	16. Excitation winding	25. Countersunk screw	35. Bearing shell
6. Cylinder head screw	17. Countersunk screw	26. Drive bearing with bearing shell	36. Gears
7. Hex nut	18. Cylinder head screw	27. Screw	37. Guide ring
8. Lockwasher	19. Carbon brush set	28. Lockwasher	38. Sleeve
9. Washer	20. Compression spring	29. Lockwasher	39. Washer shim
10. Bearing shell		30. Hex nut	40. Parts set
11. Collector bearing			

Exploded view of typical Bosch starter

noting the colors attached to each terminal. On four cylinder models, disconnect the mounting bracket at the block by removing the two bolts.

4. Remove the starter mounting bolts from the transmission and remove the unit.

STARTER OVERHAUL

Brush Replacement

1. On four cylinder starters, remove the support bracket. Remove the two screws and remove the dust cap.

2. Remove the lockwasher, shims, and gasket or seal.

3. Unscrew the pole housing through-bolts and remove the cap.

4. Lift out positive side brushes and then remove the brush plate, noting how the housing bolts pass through the locating slots in the plate.

5. Unsolder brushes from the exterior coil and brush plate and resolder new brushes connections in place.

Disassemble the starter in numbered order (typical of six cylinder starters)

Continue six cylinder starter disassembly in numbered order. See illustration above. No. 9 is the brush holder

6. Assemble in reverse order. On 630, 633, and 733 models, check end play at the front of the armature. It should be .004–.006 in. If the play is excessive, correct it by inserting additional shims under the dust cap.

Drive Replacement

1. On four cylinder starters, remove the support bracket. Then, on all starters, remove the solenoid (see below), and remove the two pole housing through-bolts.

2. Remove the engagement lever pivot screw and nut. Then, pull the front housing off the starter, maneuvering the armature and operating yoke out of the front housing. Then, pull the operating yoke out of the yoke ring.

1. Thrust ring 2. Retaining ring

Removing starter drive

3. Push the thrust ring back toward the armature coils. Remove the circlip. Then, slide the starter drive gear/clutch unit off the front of the armature shaft.

4. Replace the gear/clutch unit in reverse order, greasing the helical threads of the starter drive, and the groove in the yoke, with heavy duty, silicone grease. In reinstallation, make sure to pull the thrust ring forward over the circlip.

SOLENOID REPLACEMENT

1. With the starter out of the car, disconnect the field coil connection (at the bottom of the solenoid).

2. Unscrew the two solenoid mounting screws from the front of the front housing. Then, pull the solenoid unit upward to disengage the solenoid plunger from the shift lever, and pull the unit off the starter.

3. Install in reverse order.

Battery and Starter Specifications

All cars use 12 volt, negative ground electrical systems

Year	Model	Battery Amp Hour Capacity	Lock Test Amps	Lock Test Volts	Lock Test Torque (ft./lbs)	Starter No Load Test Amps	Starter No Load Test Volts	Starter No Load Test RPM	Brush Spring Tension (oz)	Min Brush Length (in.)
1970–71	1600-2	36	310–350	8.0	—	30–50	11.5	4000–7000	32–40	—
1970–76	2002, 2002A, 2002Tii	44	325–375	6.0	—	35–55	11.5	6500–8500	32–40	—
1977–79	320i	55	380	7.7	13.0	210	9.6	1.31①②	—	—
1970–72	2800	55	380	8	12.65	210	9.8	1.03①②	—	—
1973–74 1975–77	3.0S 3.0Si	55	380	8	15.2	270	9.1	1.82①③	—	—
1977–78 1979	530i 528i	55④	540	6.8	15.0	270	9.1	1.82①③	—	—
1977 1978–79	630CSi 633CSi	66	540	6.8	15.0	270	9.1	1.82①③	—	—
1977–79	733i	66	550	7.9	13.4	340	9.1	1.63①③	—	1512

① Figure represents horsepower—a maximum power test is given
② Maximum no-load speed is 13,000
③ Maximum no-load speed is 10,000
④ 528i—66

Positioning solenoid eyelet into engaging arm

Location of battery clamp screw—typical

NOTE: *Make sure you connect terminals + to + and − to −, or damage to the alternator will result.*

4. Apply petroleum jelly to the connections.

Battery

REMOVAL AND INSTALLATION

1. Turn the engine off. Disconnect both battery cables (Negative first).

2. Loosen the angled clamp screw, located in front of the battery. Then, shift the retaining bracket away from the battery and remove the unit.

3. To install, reverse the removal procedure, making sure the retaining bracket has the battery tightly clamped in place before tightening the clamp screw.

ENGINE MECHANICAL

Design

The two litre engines are four cylinder, in-line designs, while all larger engines are six clylinder in-line designs. The block is made of a special gray iron, while the heads are of aluminum alloy to save weight. The crankshafts are of forged steel and are nitrite har-

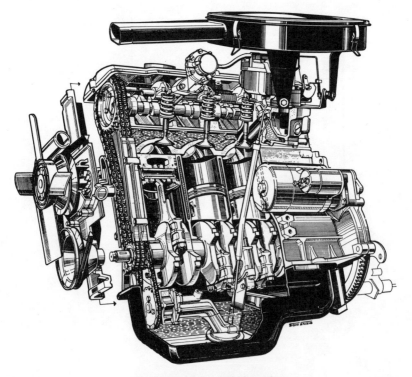

Cutaway view of 2002 engine

General Engine Specifications

Year	Engine Displacement Cu In. (cc)	Carburetor Injection Type	Horsepower (@ rpm)	Torque @ rpm (ft lbs)	Bore x Stroke (in.)	Compression Ratio	Oil Pressure @ rpm (psi)
1970–71	95.99 (1573)	Solex 38 PDSI	105 @ 5500	91 @ 3000	3.307 x 2.795	8.6 : 1	56.9 @ 4000
	121.44 (1990)	Solex 38 PDSI or PDSIT①	113 @ 5800	115.7 @ 3000	3.504 x 3.130	8.5 : 1	56.9 @ 4000
1972–74	121.44 (1990)	Kugelfisher Mechanical Injection	125 @ 5500	127 @ 4000	3.504 x 3.150	9.0 : 1	56.9 @ 4000
1972–76	121.44 (1990)	Solex 32/32① DIPTA	98 @ 5500	100 @ 3500	3.504 x 3.150	8.3 : 1	56.9 @ 4000
1970–72	170.1 (2778)	Zenith 35/40 INAT②	192 @ 6000	173 @ 3700	3.385 x 3.149	9.0 : 1	71 @ 6400
1973–74	182.16 (2985)	Zenith 35/40 INAT②	180 @ 6000	188 @ 3700	3.504 x 3.149	9.0 : 1	71 @ 6000
1975–76	182.16 (2985)	Bosch Electronic Ignition	200 @ 5500	200 @ 4000	3.504 x 3.149	9.0 : 1	71 @ 6000
1977–79	121.44 (1990)	Bosch K-Jetronic Mechanical Injection	110 @ 5800	112 @ 3750	3.504 x 3.150	8.2 : 1	57 @ 4000
1977–78	182.16 (2985)	Bosch L-Jetronic Electronic Injection	176 @ 5500	185 @ 4500	3.504 x 3.150	8.1 : 1	71 @ 6000
1977–79	196.0 (3210)	Bosch L-Jetronic Electronic Injection	177 @ 5200	195 @ 4000	3.504 x 3.386	8.4 : 1	71 @ 6000
1979	170.1 (2788)	Bosch L-Jetronic Electronic Injection	169 @ 5500	170 @ 4500	3.39 x 3.15	8.2 : 1	71 @ 6000

① 2002A
② From Chassis No. 2532752

Valve Specifications

Year	Engine Displacement Cu In. (cc)	Seat Angle (deg)	Face Angle (deg)	Spring Test Pressure (lbs @ in.)	Spring Free Height (in.)	STEM TO GUIDE CLEARANCE (in.)		STEM DIAMETER (in.)	
						Intake	Exhaust	Intake	Exhaust
1970–79	95.99 (1573) 121.44 (1990)	45	45½	64 @ 1.48	1.7126①	.0010–.0020	.0015–.0030	.3149	.3149
1970–72	170.1 (2788)	45	45⅓	64 @ 1.48	1.7126	.0010–.0020	.0015–.0030	.3150	.3150
1973–76	182.16 (2985)	45	45⅓	64 @ 1.48	1.71	.0010–.0020	.0015–.0030	.3150	.3150
1977–78	182.16 (2985)	45	45⅓	64 @ 1.48	1.71	.0010–.0021	.0015–.0027	.3149	.3149
1978–79	196.0 (3210)	45	45½	64 @ 1.48	1.71①	.0010–.0022	.0016–.0027	.3150	.3150
1979	170.1 (2788)	45	45⅓	64 @ 1.48	1.7126	.0010–.0020	.0015–.0030	.3150	.3150

① A dimension of 1.8110 applies to some springs, depending upon the manufacturer. Test pressure is the same.

Crankshaft and Connecting Rod Specifications

All measurements are given in inches

Year	Engine Displacement Cu In. (cc)	CRANKSHAFT				CONNECTING ROD		
		Main Brg Journal Dia	Main Brg Oil Clearance	Shaft End-Play	Thrust on No.	Journal Diameter	Oil Clearance	Side Clearance
1970–71	95.99 (1573)	2.1654	①	.003–.006	3	1.8898	.00090–.00272	.00158
1970–76	121.44 (1990)							
1977–79	121.44 (1990)	2.1653	.0012–.0027	.003–.007	3	1.8898	.0009–.0031	.0015
1970–72, 1979	170.1 (2788)	2.3622	.0012–.0028	.003–.007	4	1.8898	.0013–.0027	.0016
1973–76	182.16 (2985)							
1977–78	182.16 (2985)	2.3622	.0011–.0027	.003–.007	4	1.8897	.0009–.0027	.0016
1978–79	196.0 (3210)	2.3622	.0012–.0027	.003–.007	4	1.8898	.0009–.0031	.0015

① Red: .00118–.002756
Blue: .00118–.002677

Ring Gap

All measurements are given in inches

Year	Engine No. Cyl Displacement (cu in.)	Top Compression	Bottom Compression	Oil Control
1970–71	95.99 (1573)	.0118– .0197	.0118– .0177	.0098– .0157
1970–76	121.44 (1990)	.0118– .0197	.0079–① .0157	.0098– .0157
1977–79	121.44 (1990)	.012– .018	.008– .016	.010– .020
1970–72 1973–76	170.10 (2788) 182.16 (2985)	.012– .020	.008– .016	.010– .016
1977–78	182.16 (2985)	.012– .020	.008– .015	.010– .016
1979	170.1 (2788)	.012– .020	.008– .016	.010– .016
1977–79	196.0 (3210)	.012– .018	.008– .016	.010– .016

① Previous design used a clearance of .0118–.0177.

Ring Side Clearance

All measurements are given in inches

Year	Engine	Top Compression	Bottom Compression	Oil Control
1970–71 1970–76	95.99 (1573) 121.44 (1990)	.002– .003	.001– .002	.001– .002
1977–79	121.44 (1990)	.002– .004	.002– .003	.001– .002

Ring Side Clearance (cont.)
All measurements are given in inches

Year	Engine	Top Compression	Bottom Compression	Oil Control
1970–72, 1979 1973–76	170.1 (2788) 182.16 (2985)	.002–.003	.001–.002	.001–.002
1977–78	182.16 (2985)	.002–.003	.001–.002	.001–.002
1978–79	196.0 (3210)	.002–.004	.002–.003	.001–.002

Torque Specifications
All readings in ft lbs

Year	Engine Displacement Cu In. (cc)	Cylinder Head Bolts	Rod Bearing Bolts	Main Bearing Bolts	Crankshaft Pulley Bolt	Flywheel-to-Crankshaft Bolts	MANIFOLDS Intake	Exhaust
1970–71 1970–76	95.99 (1573) 121.44 (1990)	①	37.6–41.2	42.0–45.6	101–108	75.9–83.2	15–20	21.7–23.9
1977–79	121.44 (1990)	①	38–41	42–45	101–108	72–83	—	22–24
1970–72, 1979 1973–76	170.10 (2788) 182.16 (2985)	53–55	38–41	42–46	174–188 318–333②	72–83	—	22–24
1977–78	182.16 (2985)	53–56	38–40	42–46	320–330③	72–83	—	22–24④
1978–79	196.00 (3210)	56–59	38–40	42–45	320–330③	72–83	—	22–24④

① Torque in three stages following tightening sequence:
1. 25–33
2. 43–47
3. 49–52
② Use higher figure with collar type nut
③ Applies to vibration damper—pulley torque is 101
④ Thermal reactor—23–25

Piston Clearance

Year	Engine No. Cyl Displacement (cu in.)	Piston to Bore Clearance (in.)
1970–71	95.99 (1573)	.0018
1972–79	121.44 (1990)	
1970–72, 1979	170.1 (2788)	.0016
1973–76	186.16 (2985)	
1977–79	186.16 (2985)	.0015–.0018
1978–79	196.0 (3210)	.0018

dened. Four cylinder engines use eight counterweights, while sixes use 12, for optimum blanance. Four cylinder engines use five main bearings while the sixes employ seven; all main bearings are of replaceable, three layer design.

The cylinder heads employ valves located in an inverted Vee pattern, allowing the use of hemispherical combustion chambers for optimum, swirl assisted combustion with minimum heat transfer to the cylinder head. This kind of combustion chamber also allows for use of the largest possible valves. The valves are actuated by a single, nitrite hardened overhead camshaft. Since they are not located directly below the shaft, they are actuated via light alloy rockers. This makes valve adjustment procedure very simple— the only special tool required is a simple piece of wire. Valve adjustments are made via a unique cam, located in the end of the rocker arm and in effect, pinched between sections of it. Since the adjusting cams are separate from the adjusting lockbolts and nuts, and since the lockbolts are prevented from turning via a flat at one end, it is easy to tighten down on the adjustment mechanism without changing the clearance. This minimizes the time required in performing the adjustment. Other engine features that prolong life are the use of chromium plated rings and valve stems, and forged connecting rods.

The outstanding feature of BMW engines is maximum output per cubic inch. This is possible through painstaking design of camshafts, valves, and the crossflow form taken by the intake and exhaust systems; the ram-type manifolds used on later models; the use of fuel injection on later models, which permits elimination of the restricting effect of the carburetor venturi; and on all engines, the toughness and precise balance required to permit high rpm operation—all BMW engines will run up to 6,400 rpm, and are rated for a constant 6,000 rpm. The result is high performance without the fuel economy penalty usually associated with it.

Engine Removal and Installation

Most engine repair work may be performed with the engine installed in the car. The only operations that should require removal of the engine are crankshaft removal, or any extensive cylinder block overhaul. Remember that on all 1600-2 and 2002 series models, the engine and transmission should be removed as a unit.

Before setting out to tear out your engine, and tying up both yourself and your BMW, there are a few preliminary steps that should be taken. Jot down those engine and chassis numbers (see Chapter 1) and make a trip to your parts dealer to order all those gaskets, hoses, belts, filters, etc. (i.e., exhaust manifold-to-head pipe flange gasket) that are in need of replacement. This will help avoid last minute or weekend parts dashes that can tie up a car even longer. Also, have enough oil, antifreeze, transmission fluid, etc. (see "Capacities" chart) on hand for the job. If the car is still running, have the engine, engine compartment, and underbody steam cleaned. The less dirt, the better. Have all of the necessary tools together. These should include a sturdy hydraulic jack and a pair of jackstands of sufficient capacity, a chain/pulley engine hoist of sufficient test strength, a wooden block and small jack to support the oil pan or transmission, a can of penetrating fluid to help loosen rusty nuts and bolts, a few jars or plastic containers to store and identify used engine hardware, and a punch or bottle of brush paint to matchmark adjacent parts to aid reassembly. Once you have all of your parts, tools, and fluids together, proceed with the task.

1600-2, 2002

1. Open the hood and trace the outline of the hood hinge mounts on the hood.

2. Cover the fenders with fender aprons. With the help of an assistant, remove the hood hinge bolts and lift off the hood. Place the hood away from the work area or it may become damaged.

3. Open the drain cocks at the bottom of the radiator and at the rear right-hand side of the engine block. Drain the cooling system (remove the radiator cap to speed the process).

4. Place a drip pan (5 qt. capacity) under the oil pan and remove the engine oil drain plug. Drain the crankcase.

5. Place a drip pan (2 qt. capacity) under the transmission. Remove the drain plug (manual and automatic transmission) and drain the transmission.

6. Disconnect the cables and remove the battery.

7. Remove the mounting bolts, vacuum control hose(s), breather hoses and tubes, and intake air hose from the air cleaner, marking them for reassembly. Remove and disassemble the air cleaner.

8. On carbureated versions, remove the preheating air regulation housing and hose assembly from the front panel.

9. Disconnect the radiator hoses at the thermostat and water pump. On 2002A models, disconnect and plug the transmission cooler lines at the radiator. Remove the radiator retaining bolts and carefully lift out the radiator.

10. Disconnect the multiple plug from the alternator, and remove the B+ cable from the alternator and starter. Mark them for reassembly. Disconnect the coolant temperature sensor.

11. Disconnect the throttle linkage. On the 2002A, disconnect the cable from the automatic choke and the thermo-start valve. Also on the 2002A, detach the plug from the starter lock and pull the cable loom out of the retainer at the transmission. Detach the coolant hoses from the automatic choke housing. On manual choke models, disconnect the choke cable from its lever and the cable sleeve from the cable clamp and pull out the cable. On all 2002 and 2002A models equipped with the Solex 32/32 DTDTA carburetor, disconnect the wire for the electric choke, and the leads for the EGR system. On the 2002A, disconnect the downshift linkage

1. Return spring
2. Clamp spring
3. Control rod

Disconnecting throttle linkage—carbureted models

Disconnecting throttle linkage—2002Tii models

by detaching the clamp spring, return spring, lifting out the wire retainer, disconnecting the linkage ball, and pulling the torsion shaft towards the front.

12. Disconnect and plug the fuel line at the tank side of the fuel pump. On 2002 Tii models, disconnect the fuel hose at the injection pump. On Tii models, remove the main fuel filter from its mount on the front panel. Also on 2002 Tii models disconnect the fuel reflow hose.

13. On models equipped with the emission control air pump, disconnect the vacuum line from the check (non-return) valve at the intake manifold.

14. Disconnect the heater hoses at the return flow connection and cylinder head.

15. Disconnect and label the wire connector from the oil pressure switch, the distributor primary connection, and the ground strap at the engine transmission flange. On 2002

1. Clamp spring
2. Return spring
3. Wire retainer

Disconnecting downshift linkage—2002A

Connecting engine hoist

Tii models, disconnect the cable from the thermo-time switch. Also on 2002Tii models, disconnect and label the vacuum hose from the air container and the cable from the start valve. Release the cable from the cable clamps on the cam cover.

16. Disconnect the coil high-tension lead from the center of the distributor cap. On 2002Tii models, pull out the induction transmitter from the coil. On all models, remove the distributor cap and rotor.

17. On manual transmission models, remove the shifter by sliding the shifter boot up along with the foam rubber ring and inner sealing boot. Lift the leaf spring out of the selector head and push the bolt and leaf spring from the selector head. On models with a pivot-ball on the shift lever end, pull up the rubber boot and gasket to remove the snap-ring and shift lever.

18. Using a hydraulic floor jack of sufficient capacity for the car's weight, raise the front of the car, and position jackstands beneath the reinforced box members adjacent to the two front jacking points (front of each rocker panel).

CAUTION: *Before climbing under the car, make sure that the jackstands are secure. Test their stability by attempting to rock the car back and forth, forward and sideways.*

19. Disconnect the head pipe from the exhaust manifold. Disconnect the head pipe support and the front muffler mounting screws.

20. Disconnect the driveshaft from the transmission flange by releasing the self-locking nuts and bolts from the rotoflex coupling.

Tie up the driven shaft so that it does not fall out of the transmission. Disconnect the back-up light wires from their terminals, and the speedometer cable from the transmission.

21. On the 2002 series models, remove the hydraulic line bracket from the clutch housing, but do not disconnect the line from the slave cylinder. Disconnect the return spring from the throwout lever. Pull back the dust cover and remove the snap-ring from the slave cylinder. Then pull the slave cylinder forward and remove the pushrod.

22. On 1600—2 models, detach the pullrod on the intermediate shaft. Detach the bearing support from the engine support. Then remove the intermediate shaft.

23. On 2002A models, remove the selector lever. Also lift out the circlip and detach the selector rod from the selector lever. Disconnect the back-up light neutral start switch lead.

24. Support the weight of the transmission with a floor jack and a block of wood. Attach lifting eyes to strong mounting points at the front and rear of the engine. Hook up an engine hoist to the eyelets and take the slack out of the hoist chain.

25. Remove the left- and right-hand engine mount bolts. Remove the bolts retaining the driveshaft center support bearing to the body. Remove the bolts for the transmission support crossmember. The engine/transmission unit should now be free. Check to make sure that all wires, hoses, etc. are disconnected. Remove the windshield washer reservoir.

26. Carefully, tilt the transmission down and the front of the engine up. Lift the engine out with the front raised. Lower the car, and push it back out from under the engine. Lower the engine onto a stand,

Removing right hand engine mount

Adjusting clearance of engine mount

Removing left hand engine mount

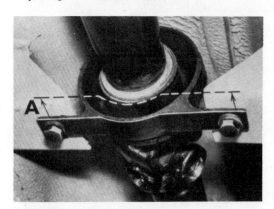

Preloading center support bearing housing

Removing transmission support crossmember

workbench, or other suitable sturdy work surface.

27. Reverse the above procedure to install, using the following installation notes:

a. When bolting the engine of the 1600-2, 2002, and 2002A in place, make sure that the right engine mount support stop is adjusted so that a 0.118 in. clearance exists as per the illustration.

b. When installing the center driveshaft support bearing mount, preload the bearing mount by adjusting it forward 0.08 in. in its eccentric bolt holes. Make sure that the driveshaft bolts are torqued to 21.8 ft lbs.

c. When connecting the pullrod to the intermediate shaft, make sure that the bearing support is aligned at a 90° angle to the engine before tightening the mounting screws.

d. When hooking up the exhaust system, make sure that the following sequence is used: first connect the head pipe to the manifold, then loosen the head pipe support mount on the transmission (2) so that it rests tension-free against the pipe, then tighten the support mount on the transmission (2) and (1) and finally tighten the support bracket on the head pipe (3).

e. Adjust the clutch free-play while the car is up in the air following the procedure given in Chapter 6.

Head pipe support bracket

f. When installing the shift lever, make sure that the gearshift pin is installed in its lever with the bolt positioned in the centering recess of the pin. Also make sure that the breather holes in the shifter dust boot face down.

g. When filling the radiator, make sure that the heater control is set to the "Hot" position.

h. When filling the automatic transmission on the 2002A, follow the instructions for filling under "Changing the Transmission Oil" in Chapter 1.

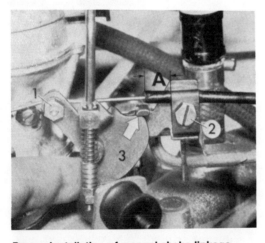

Proper installation of manual choke linkage

i. When hooking up the choke on 1969–71 1600-2 and 2002 models, make sure that the choke handle on the dash is at its bottom notch. Then press the fast idle lever (3) against the stop, and tighten the clamp screw (1). The sleeve must project exactly 0.59 in. (distance "A") for the choke flap to close fully.

Removal and installation of six cylinder engines—typical

3.0 CARBURETED MODELS

1. Scribe the hood hinge locations and remove the hood. Disconnect and remove the battery.

2. Remove the air cleaner and hoses.

3. Drain the cooling system, disconnect the hoses and remove the radiator.

4. Remove the windshield washer reservoir and the fan.

5. Disconnect the electrical wiring from the engine components, tagging them for later installation.

7. Disconnect the accelerator linkage and unbolt the exhaust pipe from the exhaust manifold.

8. Remove the front lower apron and loosen both engine mount retaining nuts.

9. On vehicles with power steering, remove the pump from the mounting brackets and move the pump out of the way. Do not remove the lines.

10. Raise and support the vehicle.

11. Remove the transmission. Refer to "Transmission Removal and Installation". See Chapter 6.

12. On manual transmission cars, remove the slave cylinder from the clutch housing, leaving the pressure hose attached.

13. Lower the car and attach a lifting sling to the engine.

14. Be sure that all wires, hoses and linkages are disconnected and remove the engine.

15. Installation is the reverse of removal. Be sure all bolt and clip connections are secure and all fluids are filled before starting the engine.

3.0 FUEL INJECTED MODELS

Follow the engine removal and installation procedures for carburetor equipped models.

The following procedures pertain specifically to fuel injection models.

1. Separate the electrical connection for the fuel injection wire loom by removing the 3 retaining screws.

2. Remove the wire leads from the relays, sensors, and switches. Mark the wire connections for installation.

3. Remove the transmission if equipped with an automatic transmission. If equipped with a manual transmission, the engine can be removed with the transmission attached.

320i

1. Raise and support the vehicle. Remove the transmission. (See "Transmission Removal and Installation" in Chapter 6.) Remove the exhaust pipe from the exhaust manifold.

2. Remove the hood, after scribing the hinge locations.

3. Drain the cooling system, disconnect the hoses and remove the radiator. Remove the intake air panel.

4. Disconnect and tag the lines to the injector valves.

5. Disconnect all electrical wires from the engine, marking them for installation.

6. Disconnect all fuel and vacuum lines and mark them for installation.

7. Disconnect the accelerator cable. Disconnect the battery cables and remove the battery.

8. Attach a lifting sling to the engine. Remove the retaining nuts from the left and right engine mounts and the upper engine damper, located on the left side of the engine.

On the 320i, red (13), blue (14), and white (15) hoses, and the heater hoses (16 and 17)

9. Carefully raise and remove the engine.

10. Installation is the reverse of removal.

528i, 530i

1. Raise and support the vehicle. Remove the transmission. (See "Transmission Removal and Installation" in Chapter 6.) Disconnect the exhaust pipe at the exhaust manifold.

2. Remove the power steering pump and place it out of the way along the inner fender panel. Leave the hoses attached.

3. Lower the vehicle, scribe the hood hinge location and remove the hood.

4. Remove the air cleaner with the duct work attached. Disconnect and remove the air volume control.

5. Disconnect and remove the battery.

6. Disconnect all electrical wires and connectors. Mark the wires and connector for installation.

Removal and installation of four cylinder engines—typical

On the 530i, hoses are coded as follows: 2-blue, 3-black, 4-white, 5-white, 6-black. Also disconnect hose 8 at the blowoff valve and hose 9 at the fuel pressure governor

7. Disconnect all vacuum hoses, marking them for installation.

8. Drain the cooling system, disconnect the hoses and remove the radiator.

9. Disconnect the accelerator linkage.

10. Install a lifting sling on the engine.

11. Remove the left and right engine mount retaining nuts and washers.

12. Carefully lift the engine from the engine compartment.

13. Installation is the reverse of removal.

630i, 630CSi, 633 CSi

1. Raise and support the vehicle and remove the transmission. (See "Transmission Removal and Installation in Chapter 6.) Disconnect the exhaust pipe at the manifold.

2. Remove the power steering pump and place it out of the way. Leave the hoses attached.

3. If equipped with air conditioning, remove the compressor and place it aside. Do not remove the hoses.

4. Scribe the hood hinge locations and remove the hood.

5. Drain the cooling system, disconnect the hoses and remove the radiator.

6. Remove the air cleaner housing at the wheelhouse.

7. Remove the electrical wires and connectors from the engine components. Tag the wires and connectors.

NOTE: *The fuel injection control box is located either in the glove box or behind the right side kick panel. Remove the plug and thread the wire and connector through the hold in the firewall and into the engine compartment.*

On the 630CSi and 633CSi, hoses are coded as follows: 3-red from EGR valve and red capped electric valve; 4-blue from EGR valve/pressure converter; 5-red from throttle housing and red capped electric valve; 6-white from collector/distributor electric switching valve

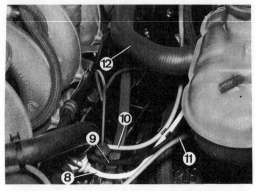

On the 630CSi and 633CSi, also disconnect the hoses shown, which are routed/coded as follows: 8-white from booster blowoff valve to white capped valve; 9-black from booster blowoff valve to blue capped valve; 10-blue from booster blowoff valve to blue capped valve; 11-red from pressure converter to EGR valve. Also detach overflow tank hose (12)

8. Install a lifting sling on the engine.

9. Remove the right and left engine mount retaining nuts and washers.

10. Remove the engine.

11. Installation is the reverse of removal.

733i

1. Raise and support the vehicle and remove the transmission. (See "Transmission Removal and Installation" in Chapter 6.) Disconnect the exhaust pipe at the exhaust manifold or thermal reactor.

2. Remove the clutch housing from the engine.

3. Remove the power steering pump and place it out of the way. Do not disconnect the hoses.

4. If equipped with air conditioning, remove the compressor and place it out of the way. Do not disconnect the hoses.

5. Remove the damper bracket from the crankcase and lower the vehicle.

6. Scribe the hood hinge locations and remove the hood.

7. Drain the cooling system, disconnect the hoses and remove the radiator.

8. Remove the windshield washer reservoir and the air filter housing located on the inner fender panel.

9. Remove the electrical wiring from the engine components. Tag all wires.

10. Disconnect and remove the battery.

11. Remove and tag all vacuum hoses.

NOTE: *Some vacuum hoses are color coded.*

12. Disconnect the throttle linkage.

Disconnect vacuum hoses (8-13) and fuel hoses (14 and 15) and pull out of harnesses

Engine Mounting Torque Chart

1600, 2002

Engine Mounting Bracket	34.0
Rubber Mounting Nuts	18.1
Gearbox Flange	18.1—M8
	34.0—M10

2800

Engine Support Bracket	34.0
Rubber Mounting Nuts	18—M8
	34—M10

3.0

Support Bracket	34.0
Rubber Mounting Nuts	18.4
Gearbox Flange	18.0

320i

Support Bracket	34.0
Rubber Mounting Nuts	18.4
Gearbox Flange	18.0

528i, 530i

Support Bracket	34
Rubber Mounting Nuts	31

630CSi

Engine Support Bracket	34
Rubber Mounting Nuts	31

633CSi, 733i

Engine Support Bracket	16—M8 (left side)
	31—M10 (right side)
Rubber Nuts on Front Axle	31
Gearbox Flange	18

13. Remove the right kick panel from the passenger compartment, remove the fuel injection control unit wire connector and thread the connector and wire through the hole in the firewall.

14. Attach a lifting sling to the engine. Remove the left and right engine mount retaining nuts and washers. Lift the engine from the engine compartment.

15. Installation is the reverse of removal.

Cylinder Head

REMOVAL AND INSTALLATION

1600-2, 2002, 320i

NOTE: *To prevent warpage, the engine must be cold (coolant temperature less than 96° F).*

1. Remove the air cleaner and disconnect the breather tube. On fuel injection engines, remove the intake manifold.

2. Disconnect the battery ground cable and drain the cooling system.

3. Remove the choke cable, if equipped.

4. Disconnect the throttle linkage. On the 2002A, disconnect the downshift linkage. On 1972–74 carbureted models equipped with the Solex 32/32 DIDTA carburetor, disconnect and mark all electrical leads. On the 2002Tii, disconnect the throttle butterfly linkage, and all electrical leads. Pull the torsion shaft towards the firewall until the ball is free of the torsion shaft.

5. Remove and tag the vacuum hoses. On 1970–72 models equipped with the emission control air pump, disconnect the vacuum hose with the non-return valve from its fitting on the intake manifold.

6. Disconnect the coolant hoses from the cylinder head. Disconnect intake manifold water hoses, if so equipped.

7. Disconnect the electrical wiring and connectors from the cylinder head and engine components.

8. On carbureted models, disconnect and plug the fuel line on the tank side of the fuel pump. On 1974 models, disconnect and plug the fuel reflow hose. On the 2002Tii, disconnect the fuel line at the injection pump.

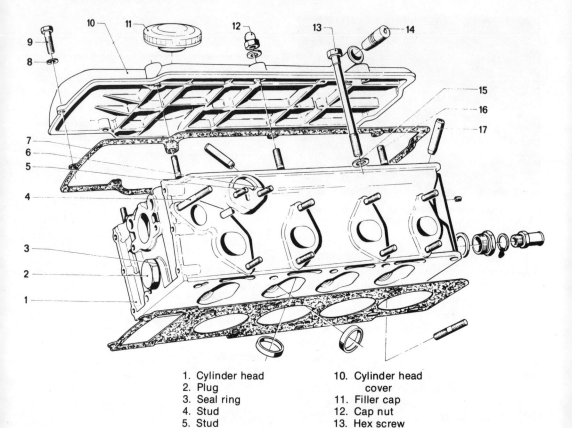

1. Cylinder head
2. Plug
3. Seal ring
4. Stud
5. Stud
6. Stud
7. Gasket
8. Lockwasher
9. Hex screw
10. Cylinder head cover
11. Filler cap
12. Cap nut
13. Hex screw
14. Jet
15. Washer
16. Stud
17. Valve guide

Exploded view of cylinder head components

9. Remove the cylinder head cover and the front upper timing case cover.

10. Rotate the engine until the distributor rotor points to the notch on the distributor body edge and the timing indicator points to the first notch on the belt pulley 320i, or second notch for the 2002, 2002A and 2002Ti models. No. 1 piston should now be at TDC on its firing stroke.

11. Remove the timing chain tensioner piston by removing the plug in the side of the block.

CAUTION: *The plug is under heavy spring tension.*

12. Open the lockplates, remove the retaining bolts and remove the timing chain sprocket from the camshaft.

NOTE: *The dowel pin hole on the camshaft flange should be in the 6 o'clock position while the notch at the top of the cam flange should be aligned with the cast projection on the cylinder head and in the 12*

Camshaft notch aligned with raised boss with the No. 1 cylinder at TDC

o'clock position for proper installation.

13. Remove the exhaust pipe from the exhaust manifold and remove the dipstick holder.

Cylinder head bolt tightening sequence—four cylinder engines

14. Unscrew the cylinder head bolts in the reverse of the tightening sequence and remove the cylinder head.

15. Installation is the reverse of removal but note the following points.

a. Tighten the cylinder head bolts in three stages, following the illustrated sequence. Adjust the valves, start the engine and bring to normal operating temperature. Stop the engine and allow it to cool to approximately 95° F (35° C). Retorque the cylinder head bolts to specifications and readjust the valves.

NOTE: *The cylinder head bolts should be retorqued after 600 miles (100 km) of driving.*

b. Check the projection of the cylinder head dowel sleeve in the cylinder block mating surface. Maximum height is 0.20 in.

c. Match the cylinder head gasket to the cylinder block and head to verify coolant flow passages are correct.

d. Adjust timing and idle speed.

e. Bleed the timing chain tensioner—see Step 20 of "Timing Chain Removal and Installation."

f. Bleed the cooling system. Set heater valve to the warm position and fill cooling system. Run the engine to normal temperature and when thermostat has opened, release the pressure cap to the first position. Squeeze the upper and lower radiator hoses in a pumping effect, to allow trapped air to escape through the radiator. Recheck coolant level and close the pressure cap to its second catch position.

2800, 3.0, 528i, 530i, 630CSi, 633CSi, 733i

1. Disconnect the battery ground cable. Drain the cooling system.

2. Disconnect/remove items for each model of car as described below:

2800

A. Disconnect throttle linkage rods running between carburetors. Disconnect water temperature sensor at the thermostat and the two electrically heated choke connectors.

B. Remove the power brake hose from the base of the front carburetor. Remove the dipstick support.

C. Disconnect heater hoses, water hoses to the intake manifold, and water heated choke hoses.

3.0

A. Disconnect and remove the air cleaner and hoses.

B. Remove the ignition high tension wire tube.

C. Disconnect the inductive switch and cable off the coil. Remove the distributor cap and disconnect the primary wire and vacuum line from the distributor.

D. Disconnect the two vacuum hoses at the rear of the intake manifold, and the two fuel lines at the fuel manifold.

E. Disconnect the water hoses for the heater at the firewall and disconnect the equalizing reservoir hose at the reservoir. Disconnect the oil pressure switch line at the plug.

530i, 630CSi, 633CSi

A. Disconnect and remove the air volume control assembly. Disconnect the ignition cable tube and wires and remove it, and disconnect the cam cover vent hose.

B. Mark locations and then disconnect the three coil connections.

C. Disconnect all 6 injection valve plugs, and the plug at the throttle switch. Disconnect the throttle linkage rod at the top and bottom.

D. Disconnect the vacuum hose from the throttle housing and disconnect the temperature sensor wire at the front of the head.

E. Disconnect the water hose at the throttle housing and the oil pressure switch wire.

F. Disconnect water hoses at the thermostat housing. Disconnect the hose going to the charcoal filter. Disconnect the fuel feed line at the filter.

G. On 530i only, remove the connector from between Nos. 2 and 3 cylinder intake tubes.

H. Disconnect the four vacuum sensing hoses from the EGR valve and collector/vacuum valve, noting color coding and locations. Disconnect the brake booster vacuum hose at the manifold.

I. Disconnect heater hoses at the firewall, noting locations. Disconnect the two air hoses at the auxiliary air valve; disconnect the two electrical connectors at the auxiliary air valve. Then, remove the auxiliary air valve wiring harness through the opening in the intake manifold.

J. Disconnect and remove the EGR filter.

733i

A. Disconnect and remove the air volume control assembly. Disconnect the ignition cable tube and wires and remove it, and disconnect the cam cover vent hose.

B. Mark locations and then remove the three coil connections. Remove the EGR filter.

C. Disconnect all 6 injection valve plugs, and the plug at the throttle switch. Detach the ground wire at the collector brace. Disconnect the throttle linkage rod at top and bottom. Pull off vacuum hoses from the throttle housing and EGR line.

D. Disconnect the water hose at the throttle housing, and loosen the clamp located on the collector mounting bracket. Disconnect the oil pressure switch.

E. Detach the hot water hose at the valve located above the rear of the engine on the firewall.

F. Pull the wires off the temperature transmitter and disconnect both water hoses at the thermostat housing. Detach the TDC position transmitter plug.

G. Mark or note locations, and then pull vacuum signal hoses off the heater valve, EGR valve electrical switch, the EGR valve pressure converter, and the collector/adapter pressure converter. Pull the electrical plug off the EGR valve pressure converter.

H. Remove the bracket connecting Nos. 2 and 3 intake pipes. Disconnect the accelerator cable and remove the holder from the collector, on automatic transmission equipped cars.

I. Detach the water hoses for the heater at the cylinder head.

J. Pull the wire connectors off the temperature switch, noting their locations. Lift the harness out of the holders and then pull it up through the intake neck.

3. Remove the cam cover.

NOTE: *Do not interchange the heater hoses.*

4. Rotate the engine so that the distributor rotor points to the notch on the distributor body edge and the timing indicator points to the notch on the belt pulley. This will place number one piston at TDC on its firing stroke.

5. Remove the upper timing housing cover after removing the distributor and thermostat housing.

6. Remove the timing chain tensioner piston.

CAUTION: *The retaining plug is under heavy spring tension.*

7. Open the camshaft sprocket bolt lockplates and remove the bolts. Remove the sprocket.

NOTE: *For installation purposes, the sprocket dowel pin should be located at the lower left, between 7 and 8 o'clock, while the upper bolt bore must align with the threaded bore of the camshaft and the cylinder head cast tab, visable through the two bores, when at the 12 o'clock position.*

8. Remove the exhaust system completely (630i), disconnect the exhaust line at the exhaust manifold, or disconnect the exhaust manifolds at the thermal reactor (733). Remove the exhaust filter.

9. Remove the cylinder head bolts in the reverse order of the tightening sequence and install locating pins in four head bolt bores to prevent the rocker shafts from turning.

10. Remove the cylinder head.

11. Installation is the reverse of removal. Note the following points.

Cylinder head torque sequence—2800, 3.0 and all 500 and 600 series cars

Cylinder head torque sequence—733i

a. Tighten the cylinder head bolts in three stages, following the illustrated sequence. Make sure bolt holes are free of oil. Adjust the valves, start the engine and bring it to normal operating temperature. Stop the engine and allow it to cool to approximately 95° F (35° C). Retorque the cylinder head bolts to specifications and readjust the valves.

NOTE: *The cylinder head bolts should be retorqued after 600 miles (1000 km) of driving.*

b. Check the projection of the cylinder head dowel sleeve in the cylinder block mating surface. Maximum height is 0.20 in. (5.0 mm).

c. Match the cylinder head gasket to the cylinder block and head to verify that the coolant flow passages are correct.

d. Run a straightedge along the head diagonally to check for warpage. Have the head, and the top of the timing cover, machined, as necessary. The head may be machined as much as .0197″ on 1600, 2002, 2800, and 3.0 models, and as much as .012″ on 320, 528, 530, 630, 633, and 733 models.

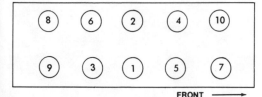

Four cylinder head torque sequence

Six cylinder head torque sequence

e. Apply sealer to the joint between the block and upper timing cover.

f. Bleed the timing chain tensioner—see Step 20 of "Timing Chain Removal and Installation."

9. Adjust the timing and idle speeds.

h. When refilling the cooling system, bleed it carefully (see Chapter 1).

Valve Guide and Seat Removal and Installation

The valve guides are shrunk-fit into the cylinder head. Therefore, this procedure is best left to a qualified automotive machine shop. The procedure is included here for reference purposes.

1. Remove the cylinder head.

2. Using a suitable valve spring compressor, compress the spring and remove the split keepers. Remove the spring and check it against specifications.

3. Check the valve stem-to-valve guide clearance by holding the valve about ⅛ in. from the valve seat and rocking it sideways.

Valve guide removal

Valve guide installation (A = .0197 in.)

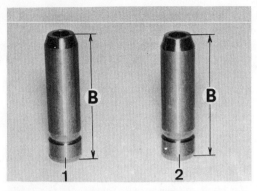

Valve guide 2 is 1.5 mm shorter than valve guide 1, but may be installed in engines originally equipped with the earlier type guide

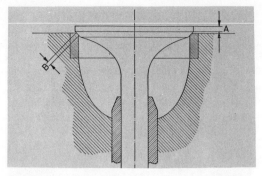

Machining valve guides. A = valve margin; B = valve seat angle

Movement of the valve head across the seat must not exceed the figure shown in the specifications.

4. If the clearance is excessive, the guide must be driven out (into the combustion chamber) with a drift of the proper diameter and replaced.

5. To install a new valve guide, the cylinder head must be heated to 450° F so the new guide can be pressed in without excessive pressure. The guide is then pressed in until it protrudes .571–.611 in. On the 3.3 litre engine, a new type of shorter guide is available, which is pressed in .511–.551 in. BMW special tool 11 1 20 incorporates a recess which provides the proper protrusion. With the shorter guide, a washer is used to create the proper dimension. After installation, the guide must be reamed out to the proper dimension.

The valve seats can be replaced in case machining will not restore proper dimensions. The head must be heated to 450 degrees F and the seats chilled to −94 degrees F to install them.

OVERHAUL

The cylinder head is generally overhauled in a conventional manner—see the Engine Overhaul section following this chapter. Note that, since the head is of aluminum, it must not be hot tanked.

Two points of importance are valve seat angles and valve margin. Note that valve seat angles must conform to the angles quoted in specifications. The seat machined surfaces must be free of any scars or marks. If the valves cannot be brought to the proper angle completely cleaned up without reducing the margin below limits specified below, they must be replaced. Margins are: Four cylinder engines—.039 in. intake; .059 in. exhaust. Six cylinder engines—.047 in. intake; .075 in. exhaust.

Rocker Shafts

REMOVAL AND INSTALLATION

1. Remove the cylinder head. See the "Cylinder Head Removal and Installation" procedure above.

2. Remove the camshaft. See the "Camshaft Removal and Installation" procedure below.

3. Slide the thrust rings and rocker arms rearward and remove the circlips from the rocker arm shafts.

4. On 4-cylinder engines:

a. Remove the distributor flange from the rear of the cylinder head.

b. Using a long punch, drive the rocker arm shaft from the rear to the front of the cylinder head.

NOTE: *Be sure all circlips are off the shaft before attempting to drive the shaft from the cylinder head.*

Removing distributor flange—2002

"E" is exhaust side, "A" intake. Order of assembly is: spring (3); washer (4), rocker arm (5), and thrust ring (6)

Align the rocker shafts so the head bolts will slide through the indentations in the rocker shafts

c. The intake rocker shaft is not plugged at the rear, while the exhaust rocker shaft must be plugged. Renew the plug if necessary, during the installation.

5. On 6-cylinder engines:

a. Unscrew the rocker shaft locking bolts from the cylinder head.

b. Install a threaded slide hammer into the ends of the front rocker shafts and remove the shafts from the cylinder head. NOTE: *Be sure all circlips have been removed from the rocker shafts before removal.*

c. Remove the end cover from the rear of the cylinder head.

6. The rocker arms, springs, washers, thrust rings and shafts should be examined and worn parts replaced. Special attention should be given to the rocker arm cam followers. If these are loose, replace the arm assembly.

The valves can be removed, repaired or replaced, as necessary, while the shafts and rocker arms are out of the cylinder head.

7. Installation is the reverse of removal. Note the following procedures.

a. Design changes of the rocker arms and shafts have occurred with the installation of a bushing in the rocker arm and the use of two horizontal oil flow holes drilled in the rocker shaft for improved oil supply. Do not mix the previously designed parts with the later designed parts.

b. When installing the rocker arms and components to the rocker shafts, install locating pins in the cylinder head bolt bores to properly align the rocker arm shafts.

c. Install sealer on the rocker arm shaft locking bolts and rear cover.

d. On the 4-cylinder engines, position the rocker shafts so that the camshaft retaining plate ends can be engaged in the slots of shafts during camshaft installation.

e. Adjust the valve clearance.

Intake Manifold

REMOVAL AND INSTALLATION

1600, 2002, 2002A, 2002Ti

1. Remove the air cleaner.

2. Remove and tag the fuel lines, vacuum lines and electrical wiring.

3. Drain the cooling system.

4. Disconnect the manual choke control cable. On the 2002A, disconnect the wire connector to the choke cover.

5. Disconnect the accelerator linkage. On 2002A, disconnect the linkage at the ball socket.

6. Disconnect the coolant lines to the manifold.

7. Disconnect the dipstick support.

8. Remove the intake manifold.

Removing intake manifold—carbureted models

9. Installation is the reverse of removal. Use new gaskets.

NOTE: *The 2 front or rear intake tubes can be removed and installed on the 2002Ti engine (four carburetors), by separating the connecting rod between the middle carburetors and removing the front or rear section as desired by using the above procedure as a guide.*

2800, 3.0

FRONT INTAKE MANIFOLD

1. Drain the cooling system.
2. Remove the air filter.
3. Disconnect and tag all fuel and vacuum lines.
4. Disconnect the throttle linkage bar and connecting bar and remove the bearing block.
5. Disconnect the manual choke cable.
6. Remove the coolant hoses to the manifold or carburetor.
7. Remove the dipstick support.
8. Remove the intake manifold with the crburetor attached.
9. Installation is the reverse of the removal. Use new gaskets.

REAR INTAKE MANIFOLD

1. Drain the cooling system.
2. Disconnect the battery ground cable.
3. Remove the air filter.
4. Disconnect and tag all fuel and vacuum lines.
5. Disconnect the accelerator thrust bar and bearing block.
6. Disconnect the electrical wire from the choke cover. Remove the choke cover with the coolant lines attached.
7. Disconnect the heater hoses from the manifold base.
8. Remove the intake manifold with the carburetor attached.
9. Installation is the reverse of the removal. Use new gaskets.

2002Tii

NOTE: *To remove the complete manifold system, first remove the resonater pipes or manifolds; then remove the intake pipe.*

INDUCTION RESONATOR PIPES (SECURED WITH CLAMPS)

1. Remove the air filter.
2. Remove and tag the fuel lines, starter valve cable, vacuum hoses and all induction resonator pipes.

3. Disconnect the throttle return spring and remove the injection pipe from No. one cylinder. Remove the injector valve.
4. Remove the bracket bolts at the throttle housing.
5. Remove the vacuum hose, auxiliary air hose and injection pipe from No. four cylinder.
6. Remove the air collector from the cylnder head.
7. Installation is the reverse of removal.

INDUCTION MANIFOLDS (SECURED WITH NUTS AND WASHERS)

1. Remove the air filter.
2. Remove the fuel line, fuel return line starter valve cable and vacuum hose from the air tube assembly.
3. Remove the bracket bolts on the throttle housing.
4. Remove the air collector support bolts at the top engine cover area.
5. Remove the nuts and washers from the bottom of the induction manifolds.
6. Remove the air collector together with the induction manifolds and the throttle housing.
7. Installation is the reverse of removal.

INTAKE PIPE

1. After removing the air collector, induction resonator pipes or the induction manifolds as outlined preceding, remove all of the remaining injection pipes from the injection valves.
2. Disconnect the coolant hoses and electrical connections at the thermostat housing switches.
3. Remove the retaining nuts and washers from the cylinder head studs and remove the intake pipe. The injector valves can be removed before or after the removal.
4. Installation is the reverse of removal. Use new gaskets and place them on the intake opening properly so as not to interfere with the air flow.

3.0 CSi

NOTE: *Combine the next 2 operations to remove both front and rear intake manifolds.*

FRONT INTAKE MANIFOLD

1. Remove the air cleaner.
2. Drain the cooling system.
3. Remove the inake air collector and the 3 front intake pipes.

4. Remove the pressure regulator and support from the intake manifold.

5. Disconnect the coolant hoses from the thermostat housing and the wiring from the coolant switches.

6. Remove the flat plugs from the injection valves by carefully pulling upward.

7. Remove the first three injection valves from the manifold.

NOTE: *Leave the circular pipe connected.*

8. Remove the retaining bolts from the intake manifold and remove it from the cylinder head.

9. Installation is the reverse of removal. Use new injection valve sealing rings.

REAR INTAKE MANIFOLD

1. Disconnect the battery ground cable.

2. Remove the air cleaner.

3. Remove the intake air collector and the 3 rear intake pipes.

4. Remove the pressure regulator and support from the intake manifold.

5. Remove the flat plugs from the injection valves by carefully pulling upwards.

6. Remove the three rear injector valves.

NOTE: *Leave the circular pipe connected.*

7. Remove and tag the electrical flat plugs and connectors from the end of the wire loom, routed through the intake manifold.

8. Carefully pull the wire loom upward through the hole in the intake manifold.

9. Remove the intake manifold from the cylinder head.

10. Installation is the reverse of removal. Always renew the injection valve sealing rings.

Pull off plugs 1, 2, and 3 and unplug or disconnect starter connections 4, 5, and 6. Note that the red cable goes to terminal 50, while the black cable goes to terminal 30

320i

1. Remove the air cleaner and drain the cooling system.

2. Disconnect the accelerator cable and remove the vacuum hoses from the air collector. Tag the hoses.

3. Remove the injection line holder from No. 4 intake tube.

4. Remove the No. 3 intake tube and disconnect the vacuum and coolant lines from the throttle housing.

5. Disconnect the hoses at the EGR valve and remove the wire plugs at the temperature timing switch.

6. Remove the cold start valve from the air collector.

7. Disconnect the vacuum hose and electrical connections at the timing valve.

8. Disconnect the remaining intake tubes at the collector. Disconnect the collector brackets at the engine and remove the collector.

9. Remove the air intake tubes from the manifold and remove the injector valves.

10. Remove the intake manifold.

11. Installation is the reverse of removal.

528i, 530i, 630i, 633i, 733i

NOTE: *Slight variations may exist among models due to model changes and updating but basic removal and installation remains the same.*

1. Disconnect the battery ground cable and drain the cooling system.

2. Disconnect the wire harness at the air flow sensor. Remove the air cleaner and sensor as an assembly.

3. Remove and tag the vacuum hoses and electrical plugs. Disconnect the accelerator linkage from the throttle housing.

4. Disconnect the coolant hoses from the throttle housing.

5. Working from the rear of the collector housing, disconnect the vacuum lines, and starting valve connector, fuel line and air line. Tag the hoses and lines for ease of assembly.

6. Remove the EGR valve and line.

7. Remove all intake pipes.

8. Remove the air collector housing from the engine.

9. Disconnect the plugs at the injector valves and remove the valves.

10. Disconnect the wire plugs at the coolant temperature sensor, the temperature time switch and the temperature switch.

11. Pull the wire loom upward through the opening in the intake manifold neck.

12. Remove the coolant hoses from the intake neck.

13. Remove the retaining bolts or nuts and remove either front, rear or both intake manifold necks.

14. Installation of the manifolds is the reverse of removal. Use new gaskets on the manifolds and air intake tubes.

Exhaust Manifold
REMOVAL AND INSTALLATION
2002 Series

1. Loosen the exhaust system supports.

2. Separate the exhaust pipe from the exhaust manifold and remove the hot air guide sleeve.

3. Remove the retaining nuts and washers from the exhaust manifold studs and remove the manifold from the cylinder head.

4. Installation is the reverse of removal. Tighten the clamps holding the exhaust pipes last to avoid having an exhaust system vibration during operation.

2800, 3.0 Series, 528i

NOTE: *Each exhaust manifold can be removed separately after the exhaust pipes are disconnected.*

1. Remove the air cleaner and manifold cover plate.

2. On automatic transmission equipped vehicles, detach the oil filler pipe at the rear of the cover plate.

3. On the 528i, disconnect the CO tap connector at the exhaust manifold. Disconnect the exhaust pipe from the manifold sections.

4. Remove the retaining nuts and wahers and remove the exhaust manifolds from the cylinder head.

5. Installation is the reverse of removal.

320i, 530i, 630i, 633i and 733i

The exhaust manifolds are referred to as exhaust gas recirculation reactors.

The removal and installation procedures are basically the same for all models. The four cylinder manifold (used on the 320i model), is a one piece, one outlet unit, while the six cylinder manifold assembly consist of a two piece, double outlet to the exhaust pipe. One piece can be replaced independently of the other.

1. Remove the air volume control and if necessary, air cleaner.

2. Disconnect the exhaust pipe at the reactor outlet(s).

3. Remove the guard plate from the reactor(s).

4. Disconnect the air injection pipe fitting, the EGR counterpressure line, EGR pressure line and any supports.

NOTE: *An exhaust filter is used between the reactor and the EGR valve and must be disconnected. Replace the filter if found to be defective.*

5. Remove the retaining bolts or nuts at the reactor and remove it from the cylnder head.

6. Installation is the reverse of removal. Use new gaskets.

Timing Gear Cover
REMOVAL AND INSTALLATION
2002 Series, 320i

There are two timing chain covers, one upper and one lower, which must be removed to service the timing chain and sprocket assemblies.

1. Remove the cam cover. Disconnect the negative battery cable. On 320i models, disconnect the air injection line at the front of the thermal reactor.

2. Remove the 8 bolts which retain the upper timing gear cover to the cylinder head and lower timing gear cover. Remove the upper cover, taking note of the placement of the alternator ground wire.

3. Drain the cooling system and remove the radiator, preheater intake air assembly (carburetor equipped cars only) and radiator hoses as outlined under "Radiator Removal and Insallation."

4. Bend back the lockplates for the fan retaining bolts. Remove the bolts and lift off the fan.

5. Loosen the alternator retaining bolts. Push the alternator toward the engine and remove the fan pulley and the altrnator drive (fan) belt. On the 320i, remove the four mounting bolts from the air pump bracket (where it attaches to the block), and remove the pump and bracket; then remove the bolt attaching the tensioning bar to the block and remove the tensioning bar.

6. Disconnect the coolant hoses from the water pump. Remove the six retaining bolts and copper sealing washers and lift off the water pump.

7. Unscrew the plug and remove the spring from the cam chain tensioner assembly, taking care to cushion the sudden release of spring tension. Remove the plunger (piston).

8. Disconnect the multiple plug and cable lead from the alternator. Remove the alternator with its bearing block and clamping strap.

9. Remove the flywheel inspection plate and block the ring gear from turning with a screwdriver.

10. Unscrew the crankshaft pulley nut and pull off the belt pulley.

11. Remove the bolts which retain the lower cover to the cylinder block and oil pan. With a sharp knife, carefully separate the lower edge of the timing cover from the upper edge of the oil pan gasket at the front.

12. Remove the lower timing cover. At this time, it is advisable to replace the timing cover seal (sealing ring) with a new one. The sealing ring is a press fit into the cover.

13. Clean the mating surfaces of the timing covers, oil pan, cylinder head, and cylinder block. Replace all gaskets (except the oil pan gasket), and seal them at the corners with sealing compound such as Permatex® No. 2.

Separating pan gasket from lower timing chain cover with knife

Sealing compound application areas

Sealing compound application areas

Tightening sequence for upper timing chain cover bolts

14. Reverse the above procedure to install, taking care to tighten the upper timing gear cover retaining bolts in the following sequence (as per the illustration): hand-tighten 1 and 2, then torque 3–8 in numerical order, and finally 1 and 2 to 6.5–7.9 ft lbs.

Timing Chain Cover

REMOVAL AND INSTALLATION

Six Cylinder Engines

NOTE: *On 630, 633, and 733 Series engines, this requires use of a special gauge, to be made to a certain dimension, as in Step 16.*

1. Remove the cam cover. Remove the distributor as described earlier in this chapter. On 530i, 630i, and all 3.3 litre models, detach the distributor guard and the air line going to the thermal reactor.

2. Drain the coolant to below the level of the thermostat and remove the thermostat housing cover.

3. Remove the eight bolts and remove the upper timing case cover with the worm drive which drives the distributor.

4. Remove the piston which tensions the

timing chain, *working carefully because of very high spring pressure.*

5. Remove the cooling fan and all drive belts.

6. Remove the flywheel housing cover and lock the flywheel in position with an appropriate special tool.

7. Unscrew the nut from the center of the pulley and pull the pulley/vibration damper off the crankshaft.

8. Detach the TDC position transmitter on 733, 633 and 630 models.

9. Loosen all the oil pan bolts, and then unscrew all the bolts from the lower timing case cover. Use a knife to separate the gasket at the base of the lower timing cover. Then, remove the cover.

10. To install the lower cover, first coat the surfaces of the oil pan and block with sealer. Put it into position on the block, making sure the tensioning piston holding web (cast into the block) is in the oil pocket. Install all bolts; then tighten lower front cover bolts evenly; finally, tighten the oil pan bolts evenly.

11. Inspect the hub of the vibration damper. If the hub is scored, install the radial seal so the sealing lip is in front of or to the rear of the scored area. Pack the seal with grease and install it with a seal installer.

12. Install the pulley/damper and torque the bolt to specifications. When installing, make sure the key and keyway are properly aligned.

13. Remove the flywheel locking tool and reinstall the cover. Reinstall and tension all belts.

14. Before installing the upper cover, use sealer to seal the joint between the back of the lower timing cover and block at the top. On 630, 633, and 733 models, there are

Fill the wells (circled) with sealer on 630CSi, 633CSi, and 733i

sealer wells which are to be filled with sealer. Check the cork seal at the distributor drive coupling, and replace it if necessary.

15. See the illustration for four cylinder engines above, and tighten bolts 1 and 2 (the lower bolts) slightly. Then, tighten bolts 3–8. Finally, fully tighten lower bolts.

16. On 630, 633, and 733 models, install the TDC position transmitter loosely. With the engine at exactly 0 degrees Top Center, as shown by the marker on the front cover, adjust the position of the transmitter with a gauge which should be made to conform to the dimensions shown in the illustration: i.e. it must fit the curve on the outside of the balancer, and incorporate a notch (for the pin on the balancer) and a ridge against which the transmitter must rest. The straight line distance between the center of the notch and bottom of the ridge must be exactly 37.5 mm. Then, tighten the transmitter mounting screw.

17. Reverse the remaining removal procedures, making sure to bleed the cooling system on six cylinder engines.

Checking alternator drive belt tension

TDC transmitter gauge. A = .197 in., B = 1.398 in., and C = .197 in. Position the gauge on the contact pin (5). Position the transmitter holder (4) on the gauge and tighten

7051

Removing cover seal with claw—type puller

TIMING GEAR COVER OIL SEAL REPLACEMENT

1. Position the engine with the No. 1 cylinder at TDC. Then, remove the flywheel housing cover and install a locking tool. Remove the bolt from the front pulley.

2. Remove all belts. With a puller, pull off the vibration damper. Remove the seal with a three prong puller.

3. Pack the new seal with grease and press it in with a special tool which works on the threads on the crankshaft. If the hub is scored, make sure the lip of the seal is in front of or behind the scored groove.

4. When installing the hub, make sure key and keyway are properly aligned. Torque the bolt to the proper value as shown in specifications.

Timing Chain and Tensioner
REMOVAL AND INSTALLATION

1. Rotate the crankshaft to set No. 1 piston at TDC, at the beginning of its compression stroke.

2. Remove the distributor (6-cylinder engines only).

3. Remove the cylinder head cover, air injection pipe and guard plate.

4. Drain the cooling system and remove the thermostat housing.

5. Remove the upper timing housing cover. See the "Timing Chain Cover Removal and Installation" procedure above.

6. Remove the timing chain tensioner piston.

NOTE: *The piston is under heavy spring tension.*

7. Remove the drive belts and fan.

8. Remove the flywheel guard and lock the flywheel with a locking tool.

9. Remove the vibration damper assembly.

NOTE: *The crankshaft woodruff key should be in the 12 o'clock position.*

10. Remove the lower timing housing cover screws and the front oil pan screws. Loosen the remaining oil pan screws.

11. Loosen the oil pan-to-timing housing cover gasket with a thin bladed tool and remove the timing housing cover.

12. Open the camshaft lockplates, remove the bolts and remove the camshaft sprocket.

13. On 4-cylinder engines:

a. Remove the bottom circlip holding the chain guide rail to the block. Loosen the upper pivot pin until the guide rail rests against the forward part of the cylinder head gasket.

b. Remove the timing chain from the sprockets and remove the guide rail by pulling downward and swinging the rail to the right.

c. Remove the chain from the guide rail and remove it from the engine.

14. On 6-cylinder engines:
Remove the chain from the lower sprocket, swing the chain to the right front and out of the guide rail and remove the chain from the engine.

15. Installation is the reverse of removal, but note the following:

16. Be sure that No. 1 piston remains at the top of its firing stroke and the key on the crankshaft is in the 12 o'clock position.

17. On 4-cylinder engines:

a. Position camshaft flange so that the dowel pin bore is located at the 6 o'clock position and the notch in the top of the flange aligns with the cast tab on the cylinder head.

b. Position the chain in the chain guide rail and move the rail upward and to the left, engaging the lower locating pivot pin and threading the upper pivot pin into the block. Install the circlip on the lower guide pin.

c. Engage the chain on the crankshaft sprocket and fit the camshaft sprocket into the chain.

d. Align the gear dowel pin to the camshaft flange and bolt the sprocket into place. Use new lockplates and secure the bolt heads.

18. On 6-cylinder engines:

a. Position the camshaft flange so that

Position the camshaft flange so the dowel pin is located as shown and the bore in the sprocket aligns with the threaded bore in the cast tab

Location of upper (4) and lower (3) guide rail retainers

the dowel pin bore is between the 7 and 8 o'clock position and the upper flange bolt hole is aligned with the cast tab on the cylinder head.

b. Position the chain on the guide rail and swing the chain inward and to the left.

c. Engage the chain on the crankshaft gear and install the camshaft sprocket into the chain.

d. Align the gear dowel pin to the camshaft flange and bolt the sprocket into place.

19. Install the chain tensioner piston, spring and cap plug, but do not tighten.

20. To bleed the chain tensioner, fill the oil pocket, located on the upper timing housing cover, with engine oil and move the tensioner back and forth with a screwdriver until oil is expelled at the cap plug. Tighten the cap plug securely.

21. Complete the assembly in the reverse order of removal. Check the ignition timing and the idle speed. Be sure the flywheel holder is removed before any attempt is made to start the engine.

Installation of the timing cover housing showing special sealing locations

Timing Chain Sprocket
REMOVAL AND INSTALLATION

1. Remove the timing chain as described above. Remove the oil pan as described below.

2. Remove the three oil pump drive sprocket mounting bolts. Then, remove the sprocket and oil pump drive chain. Remove the woodruff key from the crankshaft.

3. Pull the sprocket off the crankshaft with a puller.

4. Reverse the removal procedure to install. On six cylinder engines, when the oil pump chain is installed, check play in the oil pump drive chain and, if necessary remove the oil pump and change the thickness of the shims, as described in "Oil Pump Removal and Installation" below.

Camshaft
REMOVAL AND INSTALLATION

1. Remove the oil line from the top of the cylinder head.

NOTE: *Observe the location of the seals when removing the hollow oil line studs. Reinstall the seals in the same position.*

2. Remove the cylinder head.

3. Adjust the valve clearance to the maximum clearance on all rocker arms.

4. Remove the fuel pump and pushrod on carbureted engines.

5. On 4-cylinder engines:

Special tools (6025-1 for carbureted engines or 6025-2 for fuel injected engines) or their equivalent, are used to hold the rocker arms away from the camshaft lobes.

NOTE: *The tool 6025-2 or its equivalent, must be used on fuel injection engines to avoid distorting the valve heads.*

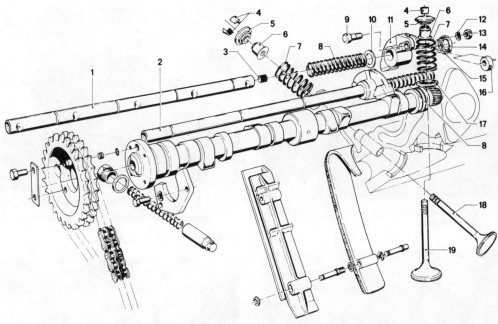

1. Rocker arm shaft, intake
2. Rocker arm shaft, exhaust
3. Plug
4. Valve cone piece
5. Upper spring plate
6. Valve seal ring
7. Valve spring
8. Spring
9. Adjusting screw
10. Washer
11. Rocker arm with bushing
12. Lockwasher
13. Hex nut
14. Snap ring
15. Washer
16. Cam
17. Lower spring plate
18. Exhaust valve
19. Intake valve

Exploded view of camshaft and valve assembly components

On 6-cylinder engines:

A special tool (11-2-060) or its equivalent, is used to hold the rocker arms away from the camshaft lobes. When installing the tool, move the intake rocker arms of No. 2 and 4 cylinders, forward approximately ¼ in. and tighten the intake side nuts to avoid contact between the valve heads. Also, in order to prevent contact between valve discs, first tighten the nuts on the exhaust side to the stop, and then tighten the intake side nuts. Reverse the sequence in removing the tool.

6. Remove the camshaft.

On 4-cylinder engines:

a. Remove the guide plate retaining bolts and move the plate downward and out of the slots on the rocker arm shafts.

b. Carefully remove the camshaft from the cylinder head.

On 6-cylinder engines:

Cylinder head installation on holding fixture No. 6025-1

Removing mechanical fuel pump pushrod

Clamping plate installed on cylinder head to off-load rocker arms

Removing camshaft guide plate

Checking camshaft axial play

Camshaft designation location—four cylinder

a. Rotate the camshaft so that the two cutout areas of the camshaft flange are horizontal and remove the retaining plate bolts.

b. Carefully remove the camshaft from the cylinder head.

c. The flange and guide plate can be removed from the camshaft by removing the lockplate and nut from the camshaft end.

7. Install the camshaft and associated components in the reverse order of removal, but observe the following:

a. After installing the camshaft guide plate, the camshaft should turn easily, or the guide plate is scored or has been installed incorrectly. Check the camshaft end play, and replace the guide plate, if necessary.

b. On four cylinder engines, the bore for the dowel pin in the camshaft flange must face downward, and the notch must align with the tab cast into the cylinder head.

c. On six cylinder engines, the

threaded bore in the flange must align with the tab cast into the head, before installing timing chain. Also, before removing the special tool, make sure cylinder No. 6 is at valve overlap position.

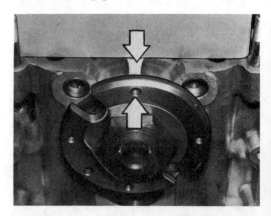

The threaded bore in the camshaft flange must align with the projection cast into the front of the block-six cylinder engines

d. Install the oil tube hollow stud washer seals properly, one above and one below the oil pipe.

e. Adjust the valve clearances.

Pistons and Connecting Rods

REMOVAL AND INSTALLATION

Pistons are removed with the engine out of the car through the top of the block. Remove the engine, remove the cylinder head, and remove the oil pan and oil pump (see appropriate procedures above and below in this chapter). Using a ridge reamer, remove the ridge from the cylinder or cylinders from which pistons are to be removed—see the Engine Rebuilding section which follows this chapter. Remove each piston/rod assembly with the crankshaft in Bottom Center position.

Note all of the following points in reassembly:

1. Connecting rods/caps must be reinstalled in the same cylinder and are so marked. Make sure markings on rod and cap are on the same side when reassembling.

The arrow on top of the piston must face forward and the oil hole in the connecting rod must face the same direction as the arrow on top. See the text for explanation of weight class ("+" or "−" markings)

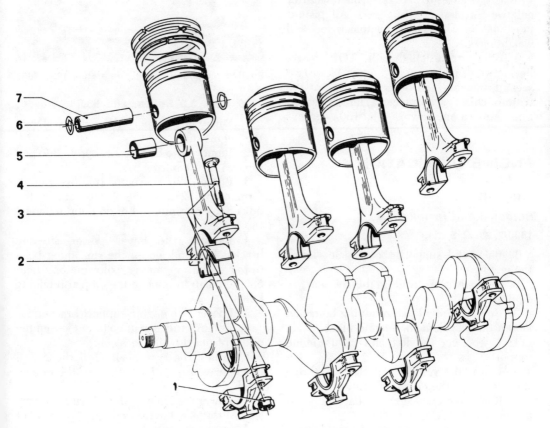

1. Hex nut
2. Bearing shell
3. Connecting rod
4. Connecting rod bolt
5. Connecting rod bushing
6. Circlip
7. Piston pin

Exploded view of piston and connecting rod assemblies—four cylinder engines

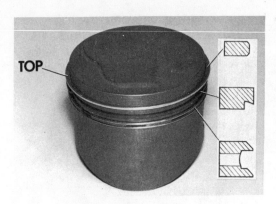

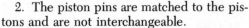

The rings are installed in positions shown. See the text

Sealing compound application areas—1600, 2002

Sealing compound application areas—1600, 2002

2. The piston pins are matched to the pistons and are not interchangeable.

3. The arrow on top of the piston must face forward (toward the timing chain). The oil hole in the connecting rod faces the same direction as the arrow on top of the piston. Pistons are also marked as to manufacturer and weight class "+" or "−"). All pistons must be of the same manufacturer and weight class.

4. Rings are installed with "TOP" markings upward, plain ring at the top, taper face second, and beveled oil control ring at the bottom. Offset each ring gap as far as possible from the next one down, i.e. at 180 degrees.

ENGINE LUBRICATION

Oil Pan

Removal and Installation

1600-2, 2002 Series

1. Raise and support the vehicle. Drain the engine oil.

2. Remove the front stabilizer bar, if equipped.

3. Remove the oil pan retaining bolts and loosen the pan from the engine block.

4. Disconnect the left and right engine supports.

5. Lower the vehicle and attach a lifting sling and raise the engine slightly.

6. Rotate the crankshaft so that the No. 4 piston is at TDC.

7. Remove the oil pan toward the front.

8. Reverse the procedure to install the oil pan, using a new gasket. Put sealer on the joints formed where the end cover and timing cover butt up against the block.

2800, 528i, 3.0 Series, and 530i

1. Raise and support the vehicle. Drain the engine oil.

2. Remove the front lower apron (3.0) and remove the stabilizer bar.

3. Loosen the alternator (remove the alternator on 528i and 530i) and remove the power steering pump, but do not disconnect the hoses.

4. Remove the lower power steering bracket bolt and loosen the remaining bolts (remove the remaining bolts on 528i and 530i) enough to remove the oil pan retaining bolts.

5. Loosen the engine support bracket.

6. Remove the oil pan bolts and loosen the oil pan from the engine block.

7. Rotate the crankshaft until the No. 6 crankpin is above the bottom of the engine block.

8. Lower the front of the oil pan, turn the rear of the pan towards the support bracket and remove the pan.

9. Reverse the procedure to install the oil pan, using new gaskets. Put the sealer on the joints formed where the end cover and timing cover butt up against the block.

320i

1. Raise and support the vehicle. Drain the engine oil.

2. Loosen the steering gear bolts and pull the steering box off the front axle carrier.

3. Remove the oil pan bolts and separate the pan from the engine block.

4. Swing the oil pan downward while rotating the crankshaft to allow the pan to clear the crankpin and remove the pan toward the front.

5. Reverse the procedure to install the oil pan, using new gaskets. Put sealer on the joints formed where the end cover and timing cover butt up against the block.

630 and 633 Series

1. Raise and support the vehicle. Drain the engine oil.

2. Remove the front stabilizer bar.

3. Disconnect the wire terminal at the oil level switch.

4. Disconnect the power steering pump, but do not disconnect the hoses. Loosen all the power steering bracket bolts, and remove the bottom bolt.

5. Remove the engine oil pan bolts, separate the oil pan from the engine block and lower the front of the pan.

6. Rotate the crankshaft until the No. 6 crankpin is above the bottom of the engine block.

7. Lift the engine slightly at the clutch housing while removing the pan to the right side.

8. Reverse the procedure to install the oil pan, using new gaskets. Put sealer on the joints where the end cover and timing cover butt up against the block.

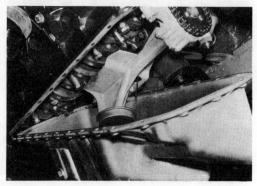

On 600 series cars, rotate the crankshaft until No. 6 connecting rod is above the crankcase sealing surface for clearance at the rear

733i

1. Raise and support the vehicle. Drain the engine oil.

2. Remove the power steering pump, but do not disconnect the hoses.

3. Remove the lower power steering bracket bolt. Loosen the upper bracket bolts in order to move the bracket away from the oil pan.

4. Disconnect the oil level switch wire terminal.

5. Remove the oil pan bolts and separate the oil pan from the engine block.

6. Disconnect the left and right engine mounts.

7. Remove the engine vibration damper.

8. Lower the vehicle and remove the fan housing from the radiator.

9. Attach a lifting sling and raise the engine until the oil pan can be removed.

10. Reverse the procedure to install the oil pan, using new gaskets. Put sealer on joints formed where the end cover and timing cover butt against the block.

Rear Main Oil Seal
REPLACEMENT

The rear main bearing oil seal can be replaced after the transmission, clutch/flywheel or the converter/flywheel has been removed from the engine.

Removal and installation, after the seal is exposed, is as follows.

1. Drain the engine oil and loosen the oil pan bolts.

2. Remove the two rear oil pan bolts.

3. Remove the end cover housing from the engine block and remove the seal from the housing.

4. Install a new seal into the end cover housing with a special seal installer or equivalent.

NOTE: *Fill the cavity between the sealing lips of the seal with grease before installing.*

5. Using a new gasket, install the end cover on the engine block and bolt it into place.

6. Reverse the removal procedure to complete the installation.

Oil Pump
REMOVAL AND INSTALLATION
1600, 2002 Series

1. Remove the oil pan as outlined under "oil Pan Removal and Installation."

Removing oil pump assembly—1600, 2002

Chain tension adjusting shim installed with oil hole properly positioned

2. Remove the 3 retaining bolts for the oil pump drive sprocket and pull off the sprocket.

3. Open the lockplates for the pickup tube mounting bolts at the main bearing cap. Remove the two bolts for the support mount and the two oil pump retaining bolts. Lower the oil pump down and out of the car, taking care not to lose the O-ring in the oil pump housing.

4. Reverse the above procedure to install, observing the following installation notes:

a. Adjust the oil pump drive chain tension so that the chain may be depressed under light thumb pressure. If the proper tension cannot be achieved with either of the replacement lengths of chain, shims (compensating plates) may be installed between the pump housing and the block to take up the slack. When installing shims, always make sure that the oil hole is not blocked. Use a new O-ring when possible.

b. After tightening the pump mounting bolts, loosen the pickup tube support

bracket and retighten the bracket bolts so that the bracket is tension-free.

320i, All Six Cylinder

1. Remove the oil pan.

2. Remove the bolts retaining the sprocket to the oil pump shaft and remove the sprocket.

3. On 4-cylinder engines:

a. Remove the oil pump retaining bolts and lower the oil pump from the engine block. This includes two bolts at the rear of the pickup.

b. Note the location of the O-ring seal, between the housing and the pressure safety line.

c. Be sure that the oil bore in the shim is correctly positioned during the oil pump installation.

4. On 6-cylinder engines:

a. Remove the oil pump retaining bolts and lower the oil pump from the engine block.

b. Do not lose the chain adjusting shims from the two mounting locations.

5. Install the oil pump in the reverse order of removal. Add or subtract shims between the oil pump body and the engine block to obtain a slight movement of the chain under light thumb pressure.

IMPORTANT: *When two shims are used, the two shim thicknesses must be the same. Tighten the pump holder at the pick-up end after shimming is completed to avoid stress on the pump.*

6. On six cylinder engines, after the main pump mounting bolts are properly torqued, loosen the bolts on the bracket at the rear of the pickup, allow the pickup to assume its most natural position so there will be no tension on the bracket and retighten the bolts.

Oil pump mounting shims used on the 600 series cars. Note that both shims must be of the same thickness and that oil holes must be in the proper position

ENGINE COOLING

Radiator

REMOVAL AND INSTALLATION

1. Remove the radiator drain cock or plug, or disconnect the lower radiator hose. Open the heater water valve by turning the control to "Hot" and remove the radiator or expansion tank cap.

2. Loosen the clamps for the upper and lower hoses and, on six cylinder engines equipped with an expansion tank, loosen the clamp for the hose to that tank; then disconnect all hoses. If the car has an automatic transmission, disconnect the transmission cooler lines at the radiator (collecting the fluid in a separate container). Disconnect any temperature sensors.

3. On carbureted models, remove the intake air preheater housing from the front panel. On cars equipped with a fan shroud, remove the attaching screws and remove it.

4. Remove the radiator retaining bolts and lift the radiator out of the car.

5. Install the radiator in reverse order. On plastic tank type radiators, be careful to avoid overtorquing the fasteners for the rubber mounts (6–7 ft-lbs). Make sure all mounts, including those on the bottom of the unit, are in good condition.

6. Bleed the cooling system. See Chapter 1.

Water Pump

REMOVAL AND INSTALLATION

All Four Cylinder Engines

1. Drain the cooling system and remove the radiator as outlined under "Radiator Removal and Installation." Disconnect the negative battery cable.

2. Bend back the lockplates for the fan bolts. Remove the fan retaining bolts and pull off the fan.

3. Loosen the alternator mounting bolts and slide the alternator toward the engine. Pull off the fan pulley and fan belt.

4. Disconnect the coolant hoses from the water pump. Remove the 7 water pump retaining bolts. Lift off the water pump, taking care not to lose the 7 copper sealing washers.

5. Reverse the above procedure to install, using a new water pump gasket. After the cooling system is filled, bleed the system as outlined in Chapter 1.

Water pump installed—four cylinder engines

All Six Cylinder Engines

1. Drain the cooling system. Remove the fan (on models equipped with a fan shroud, this will require removing the mounting screws and removing the shroud first).

2. Detach the fan mounting flange, and remove the water pump drive pulley.

3. Remove the slack adjusting plate from behind the pulley.

Remove the slack adjusting plate (1) from behind the pulley on six cylinder engines

4. Remove the water pump mounting bolts and remove the pump.

5. Reinstall in reverse of the above procedure. When refilling the cooling system, make sure to bleed it, as described in Chapter 1.

Thermostat

REMOVAL AND INSTALLATION

Four Cylinder Engines

Drain the radiator, and then loosen all three hose clamps and remove the thermostat. Replace the unit in reverse order. The angled outlet of the unit goes upward. Bleed the cooling system by running the engine hot with the radiator cap at the first notch and squeezing the hoses and check for leaks.

Six Cylinder Engines

Drain the radiator, and then remove the four bolts from the thermostat housing. Pull the housing off the engine block, and remove the thermostat. In reinstalling, make sure to replace both the conventional thermostat housing gasket and the rubber thermostat seal used in the center of it (if so equipped). Install the thermostat with the bracket facing forward (that is, so the wax pellet is toward the engine). Replace the housing and bolts. Make sure to bleed the system via the thermostat housing bleed screw as described in Chapter 1.

When replacing six cylinder thermostats, replace both the gasket (1) and seal (2)

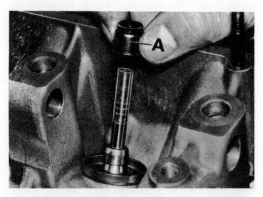

Replacing valve stem seals. Wrapping the top of the valve stem (A) with cellophane tape will help insure easy installation

Inspect the cam following pads on the rockers for looseness or excessive wear (top)

Check the camshaft axial play as shown

ENGINE REBUILDING

Most procedures involved in rebuilding an engine are fairly standard, regardless of the type of engine involved. This section is a guide to accepted rebuilding procedures. Examples of standard rebuilding practices are illustrated and should be used along with specific details concerning your particular engine, found earlier in this chapter.

The procedures given here are those used by any competent rebuilder. Obviously some of the procedures cannot be performed by the do-it-yourself mechanic, but are provided so that you will be familiar with the services that should be offered by rebuilding or machine shops. As an example, in most instances, it is more profitable for the home mechanic to remove the cylinder heads, buy the necessary parts (new valves, seals, keepers, keys, etc.) and deliver these to a machine shop for the necessary work. In this way you will save the money to remove and install the cylinder head and the mark-up on parts.

On the other hand, most of the work involved in rebuilding the lower end is well within the scope of the do-it-yourself mechanic. Only work such as hot-tanking, actually boring the block or Magnafluxing (invisible crack detection) need be sent to a machine shop.

Tools

The tools required for basic engine rebuilding should, with a few exceptions, be those included in a mechanic's tool kit. An accurate torque wrench, and a dial indicator (reading in thousandths) mounted on a universal base should be available. Special tools, where required, are available from the major tool suppliers. The services of a competent automotive machine shop must also be readily available.

Precautions

Aluminum has become increasingly popular for use in engines, due to its low weight and excellent heat transfer characteristics. The following precautions must be observed when handling aluminum (or any other) engine parts:
—Never hot-tank aluminum parts.
—Remove all aluminum parts (identification tags, etc.) from engine parts before hot-tanking (otherwise they will be removed during the process).

—Always coat threads lightly with engine oil or anti-seize compounds before installation, to prevent seizure.
—Never over-torque bolts or spark plugs in aluminum threads. Should stripping occur, threads can be restored using any of a number of thread repair kits available (see next section).

Inspection Techniques

Magnaflux and Zyglo are inspection techniques used to locate material flaws, such as stress cracks. Magnaflux is a magnetic process, applicable only to ferrous materials. The Zyglo process coats the material with a fluorescent dye penetrant, and any material may be tested using Zyglo. Specific checks of suspected surface cracks may be made at lower cost and more readily using spot check dye. The dye is sprayed onto the suspected area, wiped off, and the area is then sprayed with a developer. Cracks then will show up brightly.

Overhaul

The section is divided into two parts. The first, Cylinder Head Reconditioning, assumes that the cylinder head is removed from the engine, all manifolds are removed, and the cylinder head is on a workbench. The camshaft should be removed from overhead cam cylinder heads. The second section, Cylinder Block Reconditioning, covers the block, pistons, connecting rods and crankshaft. It is assumed that the engine is mounted on a work stand, and the cylinder head and all accessories are removed.

Procedures are identified as follows:

Unmarked—Basic procedures that must be performed in order to successfully complete the rebuilding process.

Starred (*)—Procedures that should be performed to ensure maximum performance and engine life.

Double starred (**)—Procedures that may be performed to increase engine performance and reliability.

When assembling the engine, any parts that will be in frictional contact must be pre-lubricated, to provide protection on initial start-up. Any product specifically formulated for this purpose may be used. NOTE: *Do not use engine oil.* Where semi-permanent (locked but removable) installation of bolts or nuts is desired, threads should be cleaned and located with Loctite® or a similar product (non-hardening).

Repairing Damaged Threads

Several methods of repairing damaged threads are available. Heli-Coil® (shown here), Keenserts® and Microdot® are among the most widely used. All involve basically the same principle—drilling out stripped threads, tapping the hole and installing a pre-wound insert—making welding, plugging and oversize fasteners unnecessary.

Two types of thread repair inserts are usually supplied—a standard type for most Inch Coarse, Inch Fine, Metric Coarse and Metric Fine thread sizes and a spark plug type to fit most spark plug port sizes. Consult the individual manufacturer's catalog to determine exact applications. Typical thread repair kits will contain a selection of pre-wound threaded inserts, a tap (corresponding to the outside diameter threads of the insert) and an installation tool. Spark plug inserts usually differ because they require a tap equipped with pilot threads and a combined reamer/tap section. Most manufacturers also supply blister-packed thread repair inserts separately in addition to a master kit containing a variety of taps and inserts plus installation tools.

Before effecting a repair to a threaded hole, remove any snapped, broken or damaged bolts or studs. Penetrating oil can be used to free frozen threads; the offending item can be removed with locking pliers or with a screw or stud extractor. After the hole is clear, the thread can be repaired, as follows:

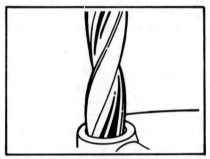
Drill out the damaged threads with specified drill. Drill completely through the hole or to the bottom of a blind hole

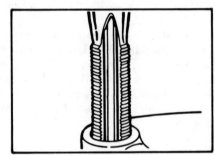
With the tap supplied, tap the hole to receive the thread insert. Keep the tap well oiled and back it out frequently to avoid clogging the threads

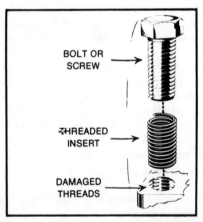

BOLT OR SCREW

THREADED INSERT

DAMAGED THREADS

Damaged bolt holes can be repaired with thread repair inserts

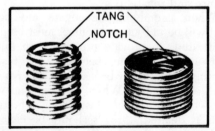

TANG

NOTCH

Standard thread repair insert (left) and spark plug thread insert (right)

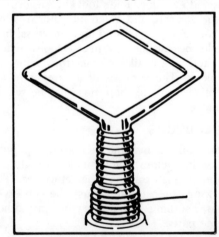
Screw the threaded insert onto the installation tool until the tang engages the slot. Screw the insert into the tapped hole until it is ¼–½ turn below the top surface. After installation break off the tang with a hammer and punch

Standard Torque Specifications and Fastener Markings

The Newton-metre has been designated the world standard for measuring torque and will gradually replace the foot-pound and kilogram-meter. In the absence of specific torques, the following chart can be used as a guide to the maximum safe torque of a particular size/grade of fastener.

- There is no torque difference for fine or coarse threads.
- Torque values are based on clean, dry threads. Reduce the value by 10% if threads are oiled prior to assembly.
- The torque required for aluminum components or fasteners is considerably less.

U. S. BOLTS

SAE Grade Number	1 or 2			5			6 or 7		

Bolt Markings

Manufacturer's marks may vary—number of lines always 2 less than the grade number.

Usage	Frequent			Frequent			Infrequent		
Bolt Size (inches)—(Thread)	Maximum Torque			Maximum Torque			Maximum Torque		
	Ft-Lb	kgm	Nm	Ft-Lb	kgm	Nm	Ft-Lb	kgm	Nm
¼—20	5	0.7	6.8	8	1.1	10.8	10	1.4	13.5
—28	6	0.8	8.1	10	1.4	13.6			
⁵⁄₁₆—18	11	1.5	14.9	17	2.3	23.0	19	2.6	25.8
—24	13	1.8	17.6	19	2.6	25.7			
⅜—16	18	2.5	24.4	31	4.3	42.0	34	4.7	46.0
—24	20	2.75	27.1	35	4.8	47.5			
⁷⁄₁₆—14	28	3.8	37.0	49	6.8	66.4	55	7.6	74.5
—20	30	4.2	40.7	55	7.6	74.5			
½—13	39	5.4	52.8	75	10.4	101.7	85	11.75	115.2
—20	41	5.7	55.6	85	11.7	115.2			
⁹⁄₁₆—12	51	7.0	69.2	110	15.2	149.1	120	16.6	162.7
—18	55	7.6	74.5	120	16.6	162.7			
⅝—11	83	11.5	112.5	150	20.7	203.3	167	23.0	226.5
—18	95	13.1	128.8	170	23.5	230.5			
¾—10	105	14.5	142.3	270	37.3	366.0	280	38.7	379.6
—16	115	15.9	155.9	295	40.8	400.0			
⅞—9	160	22.1	216.9	395	54.6	535.5	440	60.9	596.5
—14	175	24.2	237.2	435	60.1	589.7			
1—8	236	32.5	318.6	590	81.6	799.9	660	91.3	894.8
—14	250	34.6	338.9	660	91.3	849.8			

METRIC BOLTS

NOTE: *Metric bolts are marked with a number indicating the relative strength of the bolt. These numbers have nothing to do with size.*

Description	Torque ft-lbs (Nm)			
Thread size x pitch (mm)	Head mark—4		Head mark—7	
6 x 1.0	2.2–2.9	(3.0–3.9)	3.6–5.8	(4.9–7.8)
8 x 1.25	5.8–8.7	(7.9–12)	9.4–14	(13–19)
10 x 1.25	12–17	(16–23)	20–29	(27–39)
12 x 1.25	21–32	(29–43)	35–53	(47–72)
14 x 1.5	35–52	(48–70)	57–85	(77–110)
16 x 1.5	51–77	(67–100)	90–120	(130–160)
18 x 1.5	74–110	(100–150)	130–170	(180–230)
20 x 1.5	110–140	(150–190)	190–240	(160–320)
22 x 1.5	150–190	(200–260)	250–320	(340–430)
24 x 1.5	190–240	(260–320)	310–410	(420–550)

NOTE: *This engine rebuilding section is a guide to accepted rebuilding procedures. Typical examples of standard rebuilding procedures are illustrated. Use these procedures along with the detailed instructions earlier in this chapter, concerning your particular engine.*

Cylinder Head Reconditioning

Procedure	Method
Remove the cylinder head:	See the engine service procedures earlier in this chapter for details concerning specific engines.
Identify the valves:	Invert the cylinder head, and number the valve faces front to rear, using a permanent felt-tip marker.
Remove the camshaft:	See the engine service procedures earlier in this chapter for details concerning specific engines.
Remove the valves and springs:	Using an appropriate valve spring compressor (depending on the configuration of the cylinder head), compress the valve springs. Lift out the keepers with needlenose pliers, release the compressor, and remove the valve, spring, and spring retainer. See the engine service procedures earlier in this chapter for details concerning specific engines.
Check the valve stem-to-guide clearance: Check the valve stem-to-guide clearance	Clean the valve stem with lacquer thinner or a similar solvent to remove all gum and varnish. Clean the valve guides using solvent and an expanding wire-type valve guide cleaner. Mount a dial indicator so that the stem is at 90° to the valve stem, as close to the valve guide as possible. Move the valve off its seat, and measure the valve guide-to-stem clearance by rocking the stem back and forth to actuate the dial indicator. Measure the valve stems using a micrometer, and compare to specifications, to determine whether stem or guide wear is responsible for excessive clearance. NOTE: *Consult the Specifications tables earlier in this chapter.*

Cylinder Head Reconditioning

Procedure	Method
De-carbon the cylinder head and valves: 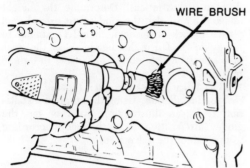 WIRE BRUSH **Remove the carbon from the cylinder head with a wire brush and electric drill**	Chip carbon away from the valve heads, combustion chambers, and ports, using a chisel made of hardwood. Remove the remaining deposits with a stiff wire brush. NOTE: *Be sure that the deposits are actually removed, rather than burnished.*
Hot-tank the cylinder head (cast iron heads only): CAUTION: *Do not hot-tank aluminum parts.*	Have the cylinder head hot-tanked to remove grease, corrosion, and scale from the water passages. NOTE: *In the case of overhead cam cylinder heads, consult the operator to determine whether the camshaft bearings will be damaged by the caustic solution.*
Degrease the remaining cylinder head parts:	Clean the remaining cylinder head parts in an engine cleaning solvent. Do not remove the protective coating from the springs.
Check the cylinder head for warpage: 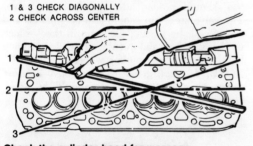 1 & 3 CHECK DIAGONALLY 2 CHECK ACROSS CENTER **Check the cylinder head for warpage**	Place a straight-edge across the gasket surface of the cylinder head. Using feeler gauges, determine the clearance at the center of the straight-edge. If warpage exceeds .003" in a 6" span, or .006" over the total length, the cylinder head must be resurfaced. NOTE: *If warpage exceeds the manufacturer's maximum tolerance for material removal, the cylinder head must be replaced.* When milling the cylinder heads of V-type engines, the intake manifold mounting position is altered, and must be corrected by milling the manifold flange a proportionate amount.
*Knurl the valve guides: 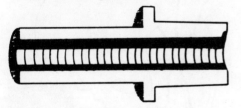 **Cut-away view of a knurled valve guide**	*Valve guides which are not excessively worn or distorted may, in some cases, be knurled rather than replaced. Knurling is a process in which metal is displaced and raised, thereby reducing clearance. Knurling also provides excellent oil control. The possibility of knurling rather than replacing valve guides should be discussed with a machinist.
Replace the valve guides: NOTE: *Valve guides should only be replaced if damaged or if an oversize valve stem is not available.*	See the engine service procedures earlier in this chapter for details concerning specific engines. Depending on the type of cylinder head, valve guides may be pressed, hammered, or shrunk in. In cases where the guides are shrunk into the head, replacement should be left to an equipped machine shop. In other

Cylinder Head Reconditioning

Procedure	Method

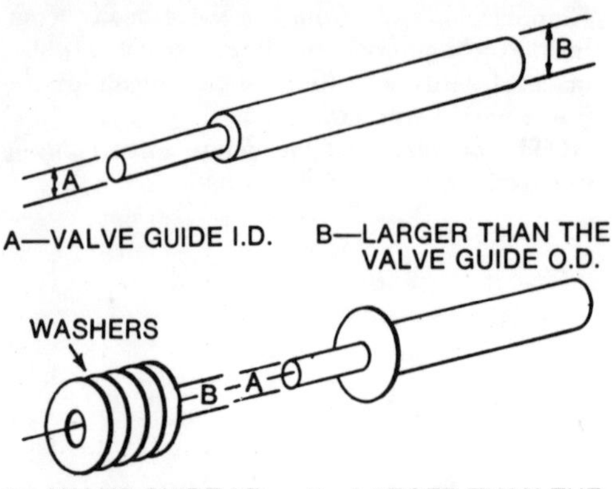

A—VALVE GUIDE I.D.　　B—LARGER THAN THE
　　　　　　　　　　　　　　VALVE GUIDE O.D.

WASHERS

B—A

A—VALVE GUIDE I.D.　　B—LARGER THAN THE
　　　　　　　　　　　　　　VALVE GUIDE O.D.

Valve guide installation tool using washers for installation

cases, the guides are replaced using a stepped drift (see illustration). Determine the height above the boss that the guide must extend, and obtain a stack of washers, their I.D. similar to the guide's O.D., of that height. Place the stack of washers on the guide, and insert the guide into the boss.
NOTE: *Valve guides are often tapered or beveled for installation.* Using the stepped installation tool (see illustration), press or tap the guides into position. Ream the guides according to the size of the valve stem.

Replace valve seat inserts:

Replacement of valve seat inserts which are worn beyond resurfacing or broken, if feasible, must be done by a machine shop.

Resurface (grind) the valve face:

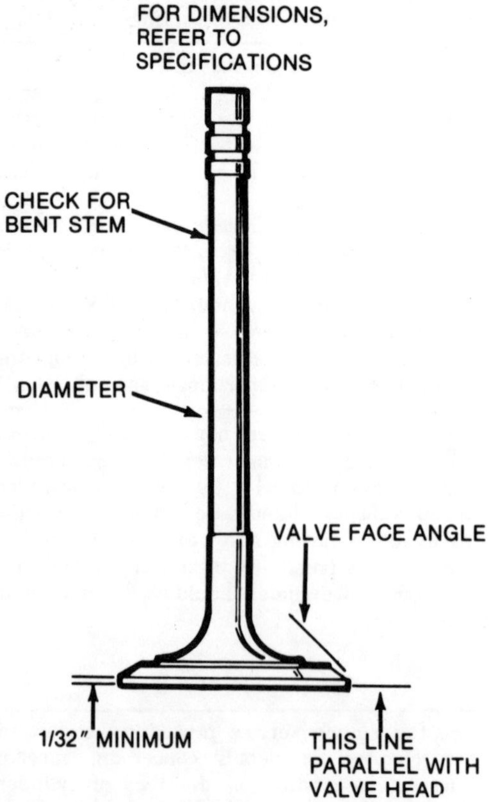

FOR DIMENSIONS,
REFER TO
SPECIFICATIONS

CHECK FOR
BENT STEM

DIAMETER

VALVE FACE ANGLE

1/32" MINIMUM

THIS LINE
PARALLEL WITH
VALVE HEAD

Critical valve dimensions

Using a valve grinder, resurface the valves according to specifications given earlier in this chapter.
CAUTION: *Valve face angle is not always identical to valve seat angle.* A minimum margin of $1/32''$ should remain after grinding the valve. The valve stem top should also be squared and resurfaced, by placing the stem in the V-block of the grinder, and turning it while pressing lightly against the grinding wheel.
NOTE: *Do not grind sodium filled exhaust valves on a machine. These should be hand lapped.*

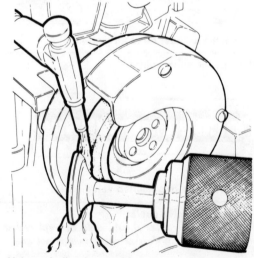

Valve grinding by machine

Cylinder Head Reconditioning

Procedure	Method

Resurface the valve seats using reamers or grinder:

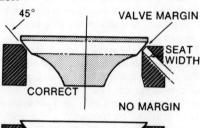

Valve seat width and centering

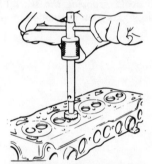

Reaming the valve seat with a hand reamer

Select a reamer of the correct seat angle, slightly larger than the diameter of the valve seat, and assemble it with a pilot of the correct size. Install the pilot into the valve guide, and using steady pressure, turn the reamer clockwise.

CAUTION: *Do not turn the reamer counterclockwise.* Remove only as much material as necessary to clean the seat. Check the concentricity of the seat (following). If the dye method is not used, coat the valve face with Prussian blue dye, install and rotate it on the valve seat. Using the dye marked area as a centering guide, center and narrow the valve seat to specifications with correction cutters.

NOTE: *When no specifications are available, minimum seat width for exhaust valves should be* $5/64''$, *intake valves* $1/16''$.

After making correction cuts, check the position of the valve seat on the valve face using Prussian blue dye.

To resurface the seat with a power grinder, select a pilot of the correct size and coarse stone of the proper angle. Lubricate the pilot and move the stone on and off the valve seat at 2 cycles per second, until all flaws are gone. Finish the seat with a fine stone. If necessary the seat can be corrected or narrowed using correction stones.

Check the valve seat concentricity:

Coat the valve face with Prussian blue dye, install the valve, and rotate it on the valve seat. If the entire seat becomes coated, and the valve is known to be concentric, the seat is concentric.

*Install the dial gauge pilot into the guide, and rest of the arm on the valve seat. Zero the gauge, and rotate the arm around the seat. Run-out should not exceed .002″.

Check the valve seat concentricity with a dial gauge

Cylinder Head Reconditioning

Procedure	Method
*Lap the valves: NOTE: *Valve lapping is done to ensure efficient sealing of resurfaced valves and seats.*	Invert the cyclinder head, lightly lubricate the valve stems, and install the valves in the head as numbered. Coat valve seats with fine grinding compound, and attach the lapping tool suction cup to a valve head. **NOTE:** *Moisten the suction cup.* Rotate the tool between the palms, changing position and lifting the tool often to prevent grooving. Lap the valve until a smooth, polished seat is evident. Remove the valve and tool, and rinse away all traces of grinding compound.

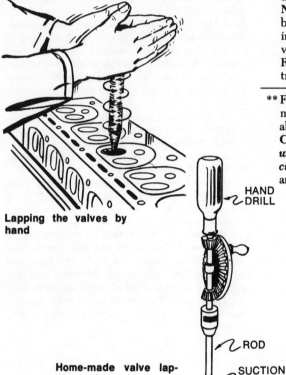

Lapping the valves by hand

HAND DRILL

Home-made valve lapping tool

ROD

SUCTION CUP

** Fasten a suction cup to a piece of drill rod, and mount the rod in a hand drill. Proceed as above, using the hand drill as a lapping tool.
CAUTION: *Due to the higher speeds involved when using the hand drill, care must be exercised to avoid grooving the seat.* Lift the tool and change direction of rotation often.

Procedure	Method
Check the valve springs:	Place the spring on a flat surface next to a square. Measure the height of the spring, and rotate it against the edge of the square to measure distortion. If spring height varies (by comparison) by more than $1/16''$ or if distortion exceeds $1/16''$, replace the spring.

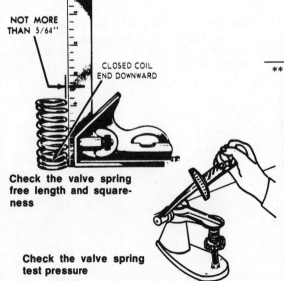

NOT MORE THAN 5/64"

CLOSED COIL END DOWNWARD

Check the valve spring free length and squareness

Check the valve spring test pressure

** In addition to evaluating the spring as above, test the spring pressure at the installed and compressed (installed height minus valve lift) height using a valve spring tester. Springs used on small displacement engines (up to 3 liters) should be $\mp$ 1 lb of all other springs in either position. A tolerance of $\mp$ 5 lbs is permissible on larger engines.

Cylinder Head Reconditioning

Procedure	Method

*Install valve stem seals:

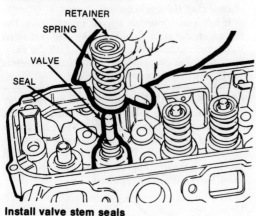

RETAINER

SPRING

VALVE

SEAL

Install valve stem seals

* Due to the pressure differential that exists at the ends of the intake valve guides (atmospheric pressure above, manifold vacuum below), oil is drawn through the valve guides into the intake port. This has been alleviated somewhat since the addition of positive crankcase ventilation, which lowers the pressure above the guides. Several types of valve stem seals are available to reduce blow-by. Certain seals simply slip over the stem and guide boss, while others require that the boss be machined. Recently, Teflon guide seals have become popular. Consult a parts supplier or machinist concerning availability and suggested usages.

NOTE: *When installing seals, ensure that a small amount of oil is able to pass the seal to lubricate the valve guides; otherwise, excessive wear may result.*

Install the valves:

See the engine service procedures earlier in this chapter for details concerning specific engines.

Lubricate the valve stems, and install the valves in the cylinder head as numbered. Lubricate and position the seals (if used) and the valve springs. Install the spring retainers, compress the springs, and insert the keys using needlenose pliers or a tool designed for this purpose.

NOTE: *Retain the keys with wheel bearing grease during installation.*

Check valve spring installed height:

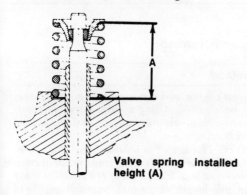

A

Valve spring installed height (A)

Measure the distance between the spring pad the lower edge of the spring retainer, and compare to specifications. If the installed height is incorrect, add shim washers between the spring pad and the spring.

CAUTION: *Use only washers designed for this purpose.*

GRIND OUT THIS PORTION

Measure the valve spring installed height (A) with a modified steel rule

Clean and inspect the camshaft:

Degrease the camshaft, using solvent, and clean out all oil holes. Visually inspect cam lobes and bearing journals for excessive wear. If a lobe is questionable, check all lobes as indicated below. If a journal or lobe is worn, the camshaft must be reground or replaced.

Cylinder Head Reconditioning

Procedure	Method
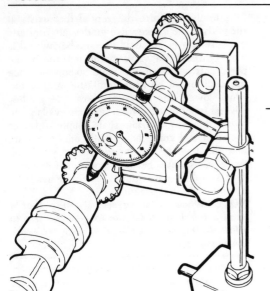 **Check the camshaft for straightness**	NOTE: *If a journal is worn, there is a good chance that the bushings are worn.* If lobes and journals appear intact, place the front and rear journals in V-blocks, and rest a dial indicator on the center journal. Rotate the camshaft to check straightness. If deviation exceeds .001″, replace the camshaft. *Check the camshaft lobes with a micrometer, by measuring the lobes from the nose to base and again at 90° (see illustration). The lift is determined by subtracting the second measurement from the first. If all exhaust lobes and all intake lobes are not identical, the camshaft must be reground or replaced. 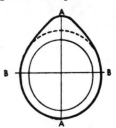 **Camshaft lobe measurement**
Install the camshaft:	See the engine service procedures earlier in this chapter for details concerning specific engines.
Install the rocker arms:	See the engine service procedures earlier in this chapter for details concerning specific engines.

Cylinder Block Reconditioning

Procedure	Method
Checking the main bearing clearance: 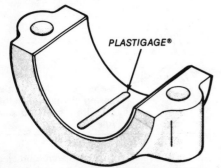 **Plastigage® installed on the lower bearing shell**	Invert engine, and remove cap from the bearing to be checked. Using a clean, dry rag, thoroughly clean all oil from crankshaft journal and bearing insert. NOTE: *Plastigage® is soluble in oil; therefore, oil on the journal or bearing could result in erroneous readings.* Place a piece of Plastigage along the full length of journal, reinstall cap, and torque to specifications. NOTE: *Specifications are given in the engine specifications earlier in this chapter.* Remove bearing cap, and determine bearing clearance by comparing width of Plastigage to the scale on Plastigage envelope. Journal taper is determined by comparing width of the Plastigage strip near its ends. Rotate crankshaft 90° and retest, to determine journal eccentricity. NOTE: *Do not rotate crankshaft with Plastigage installed.* If bearing insert and journal appear in-

Cylinder Block Reconditioning

Procedure	Method

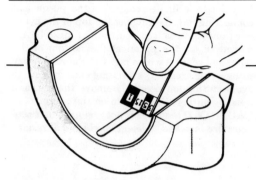

Measure Plastigage® to determine main bearing clearance

tact, and are within tolerances, no further main bearing service is required. If bearing or journal appear defective, cause of failure should be determined before replacement.

* Remove crankshaft from block (see below). Measure the main bearing journals at each end twice (90° apart) using a micrometer, to determine diameter, journal taper and eccentricity. If journals are within tolerances, reinstall bearing caps at their specified torque. Using a telescope gauge and micrometer, measure bearing I.D. parallel to piston axis and at 30° on each side of piston axis. Subtract journal O.D. from bearing I.D. to determine oil clearance. If crankshaft journals appear defective, or do not meet tolerances, there is no need to measure bearings; for the crankshaft will require grinding and/or undersize bearings will be required. If bearing appears defective, cause for failure should be determined prior to replacement.

Check the connecting rod bearing clearance:

Connecting rod bearing clearance is checked in the same manner as main bearing clearance, using Plastigage. Before removing the crankshaft, connecting rod side clearance also should be measured and recorded.

* Checking connecting rod bearing clearance, using a micrometer, is identical to checking main bearing clearance. If no other service is required, the piston and rod assemblies need not be removed.

Remove the crankshaft:

Using a punch, mark the corresponding main bearing caps and saddles according to position (i.e., one punch on the front main cap and saddle, two on the second, three on the third, etc.). Using number stamps, identify the corresponding connecting rods and caps, according to cylinder (if no numbers are present). Remove the main and connecting rod caps, and replace sleeves of plastic tubing or vacuum hose over the connecting rod bolts, to protect the journals as the crankshaft is removed. Lift the crankshaft out of the block.

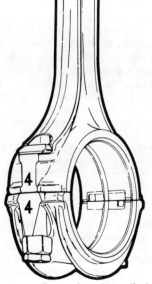

Match the connecting rod to the cylinder with a number stamp

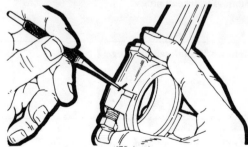

Match the connecting rod and cap with scribe marks

Cylinder Block Reconditioning

Procedure	Method
Remove the ridge from the top of the cylinder: 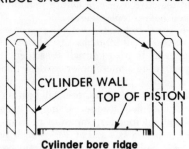 RIDGE CAUSED BY CYLINDER WEAR / CYLINDER WALL / TOP OF PISTON **Cylinder bore ridge**	In order to facilitate removal of the piston and connecting rod, the ridge at the top of the cylinder (unworn area; see illustration) must be removed. Place the piston at the bottom of the bore, and cover it with a rag. Cut the ridge away using a ridge reamer, exercising extreme care to avoid cutting too deeply. Remove the rag, and remove cuttings that remain on the piston. **CAUTION:** *If the ridge is not removed, and new rings are installed, damage to rings will result.*
Remove the piston and connecting rod: 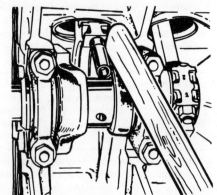 **Push the piston out with a hammer handle**	Invert the engine, and push the pistons and connecting rods out of the cylinders. If necessary, tap the connecting rod boss with a wooden hammer handle, to force the piston out. **CAUTION:** *Do not attempt to force the piston past the cylinder ridge* (see above).
Service the crankshaft:	Ensure that all oil holes and passages in the crankshaft are open and free of sludge. If necessary, have the crankshaft ground to the largest possible undersize.
	**Have the crankshaft Magnafluxed, to locate stress cracks. Consult a machinist concerning additional service procedures, such as surface hardening (e.g., nitriding, Tuftriding) to improve wear characteristics, cross drilling and chamfering the oil holes to improve lubrication, and balancing.
Removing freeze plugs:	Drill a small hole in the middle of the freeze plugs. Thread a large sheet metal screw into the hole and remove the plug with a slide hammer.
Remove the oil gallery plugs:	Threaded plugs should be removed using an appropriate (usually square) wrench. To remove soft, pressed in plugs, drill a hole in the plug, and thread in a sheet metal screw. Pull the plug out by the screw using pliers.
Hot-tank the block: NOTE: *Do not hot-tank aluminum parts.*	Have the block hot-tanked to remove grease, corrosion, and scale from the water jackets. **NOTE:** *Consult the operator to determine whether the camshaft bearings will be damaged during the hot-tank process.*

Cylinder Block Reconditioning

Procedure	Method
Check the block for cracks:	Visually inspect the block for cracks or chips. The most common locations are as follows: Adjacent to freeze plugs. Between the cylinders and water jackets. Adjacent to the main bearing saddles. At the extreme bottom of the cylinders. Check only suspected cracks using spot check dye (see introduction). If a crack is located, consult a machinist concerning possible repairs. ** Magnaflux the block to locate hidden cracks. If cracks are located, consult a machinist about feasibility of repair.
Install the oil gallery plugs and freeze plugs:	Coat freeze plugs with sealer and tap into position using a piece of pipe, slightly smaller than the plug, as a driver. To ensure retention, stake the edges of the plugs. Coat threaded oil gallery plugs with sealer and install. Drive replacement soft plugs into block using a large drift as a driver. * Rather than reinstalling lead plugs, drill and tap the holes, and install threaded plugs.
Check the bore diameter and surface: 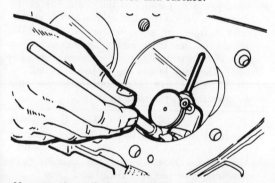 **Measure the cylinder bore with a dial gauge**	Visually inspect the cylinder bores for roughness, scoring, or scuffing. If evident, the cylinder bore must be bored or honed oversize to eliminate imperfections, and the smallest possible oversize piston used. The new pistons should be given to the machinist with the block, so that the cylinders can be bored or honed exactly to the piston size (plus clearance). If no flaws are evident, measure the bore diameter using a telescope gauge and micrometer, or dial gauge, parallel and perpendicular to the engine centerline, at the top (below the ridge) and bottom of the bore. Subtract the bottom measurements from the top to determine taper, and the parallel to the centerline measurements from the perpendicular measurements to determine eccentricity. If the measurements are not within specifications, the cylinder must be bored or honed, and an oversize piston installed. If the measurements are within specifications the cylinder may

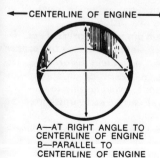

CENTERLINE OF ENGINE

A—AT RIGHT ANGLE TO CENTERLINE OF ENGINE
B—PARALLEL TO CENTERLINE OF ENGINE

Cylinder bore measuring points

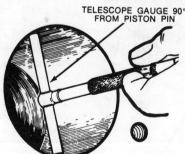

TELESCOPE GAUGE 90° FROM PISTON PIN

Measure the cylinder bore with a telescope gauge

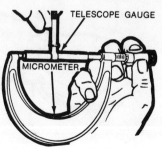

TELESCOPE GAUGE

MICROMETER

Measure the telescope gauge with a micrometer to determine the cylinder bore

Cylinder Block Reconditioning

Procedure	Method
	be used as is, with only finish honing (see below). NOTE: *Prior to submitting the block for boring, perform the following operation(s).*
Check the cylinder block bearing alignment: **Check the main bearing saddle alignment**	Remove the upper bearing inserts. Place a straightedge in the bearing saddles along the centerline of the crankshaft. If clearance exists between the straightedge and the center saddle, the block must be alignbored.
*Check the deck height:	The deck height is the distance from the crankshaft centerline to the block deck. To measure, invert the engine, and install the crankshaft, retaining it with the center maincap. Measure the distance from the crankshaft journal to the block deck, parallel to the cylinder centerline. Measure the diameter of the end (front and rear) main journals, parallel to the centerline of the cylinders, divide the diameter in half, and subtract it from the previous measurement. The results of the front and rear measurements should be identical. If the difference exceeds .005″, the deck height should be corrected. NOTE: *Block deck height and warpage should be corrected at the same time.*
Check the block deck for warpage:	Using a straightedge and feeler gauges, check the block deck for warpage in the same manner that the cylinder head is checked (see Cylinder Head Reconditioning). If warpage exceeds specifications, have the deck resurfaced. NOTE: *In certain cases a specification for total material removal (cylinder head and block deck) is provided. This specification must not be exceeded.*
Clean and inspect the pistons and connecting rods: 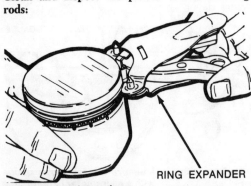 RING EXPANDER **Remove the piston rings**	Using a ring expander, remove the rings from the piston. Remove the retaining rings (if so equipped) and remove piston pin. NOTE: *If the piston pin must be pressed out, determine the proper method and use the proper tools; otherwise the piston will distort.* Clean the ring grooves using an appropriate tool, exercising care to avoid cutting too deeply. Thoroughly clean all carbon and varnish from the piston with solvent. CAUTION: *Do not use a wire brush or caustic solvent on pistons.* Inspect the pistons for scuffing, scoring, cracks, pitting, or excessive ringsgroove wear. If wear is evident, the piston must be replaced. Check the connecting rod length by measuring

Cylinder Block Reconditioning

Procedure	Method

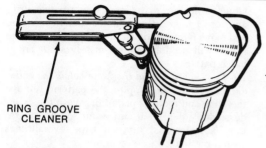

RING GROOVE
CLEANER

Clean the piston ring grooves

the rod from the inside of the large end to the inside of the small end using calipers (see illustration). All connecting rods should be equal length. Replace any rod that differs from the others in the engine.

* Have the connecting rod alignment checked in an alignment fixture by a machinist. Replace any twisted or bent rods.

* Magnaflux the connecting rods to locate stress cracks. If cracks are found, replace the connecting rod.

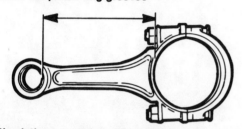

Check the connecting rod length (arrow)

Fit the pistons to the cylinders:

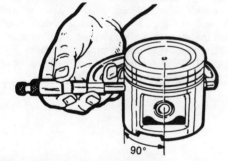

90°

Measure the piston prior to fitting

Using a telescope gauge and micrometer, or a dial gauge, measure the cylinder bore diameter perpendicular to the piston pin, 2½″ below the deck. Measure the piston perpendicular to its pin on the skirt. The difference between the two measurements is the piston clearance. If the clearance is within specifications or slightly below (after boring or honing), finish honing is all that is required. If the clearance is excessive, try to obtain a slightly larger piston to bring clearance within specifications. Where this is not possible, obtain the first oversize piston, and hone (of if necessary, bore) the cylinder to size.

Assemble the pistons and connecting rods:

Install the piston pin lock-rings (if used)

Inspect piston pin, connecting rod small end bushing, and piston bore for galling, scoring, or excessive wear. If evident, replace defective part(s). Measure the I.D. of the piston boss and connecting rod small end, and the O.D. of the piston pin. If within specifications, assemble piston pin and rod.
CAUTION: *If piston pin must be pressed in, determine the proper method and use the proper tools; otherwise the piston will distort.*
Install the lock rings; ensure that they seat properly. If the parts are not within specifications, determine the service method for the type of engine. In some cases, piston and pin are serviced as an assembly when either is defective. Others specify reaming the piston and connecting rods for an oversize pin. If the connecting rod bushing is worn, it may in many cases be replaced. Reaming the piston and replacing the rod bushing are machine shop operations.

Cylinder Block Reconditioning

Procedure	Method

Finish hone the cylinders:

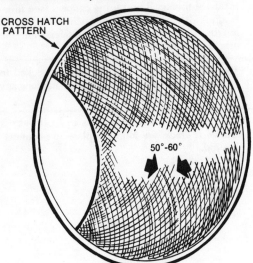

CROSS HATCH PATTERN

50°-60°

Chuck a flexible drive hone into a power drill, and insert it into the cylinder. Start the hone, and move it up and down in the cylinder at a rate which will produce approximately a 60° cross-hatch pattern.
NOTE: *Do not extend the hone below the cylinder bore.* After developing the pattern, remove the hone and recheck piston fit. Wash the cylinders with a detergent and water solution to remove abrasive dust, dry, and wipe several times with a rag soaked in engine oil.

Check piston ring end-gap:

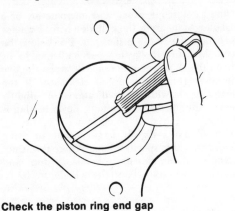

Check the piston ring end gap

Compress the piston rings to be used in a cylinder, one at a time, into that cylinder, and press them approximately 1″ below the deck with an inverted piston. Using feeler gauges, measure the ring end-gap, and compare to specifications. Pull the ring out of the cylinder and file the ends with a fine file to obtain proper clearance.
CAUTION: *If inadequate ring end-gap is utilized, ring breakage will result.*

Install the piston rings:

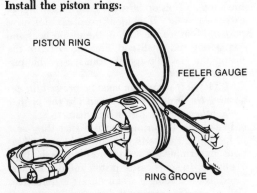

PISTON RING

FEELER GAUGE

RING GROOVE

Check the piston ring side clearance

Inspect the ring grooves in the piston for excessive wear or taper. If necessary, recut the groove(s) for use with an overwidth ring or a standard ring and spacer. If the groove is worn uniformly, overwidth rings, or standard rings and spaces may be installed without recutting. Roll the outside of the ring around the groove to check for burrs or deposits. If any are found, remove with a fine file. Hold the ring in the groove, and measure side clearance. If necessary, correct as indicated above.
NOTE: *Always install any additional spacers above the piston ring.*
    The ring groove must be deep enough to allow the ring to seat below the lands (see illustration). In many cases, a "go-no-go" depth gauge will be provided with the piston rings. Shallow grooves may be corrected by recutting, while deep

Cylinder Block Reconditioning

Procedure	Method
	grooves require some type of filler or expander behind the piston. Consult the piston ring supplier concerning the suggested method. Install the rings on the piston, lowest ring first, using a ring expander. NOTE: *Position the rings as specified by the manufacturer.* Consult the engine service procedures earlier in this chapter for details concerning specific engines.
Install the rear main seal:	See the engine service procedures earlier in this chapter for details concerning specific engines.
Install the crankshaft: 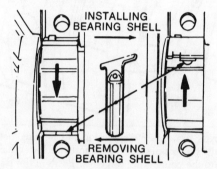 **Remove or install the upper bearing insert using a roll-out pin** 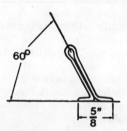 **Home-made bearing roll-out pin**	Thoroughly clean the main bearing saddles and caps. Place the upper halves of the bearing inserts on the saddles and press into position. NOTE: *Ensure that the oil holes align.* Press the corresponding bearing inserts into the main bearing caps. Lubricate the upper main bearings, and lay the crankshaft in position. Place a strip of Plastigage on each of the crankshaft journals, install the main caps, and torque to specifications. Remove the main caps, and compare the Plastigage to the scale on the Plastigage envelope. If clearances are within tolerances, remove the Plastigage, turn the crankshaft 90°, wipe off all oil and retest. If all clearances are correct, remove all Plastigage, thoroughly lubricate the main caps and bearing journals, and install the main caps. If clearances are not within tolerance, the upper bearing inserts may be removed, without removing the crankshaft, using a bearing roll out pin (see illustration). Roll in a bearing that will provide proper clearance, and retest. Torque all main caps, excluding the thrust bearing cap, to specifications. Tighten the thrust bearing cap finger tight. To properly align the thrust bearing, pry the crankshaft the extent of its axial travel several times, the last movement held toward the front of the engine, and torque the thrust bearing cap to specifications. Determine the crankshaft end-play (see below), and bring within tolerance with thrust washers.

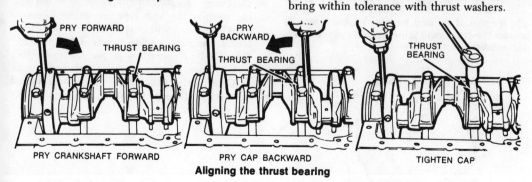

Aligning the thrust bearing

Procedure	Method
Measure crankshaft end-play:	Mount a dial indicator stand on the front of the block, with the dial indicator stem resting on the

Cylinder Block Reconditioning

Procedure	Method

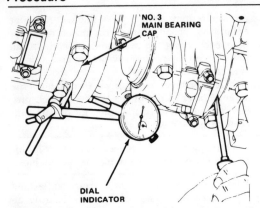

Check the crankshaft end-play with a dial indicator

Check the crankshaft end-play with a feeler gauge

nose of the crankshaft, parallel to the crankshaft axis. Pry the crankshaft the extent of its travel rearward, and zero the indicator. Pry the crankshaft forward and record crankshaft end-play.

NOTE: *Crankshaft end-play also may be measured at the thrust bearing, using feeler gauges (see illustration).*

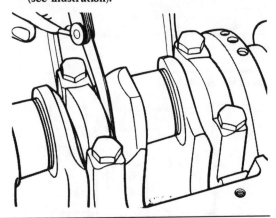

Install the pistons:

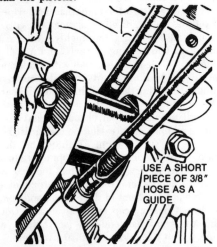

USE A SHORT PIECE OF 3/8" HOSE AS A GUIDE

Use lengths of vacuum hose or rubber tubing to protect the crankshaft journals and cylinder walls during piston installation

Press the upper connecting rod bearing halves into the connecting rods, and the lower halves into the connecting rod caps. Position the piston ring gaps according to specifications (see car section), and lubricate the pistons. Install a ring compresser on a piston, and press two long (8″) pieces of plastic tubing over the rod bolts. Using the tubes as a guide, press the pistons into the bores and onto the crankshaft with a wooden hammer handle. After seating the rod on the crankshaft journal, remove the tubes and install the cap finger tight. Install the remaining pistons in the same manner. Invert the engine and check the bearing clearance at two points (90° apart) on each journal with Plastigage.

NOTE: *Do not turn the crankshaft with Plastigage installed.*

If clearance is within tolerances, remove *all* Plastigage, thoroughly lubricate the journals, and torque the rod caps to specifications. If clearance is not within specifications, install different thickness bearing inserts and recheck.

CAUTION: *Never shim or file the connecting rods or caps.*

Always install plastic tube sleeves over the rod bolts when the caps are not installed, to protect the crankshaft journals.

RING COMPRESSOR

Install the piston using a ring compressor

Cylinder Block Reconditioning

Procedure	Method
Check connecting rod side clearance: 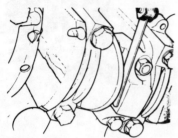 **Check the connecting rod side clearance with a feeler gauge**	Determine the clearance between the sides of the connecting rods and the crankshaft using feeler gauges. If clearance is below the minimum tolerance, the rod may be machined to provide adequate clearance. If clearance is excessive, substitute an unworn rod, and recheck. If clearance is still outside specifications, the crankshaft must be welded and reground, or replaced.
Inspect the timing chain (or belt):	Visually inspect the timing chain for broken or loose links, and replace the chain if any are found. If the chain will flex sideways, it must be replaced. Install the timing chain as specified. Be sure the timing belt is not stretched, frayed or broken. NOTE: *If the original timing chain is to be reused, install it in its original position.* See the engine service procedures earlier in this chapter for details concerning specific engines.

Completing the Rebuilding Process

Following the above procedures, complete the rebuilding process as follows:

Fill the oil pump with oil, to prevent cavitating (sucking air) on initial engine start up. Install the oil pump and the pickup tube on the engine. Coat the oil pan gasket as necessary, and install the gasket and the oil pan. Mount the flywheel and the crankshaft vibration damper or pulley on the crankshaft. NOTE: *Always use new bolts when installing the flywheel.* Inspect the clutch shaft pilot bushing in the crankshaft. If the bushing is excessively worn, remove it with an expanding puller and a slide hammer, and tap a new bushing into place.

Position the engine, cylinder head side up. Install the cylinder head, and torque it as specified. Install the rocker arms and adjust the valves.

Install the intake and exhaust manifolds, the carburetor(s), the distributor and spark plugs. Adjust the point gap and the static ignition timing. Mount all accessories and install the engine in the car. Fill the radiator with coolant, and the crankcase with high quality engine oil.

Break-in Procedure

Start the engine, and allow it to run at low speed for a few minutes, while checking for leaks. Stop the engine, check the oil level, and fill as necessary. Restart the engine, and fill the cooling system to capacity. Check the point dwell angle and adjust the ignition timing and the valves. Run the engine at low to medium speed (800–2500 rpm) for approximately ½ hour, and retorque the cylinder head bolts. Road test the car, and check again for leaks.

Follow the manufacturer's recommended engine break-in procedure and maintenance schedule for new engines.

4

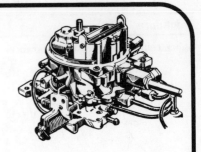

Emission Controls
and Fuel System

EMISSION CONTROLS

Crankcase Ventilation System

OPERATION

The BMW crankcase emission control system is considered a "sealed" system. Rather than purging the crankcase of blowby vapors with fresh air as is done conventionally, the blowby emissions are routed directly to the air cleaner or air collector with crankcase pressure behind them. Since the purpose of the PCV valve in conventional systems is to regulate the volume of purging air even with varying intake vacuum, this valve and the maintenance associated with it are eliminated.

TESTING

The Crankcase Emission Control System is virtually maintenance free. The connecting tube from the top engine cover to the air cleaner or air collector should be inspected during the routine maintenance services and replaced if cracked, distorted or plugged.

With the engine operating and the connecting tube disconnected, a vacuum should be noted at the air cleaner or air collector side of the hose. If vacuum is not present, an air leak or plugged air induction system may be the cause.

Evaporative Emissions Control System

OPERATION

This system stores gasoline vapors which collect above liquid fuel in the fuel tank and, on carbureted engines, in the float bowl. The system stores the vapors while the engine is off, and then allows the vacuum created in the intake manifold to draw them off and burn them when the engine is started.

Fuel tank vapors are collected by a storage tank located in the trunk. Vapor which cannot be held there, as well as float bowl vapors, are stored in a charcoal canister located in the front of the engine compartment. The charcoal has the effect of keeping the vapors in liquid form so they can be held in a minimal space. As in the case of the crankcase ventilation system, no fresh air is used in purging, eliminating the need to change an air filter in the canister.

MAINTENANCE

Inspect the hoses and hose clamps occasionally or if raw fuel odor is noticed. Tighten clamps as necessary or replace hoses which have cracked.

Under certain operating conditions, contamination or excessive vapor collection may cause the vapor canister to become saturated

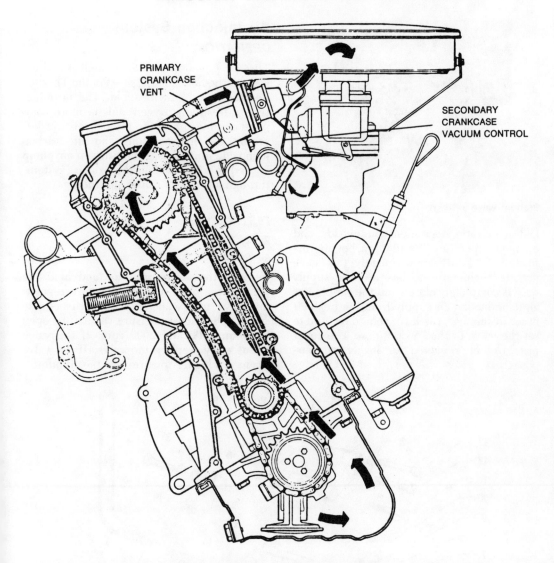

PRIMARY CRANKCASE VENT

SECONDARY CRANKCASE VACUUM CONTROL

Operation of the PCV system for 2002—1974–74

The tank vent hose is located in the trunk of the 320i

with liquid fuel. Under these conditions, the unit should be replaced, even though replacement on a routine basis is not necessary.

Automatic Air Intake Preheating Valve

CHECKING

1600 Series, 2002 Series

The automatic air induction pre-heat valve is located in a housing to the right of the radiator. Every 8000 miles, the lever should be placed in the winter (W) position and the valve's freedom of movement checked. If necessary, oil the valve. In the "W" position air drawn in at the front of the car is mixed with air preheated around the exhaust mani-

Preheat valve settings

fold in a ratio dependent on outside and engine temperatures, until it reaches approximately 86°F. At approximately this same outside temperature, the pre-heat supply hose is completely closed and the car obtains all its induction air supply from the fresh air hose. In summer, the lever should be used to set the valve to the "S" position. The cover plate can be removed for inspection purposes.

Air Injection System
OPERATION

The Air Injection system is used to add oxygen to the hot exhaust gasses in the Thermal Reactor or exhaust manifold. The introduction of fresh air (oxygen) aids in more complete combustion of the air/fuel mixture lessening the hydrocarbons and the carbon monoxide emissions. A belt driven air pump is used to force air into the exhaust system, through a series of valves and tubing.

TESTING
2002, 3.0

Air Pump

Remove the air return pipe and hold the palm of the hand over the pressure regulating valve unit while increasing the engine speed. The excess pressure valve must open between 1700 and 2000 rpm. If the valve opens early, replace the valve. If the valve opens at a higher rpm, replace the air pump.

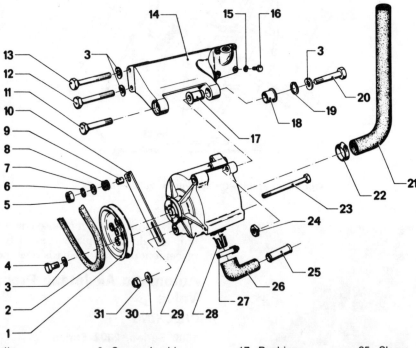

1. Belt pulley	9. Spacer bushing	17. Bushing	25. Sleeve
2. V-belt	10. Tension shackle	18. Bushing	26. Elbow
3. Lockwasher	11. Hex screw	19. Lockring	27. Hose clamp
4. Hex screw	12. Screw	20. Hex screw	28. Pressure regulator
5. Hex nut	13. Screw	21. Hose	29. Air pump
6. Spring ring	14. Bearing bracket	22. Hose clamp	30. Washer
7. Washer	15. Lockwasher	23. Hex screw	31. Hex nut
8. Rubber bushing	16. Screw	24. Square nut	

Exploded view of 2002 recombustion system air pump and related parts

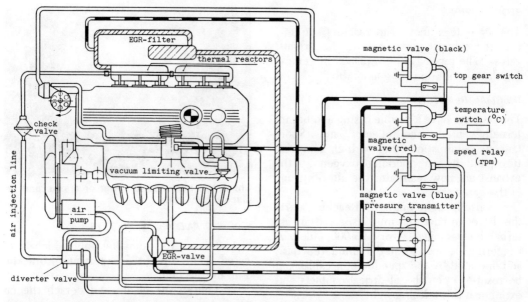

Typical six cylinder emission control system—(the black magnetic valve and high gear switch are used on California and high altitude models only)

BELT ADJUSTMENT

The air pump drive belt should have a deflection of no more than ⅜ in. measured in the middle of its longest span, when properly adjusted.

CONTROL VALVE

The control valve should be replaced if the carburetors are difficult to adjust or if the engine back-fires when the throttle is released.

CHECK VALVE

The check valve should be replaced if air can be blown through the valve in both directions. Air should move towards the manifold only.

BLOW-IN PIPES

The exhaust manifold must be removed to expose the blow-in pipes. The pipes can be replaced by unscrewing them from the manifold and screwing in new ones.

320i, 530i, 630i, 633i, and 733i

AIR PUMP

Disconnect the outlet hose and start the engine. The air velocity should increase as the engine speed increases. If not, the air pump drive belt could be slipping, the check valve or the air pump may be defective and would have to be adjusted or replaced.

BLOW-OFF VALVE

If backfiring occurs when releasing the accelerator or the air pump seems to be overloading, the blow-off valve may be defective.

The valve must release and blow-off during a coasting condition and the internal safety valve must open at 5 psi. The vacuum line must have suction when the engine is running and must allow the air to be blown off when reattached to the valve at idle.

ELECTRIC CONTROL VALVE—WHITE CAP

This control valve governs the blow-off valve and must be open at temperatures below 113° F (45° C) and closed above 113° F (45° C) of the coolant.

With the coolant temperatures above 113° F (45° C), the ignition switch on and the engine off, disconnect both vacuum hoses, attach a test hose to one nipple and blow air into the valve. The valve is functioning properly if air cannot flow through the valve. Turn the ignition switch off and blow into the valve again. Air should flow through the valve.

CHECK VALVE

The check valve must be replaced if air can be blown through the valve in both directions. Air should move towards the reactors only.

BLOW-IN PIPES

The air enters above the reactors, directly into the exhaust ports, behind the exhaust valves. The pipes can be replaced by removing the distribution tube assembly.

THERMAL REACTOR

The reactors have a double casing and has internally vented flame deflector plates. Spontaneous combustion, due to high temperatures, and the introduction of oxygen into the exhaust gas flow maintains the after-burning of the gases.

A warning light marked "Reactor" alerts the driver to have the unit inspected for external heat damage every 25,000 miles. A triggering device, located behind the dash and operated by the speedometer cable, can be reset to open the electrical contacts and extinguish the warning light.

NOTE: *Two different sized buttons are mounted side by side on the triggering device. The small button is for the reactor and the large button is for the EGR valve. Press the button to reset.*

REMOVAL AND INSTALLATION
Air Pump

1600-2, 2002

1. Disconnect inlet and outlet hoses.
2. Remove the adjusting bolt. Then, loosen and remove the front and rear mounting bolts—note that nuts will remain in the grooved portion of the housing.
3. Inspect the rubber bushings inside the mounting bracket and replace if necessary.
4. Install in reverse order; do not pry on the pump when adjusting the belt.

3201-i

1. Disconnect the hose at the back of the pump.
2. Remove the adjusting bolt and disengage the belt. Then, remove the through bolt which passes through front and rear pump brackets, being careful to retain the nut and spacer located at the rear.
3. Pull the rubber bushings (5) out of either end of the air pump mount. If the bushings are worn or cracked replace them. When reinstalling, make sure inside diameters of bushings fit over the inner spacer (6) and outside diameters fit snugly into the mount.
4. Install in reverse order.

Check the bushings for wear or cracks and replace if necessary

530i, 630 AND 633 SERIES, 733i

1. Loosen the adjusting bolt, which is located at the top of the upper pump bracket. Pull off the belt.
2. Loosen the clamp and detach the air hose at the rear.
3. Remove the three mounting bolts from the bracket at the rear of the pump and remove the bracket. Remove the single bolt from the front bracket and remove the pump.
4. Pull the rubber bushings out of the lower pump mount and inspect them. Replace them if they are worn or cracked, making sure the inside diameters fits around the inner (metal) bushing and outside diameters fit inside the mount.
5. Install the pump in reverse order.

Exhaust Gas Recirculating System
OPERATION

The EGR valve is vacuum operated by the position of the carburetor or injection system throttle plate in the throttle bore during vehicle operation. A metered amount of exhaust gas enters the combustion chamber to be mixed with the air/fuel blend. The effect is to reduce the peak combustion temperatures, which in turn reduces the amount of nitrous oxides (NO_x), formed during the combustion process.

TESTING
EGR Valve

2002, 3.0

Remove the air filter and adjust the engine idle to 900 rpm. Remove the vacuum line from the valve and using an engine vacuum source, attach the hose to the vacuum nipple. The engine speed should drop 500–600 rpm

EGR valve cyclone filter location—to be replaced at 56,000 mile intervals on 1973–74 2002

if the valve is operating properly. If little or no change of engine speed is noted, the recirculation pipes, the cyclone filter or the EGR valve may be plugged or defective.

320i

1. Start the engine and let it idle. Disconnect the blue hose at the EGR valve, and leave both ends open. The engine speed should remain the same. If the engine speed changes, the throttle blade opens too far at idle or the EGR valve is sticking open.

2. Leave the blue hose detached and disconnect the black hose at the intake header. Detach the red hose at the throttle housing and connect it to the open port on the intake header. The engine speed should drop considerably, or the EGR valve is defective and must be replaced.

3. Detach the black hose at the header. Detach the red hose at the temperature sensing valve and connect it to the open port on the intake header. If the engine speed drops, the EGR valve is sticking open or the pressure converter is defective. To check the pressure converter, detach red and blue hoses and check for vacuum at the open converter ports (engine running). If there is no vacuum at the ports, but the white hose to the converter has vacuum, the converter is defective.

530i

1. With the engine idling and hot, disconnect the black hose at the tee leading into the vacuum control valve.

2. Disconnect the hose at the vacuum limiter, and connect its open end with the open end of the black hose. The engine speed should drop about 100 rpm. Reconnect the black hose to the tee.

3. Disconnect the blue hose at the vacuum control valve and connect its open end to the open end of the hose disconnected from the vacuum limiter in Step 2. The engine speed should now drop about 200 rpm. If either test is failed, replace the EGR valve.

630CSi 633CSi, 733i

1. Bring the engine to operating temperature at idle speed. Detach the blue hose at the EGR valve—do not plug either the open end of the hose or the fitting on the valve. The engine speed should stay the same. If the engine speed drops, check the red hose from the throttle housing for vacuum. If there is vacuum there, adjust the idle position of the throttle. If there is no vacuum, the EGR valve is defective.

2. Detach the blue hose at the EGR valve. On 600 Series cars, remove the plug from the intake collector, On the 733i, disconnect the white hose at the collector. Pull the red hose off the throttle housing and attach it to the open fitting on the intake collector. If the engine speed does not drop considerably, the EGR valve, coolant temperature switch, or red electric switching valve is defective. If the engine speed does drop, go to Step 5.

3. To test the coolant temperature switch, turn on the engine with the engine stopped and cold (temperature below 113 degrees F.). Pull the connector plug off the red magnetic valve and connect the test lamp between the two open terminals on the valve. The test lamp should not come on. If the test lamp does come on, test the speed switch as described in the next step.

4. To test the speed switch, remove the electrical connector from the blue switching valve with the engine idling. Connect a test lamp between the two leads. If it lights, the speed switch is defective. If not, make sure the valve is properly grounded and, if so, replace the speed switch. If the engine speed did not drop in Step 2, and you have made the tests described in Steps 3 and 4, test the red cap electric control valve (see below) before condemning the EGR valve.

5. Connect the blue hose back to the EGR valve. Leave the red hose connected as in Step 2. Engine speed should have dropped slightly from normal idle. If the idle speed drops considerably from normal idle, there are leaking hoses, a defective pressure con-

verter, or a bad EGR valve. Restore all hoses to their normal positions. Check for leaks. If there are no leaks, detach the red hose at the pressure converter with the engine idling and hot. There should be back pressure. Then, detach the white hose to make sure there is intake vacuum. Repair broken or loose red or white hoses, if necessary. Then, reinstall the white hose, pull off the blue hose, and check for vacuum at the blue pressure converter connection. If there is no vacuum, replace the pressure converter; otherwise, replace the EGR valve.

REMOVAL AND INSTALLATION OF EGR VALVE

1. Note color coding of vacuum hoses and disconnect them.
2. On 320i, loosen the clamp and disconnect the hose running into the side of the valve.
3. Unscrew the nut at the bottom of the valve with a spanner wrench. On six cylinder engines, remove the two mounting bolts for the EGR valve holding bracket from the intake pipes, and pull the valve free of the recirculation hose.
4. Install in reverse order, coating O-rings with grease for easy installation.

Electric Control Valve—Red Cap
530i, 630CSi, 633CSi, 733i

The electric control valve should stop the EGR valve operation at coolant temperatures below 113° F. (45° C.), and speeds above 3000 rpm. Tag and disconnect both vacuum hoses at the control valve with the engine off and the coolant temperature below 113° F. (45° C.). Connect a test hose to one of the nipples and blow through the hose. The valve is functioning properly when there is air flowing through the valve with the ignition OFF and no air flow through the valve with the ignition ON.

Electronic control valves—Black (1), Red (2), and Blue (3)

Testing the electronic control valve (1), coolant temperature switch (2), and the speed switch (3). Tests are similar for remaining switches

Connect the vacuum hoses to the valve and operate the engine until the coolant is heated over 113° F. (45° C.). Disconnect the hoses and check for air flow through the valve. Air should now flow through the valve.

Coolant Temperature Switch and Control Relay

1. With the coolant temperature below 113° F. (45° C.), turn the ignition ON, but do not start the engine. Remove the wire plug at the control valve and connect a test lamp to the plug.
   a. The test lamp should light. If the test lamp does not light, connect the test lamp to ground. If the lamp now operates, the ground wire to the control valve has an open circuit.
   b. If the test lamp still does not light, disconnect the wire terminal at the coolant temperature switch and connect it to ground. If the test lamp still does not light, replace the control valve.
2. With the coolant temperature above 113° F. (45° C.), turn the ignition switch ON but do not start the engine. Disconnect the wire terminal plug at the control valve and connect a test lamp. The lamp should be off. If the lamp is on, the coolant temperature switch or control relay is defective.
3. With the engine running at temperatures above 113° F. (45° C.), connect the test light to the disconnected plug of the control valve. The test lamp should be on over an engine speed of 3000 rpm. If the test lamp does not light, the speed switch is defective.

EGR WARNING LIGHT

A warning light marked EGR is triggered at 25,000 miles, to alert the driver to service the exhaust gas recirculation system filter.

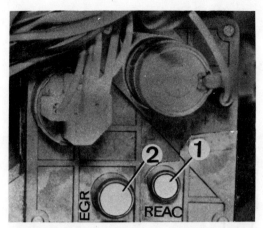

Triggering device showing reactor (1) and EGR (2) resetting devices

A triggering device, located under the dash and driven by the speedometer cable, can be reset to open the electrical contacts and extinguish the EGR warning light.

NOTE: *Two different sized buttons are mounted side by side on the triggering device. The small button is for the reactor light and the large button is for the EGR light. Press the button to reset.*

Oxygen Sensor (528i only)

OPERATION

The 528i employs a three way catalytic converter for emission control. No exhaust gas recirculation is required. Incompletely burned fuel, in the form of carbon monoxide, is utilized, within the catalyst, to remove oxygen from the nitrogenoxide emissions, leaving them in their normal state (as nitrogen). This can only be accomplished, however, if the fuel/air ratio of the engine is kept precisely at the optimum level—that is with absolutely no excess air or oxygen. A sensor located in the exhaust gas stream constantly regulates the fuel/air ratio provided by the injection system according to the amount of air in the exhaust.

SERVICE

Every 25,000 miles, an "Oxygen Sensor" warning light appears on the dash. This must be replaced with a new unit by unplugging the old unit, unscrewing it from its location on the exhaust pipe just downstream from the exhaust pipe connection at the exhaust manifold, and screwing in and plugging in the new unit. The warning light is then extinguished by depressing the reset button located on the service interval switch. This unit is under the dash and is driven by the speedometer cable.

Distributor Advance/Retard Units

OPERATION

A vacuum advance and retard unit is attached to the distributor and is controlled by engine vacuum. The advance can be checked with a strobe light and increasing the engine speed while observing the action of the timing mark during the increase in engine speed. The retard side can be checked at idle by removing the retard vacuum line and noting the increase in engine speed of at least 300 rpm.

NOTE: *Models 733i, 633i, 320i California and High Altitude vehicles equipped with manual transmissions, have the vacuum advance in operation only when the high gear is engaged. This is controlled by an electrical switch connected to the shifting linkage. Automatic transmission 633i for California and High Altitude, have the vacuum advance inoperative. Late model 530i and 630i vehicles are equipped with a vacuum retard unit only. The 528i has both advance and retard.*

TESTING

Electric Control Valve (Black Cap)—California Equipment Only

This control valve stops the retard distributor control over speeds of 3000 rpm.

Remove the outer hose (to distributor) and start the engine. At engine rpm lower than 3000 rpm, vacuum should be present in the distributor retard unit hose and not present when the engine speed is increased above 3000 rpm.

Disconnect the wire terminal end at the control valve and have the engine operating at idle. Connect a test lamp to the terminal and check for the presence of current. If current is present, the speed switch is defective.

Increase the engine speed to 3000 rpm or above, and the test lamp should light. If the test lamp does not light, the speed switch is defective.

Carburetor Dashpot

OPERATION

A dashpot is used to slow the carburetor throttle return while the vehicle engine is

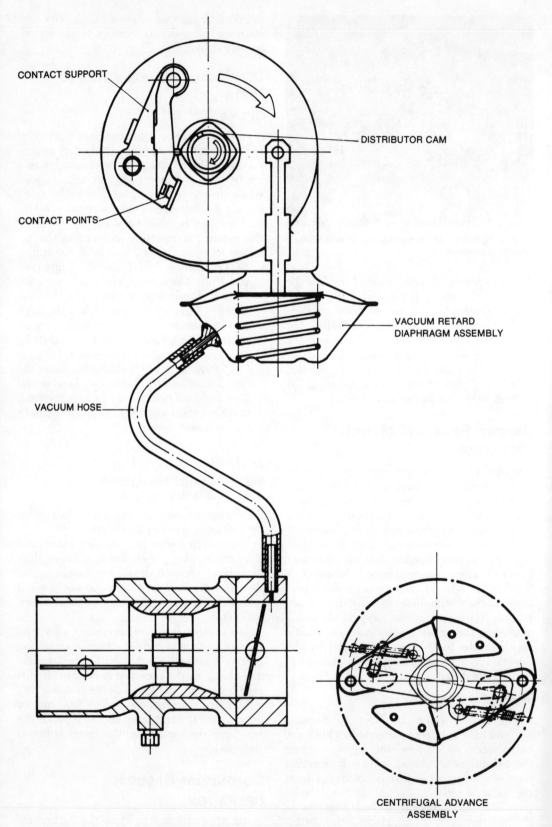

CONTACT SUPPORT

DISTRIBUTOR CAM

CONTACT POINTS

VACUUM RETARD
DIAPHRAGM ASSEMBLY

VACUUM HOSE

CENTRIFUGAL ADVANCE
ASSEMBLY

Four cylinder ignition retard system schematic—1974

above 1800 rpm on carbureted engines. An electrically controlled set of relays and magnetic switches are used to direct engine vacuum to release the dashpot at engine speeds under a certain rpm.

TESTING

Operate the engine at 2500 rpm and slowly decrease the speed to approximately 1800 rpm. The dashpot plunger should contact the throttle linkage at the 1700–1900 rpm mark (2002—1550 minimum). Adjust the dashpot plunger if necessary.

The plunger must be free of the throttle linkage under 1700 rpm minimum (2002—1550 minimum) when the engine vacuum is directed through the magnetic valve to the dashpot.

If no vacuum is present at the dashpot hose under 1700 rpm, check the engine speed relay connector. Remove the terminal end from the magnetic valve and increase the engine speed to 2000 rpm. If voltage is present at the terminal, the magnetic switch is defective and if no voltage is present, the speed sensitive relay must be replaced.

FUEL SYSTEM

Mechanical Fuel Pump (Carbureted Engines)
REMOVAL AND INSTALLATION

1. Remove the air cleaner. Disconnect and plug the two fuel lines.
2. Remove the two retaining nuts and pull the pump off the cylinder head. Pull the insulator block off and the pushrod out.
3. If there is much evidence of wear, check the length of the pushrod. It should be 3.468 in. on four cylinder cars and 4.7133 on six cylinder cars.
4. Install in reverse order. Do not use sealer on the insulator block, as this will change the effective length of the pushrod.

TESTING

Insert a tee in the fuel pump discharge line where it enters the carburetor. Connect a gauge rated at about 10 psi to the open end of the tee. Run the engine at 4,000 rpm. The pressure should be 2.99–3.56 psi.

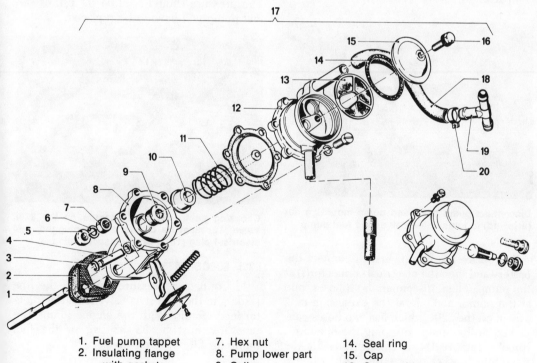

1. Fuel pump tappet
2. Insulating flange with gaskets
3. Circlip for axle
4. Axle
5. Insulating bushing
6. Lockwasher
7. Hex nut
8. Pump lower part
9. Collar
10. Hold-down
11. Diaphragm spring
12. Pump upper part
13. Fuel strainer
14. Seal ring
15. Cap
16. Screw with gasket
17. Fuel pump
18. Fuel hose
19. Distributing piece
20. Hose clamp

Exploded view of mechanical fuel pump components—four cylinder

Removing mechanical fuel pump

Electrical Fuel Pump

REMOVAL AND INSTALLATION

On all electric pump (fuel injection) equipped cars but the 320i, the fuel pump is mounted together with the expansion tank for the evaporative emissions control system. The pumps which are mounted together with the expansion tank are located under the rear of the car. The 320i pump is in the engine compartment.

Disconnect pump hose and pump mounting nut (arrowed) to remove the 600 series fuel pump

To replace the pump, first disconnect the battery and then the electrical connector(s) at the pump. Then, disconnect both hoses, one at the pump, and one at the expansion tank except on the 320i (which has two hoses connected to the pump) and plug the openings. Finally, remove the attaching nuts for the mounting bracket or, on the 320i, remove the bolt from the clamp and remove the pump. On models other than the 320i, loosen the clamp bolt, and separate the pump from the pump/expansion tank mounting bracket. Install in reverse order.

PRESSURE CHECKING

2002Tii

Connect a pressure gauge to the union at the front of the injection pump. Idle the engine. The pressure should be 28.5 psi. If pressure is low, check the pump ground. If that is ok and pressure is still low, replace the pump.

3.0

1. Install a pressure gauge in the line between the fuel filter and the injector feed circuit. The pressure must be 31.2. If not, see the adjustment procedure below or, if that will not correct low pressure, replace the pump.

320i

1. Connect a pressure gauge in the line leading from the fuel distributor on top of the injector pump to the warm up regulator. Plug the open end of the line leading to the warm up regulator, and make sure the gauge will read the pressure coming from the distributor.

2. Disconnect the wire plug on the mixture control unit, and turn on the ignition. The pressure should read 64–74 psi, or the fuel pump will have to be replaced.

Checking pump delivery pressure on the 320i. Valve (12) must be closed or line plugged, and electrical plug (15) must be disconnected

530i, 630CSi, 633CSi, 733i

1. Connect a pressure gauge in the line leading to the cold start valve from the injector feed circuit. With the engine idling, the pressure must be 33–38 psi, or the fuel pump (or filter) is defective.

ADJUSTMENT

3.0 Series

The fuel pressure regulator is located in the circuit which feeds all the injectors between

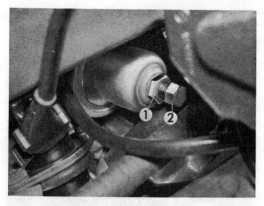

Loosen the locknut (1) and adjust the pressure (2) on the 3.0 pressure regulator

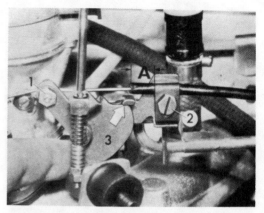

Proper choke cable installation—1600, 2002

two of the injectors. An adjusting bolt and locknut protrude from the top. To adjust it, connect a pressure gauge and idle the engine as described in the pressure check above, loosen the locknut, turn the bolt in or out until the pressure is correct, and then re-tighten the locknut.

Carburetors

APPLICATIONS

The 1970–71 1600-2 uses a single barrel downdraft Solex 38 PDSI carburetor. This unit has a manual choke.

The 1970–71 2002, up to chassis no. 2 583 405 uses a Solex 40 PDSI, which also uses a manual choke. The 1970–71 2002A (up to chassis no. 2 532 752 uses a Solex 40 PDSIT unit with a water heated automatic choke.

Later 2002 and 2002A models use a Solex 32/32 DIDTA carburetor with the water heated choke, to which was added an electric heating element in 1974. Later models also incorporate a float bowl return valve to re-duce vapor lock. The 2002TI uses two sepa-rate Solex 40 PHH carburetors, which have two progressively activated barrels each.

The 2800 and 3.0 use two Zenith 35/40 two stage carburetors.

REMOVAL AND INSTALLATION

1600-2, 2002 (Manual Choke)

1. Remove the air cleaner assembly, marking the vacuum lines, breather hoses, and air intake hose for reassembly.

2. Disconnect the fuel feed line at the car-buretor.

3. Loosen the clamp screw (1) and clamp (2), and disconnect the choke cable.

4. Lever off the clamp spring connecting the accelerator rod to the carburetor and dis-connect the throttle linkage.

5. Label and remove the vacuum line(s) from the carburetor.

6. Remove the two carburetor attaching nuts, and lift the carburetor from the mani-fold. Remove the flange gaskets and carbu-retor spacer, taking note of their placement.

7. Reverse the above procedure to install, taking care to adjust the choke cable in the following manner: push the choke knob on the dash into the bottom notch. Press the fast idle cam (3) against its stop so that the outer choke cable projects 0.6 in. (distance A) in front of the cable clamp, and tighten the clamp screw (2) in this position. Adjust the idle speed. Tighten the attaching nuts to 7.23–10.12 ft lbs.

2002-A, 2002 with Automatic Choke

1. Remove the air cleaner assembly, marking the vacuum lines, breather hoses, and air intake hose for reassembly.

2. Disconnect the fuel feed line at the car-buretor.

3. Disconnect the electrical cable for the thermostat valve. Drain the radiator.

4. Remove the 3 retaining screws and lift the choke mechanism cover from the carbu-retor body.

5. Remove the safety clip (1) from the ball socket at the throttle linkage connection to the carburetor. Press the throttle and down-shift rotary shaft downward and rearward and disconnect the throttle linkage.

6. Label and remove the vacuum line(s) from the carburetor.

7. Remove the two carburetor attaching nuts, and lift off the carburetor from the manifold. Remove the flange gaskets and car-

Disconnecting throttle linkage—Solex 40 PDSIT

Automatic choke adjustment

ifold studs. Disconnect the rod from the rotating shaft.

6. Remove the remaining mounting nuts and remove the carburetors. Remove all gaskets.

7. To install, reverse the removal procedure, bearing the following points in mind:

On the 2002TI, make sure the torsion spring is in the proper position. See text

A. Before installing the carburetor on the right side, position the prong on the choke butterfly lever so it engages with the hole in the linkage of the left hand carburetor by rotating the linkage on the left hand carburetor as necessary.

B. Make sure the torsion spring on the carburetor synchronizing portion of the throttle mechanism is in the proper position.

C. Push the choke knob in to the first notch. Open the choke mechanism on the carburetors all the way. Then, clamp the choke cable snugly in place, making sure the cable sheath does not protrude more than .6 in.

buretor spacer, taking note of their placement.

8. Reverse the above procedure to install, taking care to insert the automatic choke engaging arm in the eyelet for the bimetallic spring. The choke must be adjusted so that the notch on the choke cover and the projection on the choke housing align. Adjust the idle speed. Tighten the attaching nuts to 7.23–10.12 ft lbs.

2002Ti

1. Remove the air cleaner, labeling all hoses.

2. Disconnect the choke cable at the carburetor end and remove the cable from the bracket.

3. Loosen the dipstick retainer clip.

4. Pull off fuel hoses.

5. Remove the throttle tensioning spring. Remove the two carburetor mounting nuts which fasten the mounting bracket for the rotating shaft, and pull the bracket off the man-

2800, 3.0

1. Drain the radiator, and remove the air cleaner.

2. Disconnect fuel, vacuum, and water lines.

3. Disconnect and remove the choke cables. Disconnect the fuel return hose at the carburetor, on cars so equipped.

4. Disconnect throttle rod at the carburetor. Remove the carburetor mounting nuts from the studs, and remove the carburetor.

5. Install in reverse order, noting that the flange gasket must be in position so the smaller opening is situated toward the cylinder head, and the coated side faces down.

Synchronize the carburetors and bleed the cooling system when filling it.

THROTTLE LINKAGE ADJUSTMENT

Throttle linkage adjustments are generally not necessary except that, if synchronization of the Zenith 35/40 units proves difficult, the adjustable link connecting the two throttle linkages should be adjusted to a center-to-center length of 1.57 in.

Dimension "A" should be 1.57 in. on Zenith 35/40 units

FLOAT LEVEL ADJUSTMENT

38 PDSI, 40 PDSI, 40 PDSIT

1. Run the engine until it reaches operating temperature. Shut the engine off.
2. Disconnect the fuel feed line from the carburetor.
3. Remove the carburetor top cover and seal.
4. Using a depth gauge, the level of fuel in the bowl must be 0.7–0.75 in.
5. Adjust, as necessary, by varying the number of or thickness of the seals(s) underneath the float needle valve.

Solex 38 PDSI, Solex 32/32 DIDTA

The float level cannot be adjusted without the carburetor completely assembled, and, therefore, this adjustment cannot be accomplished without a special sightglass and equipment for adjusting the amount of fuel in the bowl.

Zenith 35/40

The float level is not adjustable, but depends upon the condition of various parts only, especially the gasket used under the float valve, which must be .04 in. thick.

Checking pulldown clearance

FAST IDLE ADJUSTMENT

2002, 2002A With Automatic Choke

1. Start the engine and bring it to operating temperature.
2. Operate the accelerator rod until the choke plate can be closed by hand. Then, close the choke plate until only 0.25 in. (6.5 mm) clearance exists between the plate and the carburetor air horn. This will bring the stop lever into the fast idling speed position. Once this clearance is set, do not disturb the accelerator rod.
3. Using the adjusting nuts (1 and 2) at the choke connector rod, adjust the fast idle speed to 2100 rpm. To increase engine speed, increase the rod length. To decrease engine speed, decrease the rod length.

Adjusting the fast idle (40 PDSIT)

2800, 3.0

1. Make sure the engine is hot, the air cleaner is removed, the carburetors are synchronized (see Chapter 2), and that idle speed is 900 rpm.

2. Where the distributor has two hoses going to the diaphragm (both advance and retard), remove the retard hose (connected on the distributor side of the diaphragm).

3. Switch off the engine and disconnect the choke rod at the rear carburetor.

4. Get a drill with .095 in. diameter and insert it between the lower edge of the choke butterfly and the throttle bore. Open the throttle slightly and then close the choke to touch the drill, and pin it against the throttle bore. This will set the fast idle mechanism on the second step. Then, release the choke.

5. Without touching the throttle linkage, start the engine. If the rpm is not 1,400, note exactly how far off and which direction from the speed.

6. If the speed must be readjusted, stop the engine, open the throttle all the way, and adjust the screw on the choke housing inward to speed the idle up or outward to slow it down, about 1 turn for each 300 rpm.

7. Repeat 4–6 until idle speed is at 1,400.

8. Open the throttle to open the rear choke. Then repeat Steps 4–6 for the front carburetor.

9. Finally, repeat Step 4 for both front and rear chokes. Both chokes must be set to the proper position while the throttle is held open. Then, both chokes must be held there as the throttle is released. Remove the drills, release the chokes, and start the engine. RPM must be 1,800–2,000.

AUTOMATIC CHOKE AND CHOKE UNLOADER ADJUSTMENT

2002, 2002A

1. Be sure the choke valve shaft will rotate freely in its bore and that the choke cap aligning notch is aligned with the lug on the choke valve housing.

2. Depress the accelerator to allow the choke valve to close under spring tension.

NOTE: *The choke valve should close if the ambient temperature is below 68° F. (20° C).*

3. If adjustment is needed, remove the choke cap with the water hoses attached.

4. Depress the choke rod (the vertical shaft inside choke housing) downward to its stop and check the choke valve clearance between the choke valve and the throttle bore. The gap should be 0.251–0.267 in.

5. An adjusting screw and locknut (1) is located under the choke housing and controls the height of the choke rod. Loosen the lock-

Pressing choke rod down to stop—2002

Adjusting clearance "1"

nut and move the screw (arrowed) in or out to change the choke valve gap.

6. Reposition the choke cover on the carburetor. Be sure the choke arm engages the coil spring loop in the choke cover. Align the notch on the cover with the lug on the choke housing.

7. Connect the heating coil wire terminal to the housing.

NOTE: *Current flow should be approximately 1 amp at 12 volts.*

8. Adjust the fast idle speed to 2,000–2,200 rpm with the engine at normal operating temperature.

9. With the choke valve set at a gap of 0.25 inch, adjust the choke connector rod nuts to set the fast idle. Shorten the rod to reduce the rpm and lengthen the rod to increase the rpm.

2800, 3.0

1. Remove the choke cover, leaving water hoses attached.

2. Open the throttle and close the choke butterfly.

3. Loosen the lockscrew on the pivot unit at the top of the choke rod. Make sure the adjusting screw inside the choke housing points to the high step of the actuating cam.

4. Raise and lower the rod until the gap between the lower end of the rod and the actuating cam is .059 in. Then, tighten the lockscrew and press the clamping ring on the rod up against the pivot unit.

5. Then, push the rod upward and push the actuating cam against the rod.

6. Check the gap between the lower edge of the choke butterfly and the throttle bore. It should be .118 in. If not, loosen the locknut and turn the adjusting screw on the choke unloader until the dimension is correct. Tighten the locknut and apply sealer.

Accelerator Pump Adjustment

A special metering cup is used to measure accelerator pump stroke and performance. If this is not available, the pump stroke (and fuel delivery) can be adjusted: on the 2002 Series by adjusting the position of the locknuts on the pump lever; on the 2800 and 3.0 Series by bending the plunger lever (located under the float bowl cover) at the pivot point. Make sure, before making adjustment, that idle mixture and ignition timing are correct, that the carburetor is clean, and that the plunger and check valves in the accelerator pump system are in good condition.

On the 2800 and 3.0, adjust the accelerator pump at the arrowed bending point. A special metering cup ("7040") is available for checking pump performance

OVERHAUL

Carburetor repair kits are recommended for each overhaul. Kits contain a complete set of gaskets and new parts to replace those that generally deteriorate most rapidly. Not substituting *all* of the new parts supplied in the kits can result in poor performance later.

Zenith/Solex carburetor repair kits are of three basic types—repair, Vit, and gasket. The following summarizes the parts in each type:

Vit kits
all gaskets
float needle valve
volume control screw
all diaphragms
spring

Repair kits
all jets and gaskets
all diaphragms
float needle valve
volume control screw
spring for pump diaphragm
pump ball valve
main jet carrier
float
complete intermediate rod
intermediate pump lever
complete injector tube
some cover hold-down screws and washers

Gasket kits
all needed gaskets

Carburetor overhaul should be performed only in a clean, dust-free area. Disassemble carburetor carefully keeping look-alike parts separated to prevent accidential interchange at assembly. Note all jet sizes. When reassembling, make sure all screws and jets are tight in their seats. Tighten all screws gradually, in rotation. Do not tighten needle valves into seats. Uneven jetting will result. Use a new flange gasket.

Wash carburetor parts—except diaphragm and electric choke units—in a carburetor cleaner, rinse in solvent, and blow dry with compressed air. Carburetors have numerous small passages that can be fouled by carbon and gummy deposits. Soak metal parts in carburetor solvent until thoroughly clean. The solvent will weaken or destroy cork, plastic, and leather components. These parts should be wiped with a clean, lint-free cloth. Clean all fuel channels in float bowl and cover. Clean jets and valves separately to avoid accidental interchange. Never use wire or sharp objects to clean jets and passages as this will seriously alter their calibration.

Check throttle valve shafts for wear or

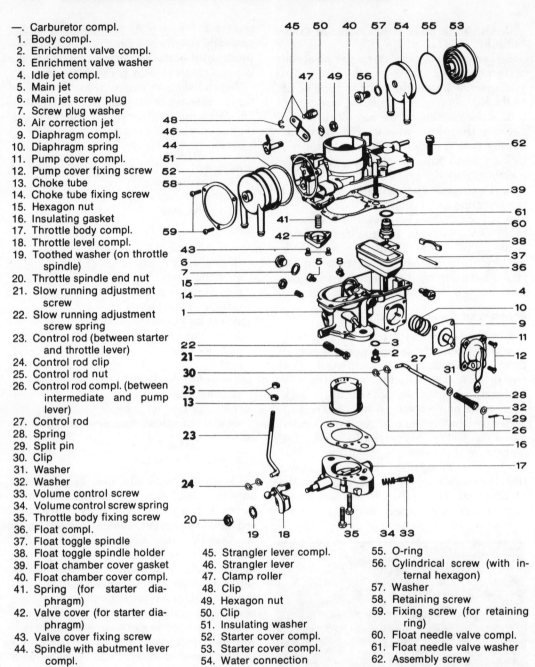

—. Carburetor compl.
1. Body compl.
2. Enrichment valve compl.
3. Enrichment valve washer
4. Idle jet compl.
5. Main jet
6. Main jet screw plug
7. Screw plug washer
8. Air correction jet
9. Diaphragm compl.
10. Diaphragm spring
11. Pump cover compl.
12. Pump cover fixing screw
13. Choke tube
14. Choke tube fixing screw
15. Hexagon nut
16. Insulating gasket
17. Throttle body compl.
18. Throttle level compl.
19. Toothed washer (on throttle spindle)
20. Throttle spindle end nut
21. Slow running adjustment screw
22. Slow running adjustment screw spring
23. Control rod (between starter and throttle lever)
24. Control rod clip
25. Control rod nut
26. Control rod compl. (between intermediate and pump lever)
27. Control rod
28. Spring
29. Split pin
30. Clip
31. Washer
32. Washer
33. Volume control screw
34. Volume control screw spring
35. Throttle body fixing screw
36. Float compl.
37. Float toggle spindle
38. Float toggle spindle holder
39. Float chamber cover gasket
40. Float chamber cover compl.
41. Spring (for starter diaphragm)
42. Valve cover (for starter diaphragm)
43. Valve cover fixing screw
44. Spindle with abutment lever compl.

45. Strangler lever compl.
46. Strangler lever
47. Clamp roller
48. Clip
49. Hexagon nut
50. Clip
51. Insulating washer
52. Starter cover compl.
53. Starter cover compl.
54. Water connection

55. O-ring
56. Cylindrical screw (with internal hexagon)
57. Washer
58. Retaining screw
59. Fixing screw (for retaining ring)
60. Float needle valve compl.
61. Float needle valve washer
62. Assembly screw

Exploded view of Solex 40 PDSIT carburetor

scoring that may allow air leakage affecting starting and idling. Inspect float spindle and other moving parts for wear. Replace if worn. Replace float if fuel has leaked into it. Accelerator pump check-valves should pass air one way but not the other. Test for proper seating by blowing and sucking on valve and replace if necessary. Wash valve again to remove breath moisture. Check bowl cover with straight edge for warped surfaces. Closely inspect valves and seats for wear and damage.

Rebuild kits contain complete, step by step disassembly and assembly instructions, so they are not included here.

Fuel Injection

BMW 2002Tii models use the Kugelfischer mechanical fuel injection system, in which

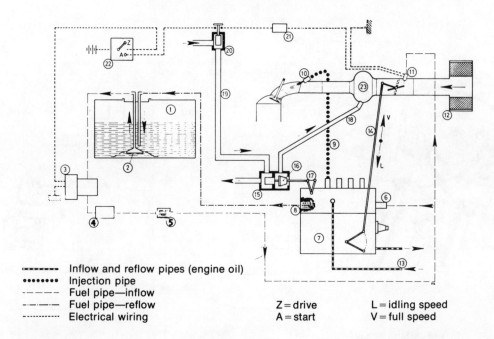

---------- Inflow and reflow pipes (engine oil)		
•••••••• Injection pipe		
– – – – Fuel pipe—inflow		
–·–·–· Fuel pipe—reflow	Z = drive	L = idling speed
---------- Electrical wiring	A = start	V = full speed

1. Fuel tank with induction unit
2. Fine-mesh filter
3. Fuel pump
4. Pressure regulator
5. Main fuel filter
6. Fine-mesh filter—fuel intake
7. Injection pump
8. Fuel return line with pressure valve
9. Injection pipe
10. Injection valve
11. Starter valve
12. Air cleaner
13. Engine oil line
14. Adjustment of engine idling and top speed (by accelerator pedal)
15. Warmup runner with expansion element
16. Air adjustment cone
17. Lever for eccentric shaft
18. Intake pipe for additional air
19. Coolant line
20. Temperature switch
21. Retard Switch
22. Ignition switch
23. Plenum chamber

2002Tii fuel injection system schematic

fuel and air are inducted separately through the injection pump and the throttle manifold butterfly. Fuel and air are mixed in the intake manifold.

Fuel is injected into the intake manifold behind the open intake valve under high pressure.

The electric fuel pump pumps fuel from the tank through a fine-mesh filter in the tank and a filter in the fuel line. The fuel flows through the expansion container, the main fuel filter, and into the injector pump at 21.7–36.2 psi. Excess fuel and any air bubbles are routed back to the tank via a return line. This ensures that the fuel is always kept cool and free of bubbles.

The injection pump camshaft is belt-driven from the engine crankshaft. Four pumping pistons, operating in firing order sequence, inject the required amount of fuel. The amount of fuel injected depends on engine load and speed.

Fuel injection volume is regulated by engine load. The accelerator pedal is con-

nected with the throttle butterfly and the lever on the injection pump. When the pedal is depressed, the throttle butterfly moves and the stroke length of the pump piston is governed by the regulating cam, depending on throttle opening.

Fuel injection volume is also regulated by engine speed. The stroke of the pump piston is governed by the injection pump governor.

During cold engine operation, the air/fuel mixture is enriched until the engine temperature reaches 140–149° F. A temperature switch in the coolant also regulates the piston pump stroke. Additional air, which does not pass through the throttle butterfly, is metered into the manifold plenum chamber.

When the engine is started, fuel is injected into the intake manifold by a solenoid valve. The duration time of injection depends on the coolant temperature.

When the injection pump pressure reaches 435–551 psi, each injection valve opens. Intake air flows through the air cleaner and the throttle manifold butterfly to

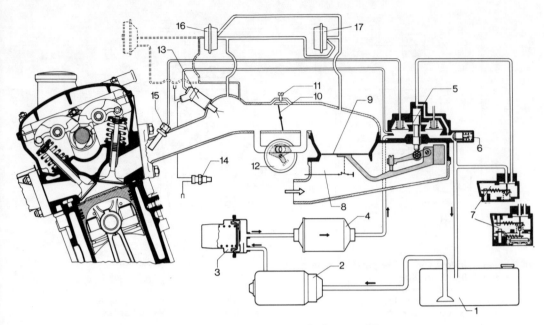

1. Fuel tank with pre-fuel pump
2. Fuel delivery pump
3. Fuel accumulator
4. Fuel filter
5. Fuel distributor
6. System pressure regulator and topping point valve
7. Warming-up regulator
8. Airflow meter
9. Sensor plate
10. Throttle butterfly
11. Idle adjustment screw
12. Aux. air device
13. Electric starting valve
14. Thermo-time switch
15. Injectors
16. Vacuum limiter
17. Start air valve

Schematic of the K-Jetronic fuel injection system used on the 320i

the manifold plenum chamber, and from there through the four manifold branches to the combustion chambers.

The 320i models are equipped with a continuous injection system called the "K-Jetronic." All the air drawn through the intake passes through a very large venturi. There is a sprung sensor plate inside the venturi which moves up or down as airflow (and therefore the pressure on it) increases or decreases. This motion is mechanically transferred to a piston located in the distributor, nearby. The electric fuel pump supplies fuel to the distributor via a warm up regulator. Pressure to the warm up regulator is regulated to a constant pressure by the system pressure regulator in the base of the distributor. Then, the warm up regulator receives signals indicating outside air and engine water temperatures and further regulates the pressure accordingly. The distirbutor also divides the fuel flow four ways to deliver it in equal amounts to the injectors, which will not open until there is at least 47 psi, thus ensuring delivery of a constant flow of properly atomized fuel to the intake ports.

A thermo-time switch also measures water temperature and opens the cold start valve, located on the intake header, a varying amount each time the engine is started, depending on the conditions.

The L-Jetronic system used on six cylinder engines employs a pressure regulator (adjustable only on the 3.0) which maintains a constant pressure above the level of vacuum in the intake manifold. Six fuel injectors are located at the intake ports and inject fuel simultaneously, once each engine revolution. Readings of temperature from the air intake and engine water jacket compensate for temperature changes. An intake throttle housing contains a flapper valve working against a spring which, through a slight venturi action, shifts its position as flow through the engine changes. This operates a "potentiometer" which generates an electric signal representing total airflow. On the 3.0, this unit is replaced by a pressure sensor. The system receives a signal from the primary side of the distributor (2.8 and 3 liter engines) or a timing TDC Position transmitter (3.3 liter engines), thus enabling total airflow to be

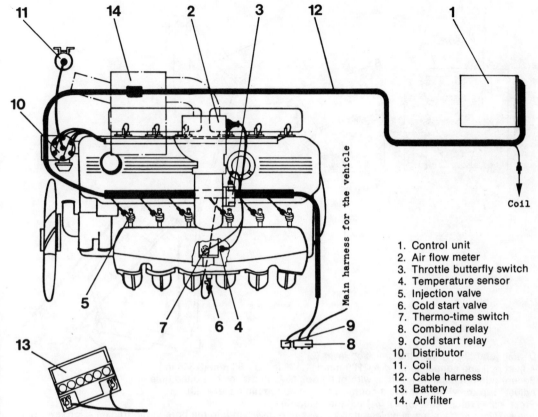

1. Control unit
2. Air flow meter
3. Throttle butterfly switch
4. Temperature sensor
5. Injection valve
6. Cold start valve
7. Thermo-time switch
8. Combined relay
9. Cold start relay
10. Distributor
11. Coil
12. Cable harness
13. Battery
14. Air filter

The L-Jetronic fuel injection system used on six cylinder engines

divided up into an appropriate number of individual "shots" of fuel required, which depends upon engine rpm. Fuel is injected simultaneously once each engine revolution. If air flow is lower, as when the throttle is nearly closed, the system's computer opens the injector valves for a shorter length of time at a given rpm; if air flow is higher, injection time is increased proportionately.

Cold starting is aided just as in the K-Jetronic system.

In the 528i, which must run at a mixture ratio which gives only the amount of air required to fully burn the fuel, an oxygen sensor located in the exhaust pipe also influences the time signal the computer sends to the injection valves. If too much air is present, the fuel amount is increased, and vice-versa.

REMOVAL AND INSTALLATION

Air Container and Throttle Valve Stub Assembly Removal and Installation (2002Tii)

1. Label and disconnect all hoses from the air cleaner. Remove the air cleaner.

2. Disconnect the fuel hose (1) and cable for the start valve (2) from the throttle valve stub. Disconnect the vacuum hose (3) from the air container.

3. Loosen all hose clamps and remove the four induction pipes.

4. Unhook the return spring from the throttle valve stub linkage. Disconnect the retaining screw for the linkage bracket.

5. Taking care to support the pipe connection while loosening, disconnect the injection pipe at no. 1 cylinder. Remove the injection valve.

6. Remove the two retaining bolts (7, 8) for the throttle valve stub support bracket. Disconnect the vacuum hose (9) from the valve stub and the auxiliary air hose (10) from the air container.

7. Again taking care to support the pipe connection while loosening, disconnect the injection pipe (11) from no. 4 cylinder.

8. Remove the six nuts retaining the air container to the cylinder head and lift off the air container and throttle valve stub assembly.

9. Reverse the above procedure to install, taking care to install new gaskets at the cylin-

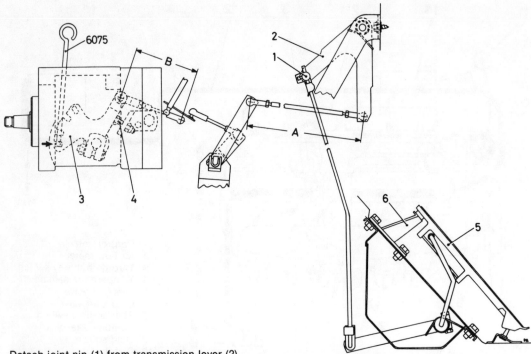

Detach joint pin (1) from transmission lever (2).
Adjust pull and connecting rod A = 289 mm (11.378 in.) B = 85 mm (3.346 in.).
Secure pump regulating lever (3) with pull hook 6075 in the lower slotted hole.
Adjust stop screw (4) that it just contacts the pump regulating lever (3).
Press accelerator pedal (5) against full load stop (6).
Adjust joint pin (1) in a way which allows stress-free insertion into the bore in the transmission lever (2).
Secure joint pin and remove pull hook 6075.

Fuel injection system throttle linkage and full load stops adjustments

Air container and throttle valve stub assembly installed with air cleaner removed

der head flange and new cord rings at the induction pipes, if necessary. Check the tightness of the induction pipes by spraying water at the pipe connections. If there is an air leak, the engine will idle unevenly.

Injection Pump Removal and Installation (2002Tii)

1. Drain the cooling system.
2. Label and disconnect all hoses from the air cleaner. Remove the air cleaner.

3. Disconnect the four injection lines and fitting rings at the pump, noting their placement for installation. Plug the pressure valves with dust caps.

4. Disconnect the fuel reflow hose, oil feed hose, water inflow hose and the oil dipstick support bracket from the pump.

5. Disconnect the water return hose (4), oil return hose (5) and the hose for the auxil-

Disconnecting hoses and bracket from throttle valve stub assembly

Removing air container and throttle valve stub assembly

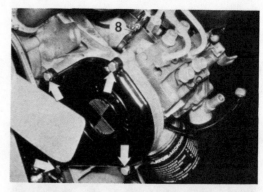

Disconnecting connecting rod (8) and removing dust cover retaining bolts

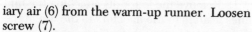

Disconnecting hoses and loosening screw (7) from rear of pump housing

Aligning pump and pulleys at top dead center

iary air (6) from the warm-up runner. Loosen screw (7).

6. Disconnect the connecting link from the pump lever.

7. Remove the four retaining bolts for the injection pump drive belt dust cover and remove the cover.

8. Rotate the engine until no. 1 cylinder is at Top Dead Center. At this point, the notch in the drive belt pulley is aligned with the projection on the lower section of the drive belt dust cover, and the distributor rotor is pointing to the spark plug wire connection for no. 1 cylinder (cap removed). Also, the notch in the cogged belt pulley is aligned with the cast-in projection on the pump housing. With the engine at TDC, remove the pump drive pulley retaining nut.

9. Using a puller, remove the pump drive pulley, taking care not to misplace the woodruff key. Remove the cogged belt.

10. Remove the two bolts retaining the injection pump to the timing case cover. Then, pull out the pump to the rear so that the intermediate shaft may be lifted out at the

warm-up senser housing. Lift out the injection pump.

11. Reverse the above procedure to install.

Cogged Belt (2002Tii)

1. Remove the front air filter hood and the upper dust cover on the pump assembly.

2. Rotate the engine so that the No. 1 piston is at TDC on its compression stroke. The crankshaft pulley must point to the mark on the dust cap and the pump pulley must align with the casting mark on the pump body.

3. Loosen the alternator and remove the belt.

4. Mark the location of the V pulley on the crankshaft and remove the retaining bolts from the pulley.

5. Remove the pulley and do not turn the engine, due to the pulley fitting at 180°.

6. Loosen the upper dust cover bolt, remove all the other retaining bolts for the lower dust cover and remove the cogged belt by pulling the dust cover to the front and

Alignment of crankshaft pulley and injector pump timing marks

Detach upper housing (10). Remove the bolts (arrowed). Make sure to replace the gasket (11) in reassembly

pulling the cogged belt out between the hub and the front dust cover.

7. Be sure of the pulley alignment for both the crankshaft and the injector pump and reverse the removal procedure to install the cogged belt.

Injection Valve (2002Tii)

1. Disconnect the feed line to the injector with fitting wrenches to avoid damage to the threaded areas.

2. Unscrew the injector valve from the induction sleeve.

3. During installation, use new sealing rings.

Mixture Control Unit (320i)

1. Disconnect the large intake pipe (made of rubber) from the unit by loosening the clamp and pulling it off.

2. Loosen the three screws in the top of the fuel distributor. Open the clips holding the fuel line to the extreme control unit, and remove the clamp linking the four fuel lines together.

2. Lift the distributor off the control unit, using tape to hold the piston up inside the unit, and move it aside.

3. Disconnect the electrical plug at the air horn, and the small vacuum hose and large air line connected to the vacuum regulator, mounted near the rear of the mixture control unit.

4. Loosen the two mounting nuts located on the wheel well side of the unit and lift it out.

5. Remove the bolts in the flange holding upper (10) and lower (11) sections of the unit together. Then remove the six bolts (three located inside the lower housing) which re-

tain the air cleaner housing to the mixture control unit.

6. Replace the mixture control unit lower and upper housings together with an entire new unit. The new unit will have to be split (top and bottom sections separate at the flange). This will permit the air cleaner bolts to be attached from inside. Use a new gasket, and reassemble the upper and lower sections of the new mixture control unit after the air cleaner housing is attached; then, reverse the remaining procedures to install it, using a new seal under the fuel distributor.

Fuel Distributor (320i)

1. Remove the four nuts attaching the fuel lines leading to the injectors to the top of the distributor (1 through 4). Unscrew the union nut and disconnect the line leading to the warm-up regulator (5) (at the front).

2. Disconnect the two, large low pressure fuel lines coming from the fuel filter (6 and 9) (at the front) and going back to the tank (at the wheel well side), by removing the attaching bolts. Also disconnect the two high

Numbered locations of fuel distributor lines for the 320i. See text

pressure (small) lines (7 and 8) from the side of the unit (front to warm up regulator, and the rear line going to the start valve) in a similar manner.

3. Remove the three screws from the top of the distributor unit. Then, lift the unit off the top of the mixture control.

4. Install in reverse order. Clean the control piston in gasoline and replace it if it is damaged. Use a new gasket where the distributor fits onto the top of the mixture control unit.

Injection Valves (320i)

1. Remove the rubber intake hose leading from the mixture control unit to the throttle unit. Remove the four retaining nuts for each, and then remove No. 2 and No. 3 (the two center cylinders) intake pipes.

2. The injector valves incorporate union nuts and a flatted section on each valve to permit the lines to beattached to the valves. However, the injection lines *need not* be disconnected to remove the valves, which are simply pressed into the intake ports. To remove each valve, simply pass a screwdriver blade downward between the intake header and the cam cover, insert the blade into the

Using a screwdriver to remove 320i injection valves

groove between the fuel line nut and flatted portion of the injection valve, and pry out. After the valve is out of the port, hold the flatted section of the valve with a wrench, use another wrench to unscrew the union nut, and disconnect the fuel line.

3. On installation, first press the white insulating bushing back into the intake port, if it came out with the valve. Then, press the rubber seal into the groove. Finally, snugly press in the injection valve. Reinstall the intake pipes, using new gaskets.

Warm-Up Regulator (320i)

1. Remove the union nuts for the fuel inlet and outlet lines and pull them off the unit. Unplug the electrical connector.

2. Remove the mounting bolts top and bottom, and remove the unit. Installation is the reverse of the removal procedure.

Control Unit

3.0 Si

1. Remove the rear seat and remove the control unit from the floor panel.

2. Open the wire connector clamp and pull out the cover slide.

3. Carefully remove the connector from the control unit.

4. During the installation, a matched pressure sensor should be replaced also. Random pairing can result in excessive fuel consumption and poor engine operation.

5. Permissible combinations are;

Pressure sensor	Control unit
a. With-out paint dot	With-out paint dot
b. Blue dot	Blue dot
c. Red dot	Red dot

528i, 530i, 630i, 633i AND 733i

1. The contol unit is located behind the glove box on models 528i, 530i, 630i and 633i, and behind the right side cowl cover on the 733i.

2. Push the lock lug towards the wire loom or press the circlip rearward and pull the multiple terminal plug to the right. Disconnect the individual plug, if connected.

3. Remove the control unit from the body.

4. When installing the control box, connect the individual connector if the vehicle is to be used in high altitude operation.

NOTE: *When the individual connector circuit is complete, the fuel injection time is reduced, resulting in a 6% leaner air/fuel mixture necessary for high altitude operation. This is not necessary on 528i models.*

Pressure Sensor

3.0Si

1. The pressure sensor is located near the firewall on the left side of the engine compartment.

2. Remove the vacuum hose from the pressure sensor.

3. Remove the base plate from the bearing block and if equipped with automatic transmission, remove the starter locking relay.

4. Invert the base plate and remove the pressure sensor retaining bolts.

5. Install the pressure sensor in the reverse order.

NOTE: *Refer to the steps 4 and 5 under the 3.0Si control unit removal and installation for proper part replacement.*

Air Flow Sensor

530i

1. Disconnect the multiple connector, and then loosen the air hose clamps at either end of the unit.

2. Remove the air cleaner. Lift the volume control out of the bracket.

3. Remove the three mounting bolts, and pull the unit out of the bracket.

4. Install in reverse order.

528i, 630CSi, 633CSi, 733i

1. Disconnect the multiple connector. Loosen the air hose clamps at either end of the unit, and detach the hose on the engine side.

2. Remove the two air cleaner mounting nuts and remove the air cleaner and airflow sensor. Then, remove the three nuts attaching the airflow sensor to the base of the air filter, detach the hose from the air cleaner, and remove the unit. Install in reverse order.

Remove the three (arrowed) nuts attaching the airflow sensor to the base of the air filter

Coolant Temperature Sensor

ALL MODELS WITH ELECTRONIC INJECTION

Partially drain the cooling system. Then, disconnect the electrical terminal plug and unscrew the coolant temperature sensor. Install in reverse order, refilling and bleeding the cooling system.

Injection Valves

3.0Si

1. Remove the electrical plug from the injection valves.

2. Loosen and remove the injection valve from the ring line.

3. Remove the retaining bolts and pull the injector from the manifold.

4. To install, replace the rubber ring and do not damage the nozzle jet during the installation.

528i, 530i, 630CSi AND 633i

1. With the air collector removed, disconnect the electrical connector plugs from the 6 injection valves.

2. Remove the valve retaining bolts and remove the injector tube with all the valves attached.

3. Remove the retaining clamps and remove the valves from the injector tube.

4. To install, reverse the removal procedure.

633CSi, 733i

1. With the injector tube and injector valves removed from the engine, cut the metal hose clamp sleeve and remove the sleeve.

2. Heat the hose with a soldering iron and remove the injector hose from the tube.

3. To install the injector valve assembly on the tube, clean the tube adapter and coat the inside of the hose with fuel.

4. Install the fuel injector hose with the hose sleeve on the injector tube and push against the stop, with the electrical terminal facing up.

5. Complete the installation in the reverse of the removal procedure.

Air Intake Temperature Sensor

3.0Si

The temperature sensor can be unscrewed from the air collector after disconnecting the electrical plug.

Temperature Timing Switch

528i, 530i, 630CSi, 633CSi AND 733i

Partially drain the coolant and disconnect the electrical connector plug. Unscrew the temperature timing switch. After installation, bleed the cooling system.

Throttle Valve Switch

ALL MODELS WITH L-JETRONIC ELECTRONIC INJECTION

1. Remove the terminal plug from the throttle valve switch.

2. Remove the switch retaining screws and remove the switch from the throttle shaft.

3. To install the switch, engage the throttle shaft into the switch orifice. Install the retaining screws and terminal plug.

Cold Start Valve

ALL MODELS

1. Remove the electrical connector and the fuel line to the valve.

2. Remove the retaining bolts and pull the valve assembly from the air collector.

3. Replace the rubber sealing ring during installation.

TESTING

Warm-Up Sensor—2002Tii

NOTE: *The warm-up sensor adjustment must be made before the engine is warmed up.*

1. Remove the air filter housing.

2. Press out the air regulator cone with a screwdriver, until special tool 6073 or equivalent can be inserted in the groove of the air regulator cone.

3. A distance of 0.102 ± 0.012 in. should exist between the grub screw and the stop screw (distance A). Adjustments can be made at the plate nut (1).

4. After the engine is at normal operating temperature, the air regulator valve cone must project $0.35 - 0.39$ in. (distance A). The plate washer must project above the lever by

. Plate nut
. Special tool to lift air regulator cone
. Clearance between grub screw and stop screw

arm-up sensor adjustment—2002Tii

1. Grub screw   2. Stop screw
A. Projection of air regulator come above the valve body
B. Projection of plate washer above lever

Air regulator valve cone adjustment—2002Tii

0.157 in. (distance B) and the grub screw must be in full contact with the stop screw.

5. If these specifications are not obtained, the warm up sensor must be replaced.

320i Fuel System Pressure Testing

Install a shut-off valve and an oil pressure gauge between the control pressure line and the fuel distributor, with the pressure gauge next to the fuel distributor.

Cold Engine Pressure Test—320i

1. Disconnect the terminal plug at the mixture control unit to avoid excessive heat.

2. Open the valve for fuel flow and turn on the ignition switch to operate the fuel pump, but do not start the engine.

3. Control pressures depend upon the engine coolant temperature. At a temperature of 50° F. (10° C.), fuel pressure should be 10–11 psi and at 77° F. (25° C.), oil pressure should be 22.0 psi. At coolant temperature of 104° F. (40° C.), the pressure should be over 29.4 psi.

NOTE: *Oil pressure to low—warm-up regulator defective. Oil pressure to high— Fuel return flow insufficient or defective warm-up regulator.*

4. Turn the ignition OFF.

Warm Engine Control Pressure—320i

1. Open the shut-off valve for fuel flow. Disconnect the mixture control terminal plug and turn the ignition ON to start the fuel pump. Do not start the engine.

2. The control pressure should be 48–54 psi after three minutes, with the engine coolant at operating temperature. If the control pressure does not rise, check the wire plug

terminal for current at the warmup regulator. If current is present, the heating coil may be defective and would necessitate the replacement of the warm-up regulator.

Air Intake Temperature Sensor—3.0

The desired resistance is listed in the following chart depending on temperature readings.

Degrees F (C)	Resistance (Ohms)
14 (− 10)	9.6
32 (0)	6.4
50 (+ 10)	4.3
68 (20)	3.0
86 (30)	2.1
104 (40)	1.5
122 (50)	1.0
140 (60)	0.79

NOTE: *Allowable variation of resistance* ± *10%.*

Coolant Temperature Sensor

3.0Si

The desired resistance is noted in the following chart depending on the temperature reading.

Degrees F (C)	Resistance (Ohms)
14 (− 10)	9.2
32 (0)	5.9
50 (+ 10)	3.7
68 (20)	2.5
86 (30)	1.7
104 (40)	1.2
122 (50)	0.84
140 (60)	0.60
158 (70)	0.43
176 (80)	0.32
194 (90)	0.25
212 (100)	0.20

528i, 530i, 630CSi, 633CSi, 733i

The coolant temperature sensor can be checked with a test lamp. The circuit should open at temperatures above 113° F. (45° C.) and closed below 113° F. (45° C.).

Temperature Timing Switch

With the use of a test lamp, the switch can be tested at various temperatures for continuity. The operating time is eight seconds at −4° F.

(−20 C.) and declines to 0 seconds at + 59° F (+ 15 C).

Cold Start Valve

3.0Si

The cold start valve should only receive current when the starter or the timer switch is in operation. The use of a test lamp on the terminal end of the starter valve and to ground, will indicate current presence to the switch when starting. The current should stop flowing no longer than eight seconds after the starter is stopped. The temperature timing switch is operable under temperatures of 41° F. (5° C.)

528i, 530i, 630CSi, 633CSi, 733i

1. Remove the cold start valve from the air collector but do not remove the fuel hose or the electrical connector.

2. Remove the connector plug from the air flow sensor.

3. Install a jumper wire between plug #36 and #39 on the air flow sensor connector.

4. Remove the connector from the cold start relay.

5. Connect a jumper wire from terminal #87 to #30 of the cold start relay connector.

6. Turn the ignition switch ON. The cold start valve should eject fuel.

Cold Start Relay

528i, 530i, 630CSi, 633CSi, 733i

1. Connect a ground wire to terminal #85.

2. Connect a positive lead to terminal #30 and #86C.

Cold start relay contact points

3. The relay is good when the test lamp operates when probed to terminals #87 and #86.

ADJUSTMENTS

Synchronizing Throttle Valve with Injection Pump (2002Tii)

1. First make sure that the connecting rod (linkage) between the pump and the throttle valve is adjusted to 3.346 in. The length of the connecting rod is measured from the centers of the ball sockets of the connecting rod.

2. Remove the two screws for the throttle valve cover and lift off the cover. Rotate the idling speed screw (1) until it is not in contact with the eccentric. Loosen the two clamping screws (2).

3. Using a four inch long piece of metal rod (approximately 0.15 in. thick in diameter) bent at a 90 degree angle at the end (such as BMW special tool 6075), insert the rod through the upper slotted hole of the regulating lever so that the rod seats in the bore of the injection pump housing (see the illustration).

4. Insert a 0.157 in. (4mm) diameter drift pin (such as BMW 6077) into the bore of the throttle valve section (see the illustration). Then, with the regulating lever set in position with the metal rod and the throttle valve eccentric pressed against the drift pin, tighten the two clamping screws (2).

5. Remove the drift pin and metal rod and check the synchronization. The synchronization is correct when the eccentric partially overlaps the bore (B) in the throttle valve section.

6. Finally, adjust the idle speed using screw (1) to 900 rpm plus or minus 50 rpm.

7. Check the synchronization at full load setting. Disconnect the induction pipe from no. 1 cylinder. Using the metal rod, insert

Using metal rod (such as BMW 6075) to align top hole of regulating lever with pump housing hole

Correct synchronization shown by eccentric partially overlapping bore (B) of throttle valve

Inserting drift pin (BMW 6077) into hole in throttle valve section (left); loosening clamping screws (2) (right)

Using metal rod (such as BMW 6075) to align lowest hole of regulator lever with pump housing hole to adjust full load setting clearance with stop screw (3)

the rod through the lowest slotted hole of the regulator lever so that the rod seats in the bore of the injection pump housing. Then, adjust stop screw (3) so that the pump lever is barely contacted.

Start Valve—2002Tii

1. Remove the start valve from the throttle valve section.
2. Turn the ignition switch to ON to obtain fuel pressure from the pump, but do not start the engine.
3. Connect a positive current jumper wire to the "SV" connection of the time switch.
4. If fuel is ejected from the start valve, the valve and the feed pipe are considered to be good.

NOTE: *The valve must not drip fuel with the current OFF.*

Thermo-Time Switch—2002Tii

1. Remove the wire terminal from the thermo-time switch.
2. Connect a test lamp to a positive terminal and the "W" terminal of the thermo-time switch.
3. The lamp should light at coolant temperature below 95° F. (35° C.).
4. Leave the test lamp attached to the "W" terminal and connect a positive jumper wire to terminal "G".
5. The internal bi-metal control should open after a short time and the light should then go out. If not, replace the thermo-time switch.

Time Switch—2002Tii

1. Remove the time switch from the firewall.
2. Connect a test lamp between ground and the "SV" terminal of the time switch.
3. Remove the No. 4 wire from the ignition coil and actuate the starter. The test lamp should go out after a short time.

NOTE: *The injection time period of start valve is as follows:*

At 4° F.(−20° C.)   9 to 15 seconds
At 32° F. (0° C.)   4 to 10 seconds
At 95° F. (35° C.)   1 second

4. Remove the terminal plug from the thermo-time switch. Actuate the starter; the light should go on for one second and then go out.
5. Connect a test lamp between the "TH" terminal and ground. The test lamp must light up as long as the starter is actuated.

Adjusting 320i basic throttle setting

Basic Throttle Setting—320i

1. Disconnect the accelerator cable and loosen the throttle stop screw.
2. Adjust the distance between the throttle lever (2) and the stop (1) to 0.039–0.058 in. clearance. Do this with screw (3).
3. Loosen the throttle lever clamping screw (4) and position the throttle valve in the housing to zero play. Tighten the clamping screw.
4. Tighten the throttle stop screw one complete turn and lock it in place.
5. Adjust the accelerator cable to the throttle lever and attach.

Auxiliary Air Regulator—320i

1. Disconnect the electrical terminal plug and the two air hoses at the auxiliary air regulator.
2. Voltage must be present at the terminal plug with the ignition switch ON.
3. Check the air bore of the regulator. With the engine temperature approximately 68° F. (20° C.), the air bore should be half open.
4. Connect the terminal plug and the two air hoses to the auxiliary air regulator.
5. Start the engine and the auxiliary air regulator bore should close within five minutes of engine operation by the cut-off valve.

Mixture Control Unit and Sensor Plate Adjustment—320i

NOTE: *49 state and California control units are not interchangeable.*

1. Remove the air intake cowl at the mixture control unit and throttle housing.
2. Turn the ignition ON for approximately five seconds, and during this time, slowly raise the sensor plate with a magnet. Turn the ignition switch OFF.

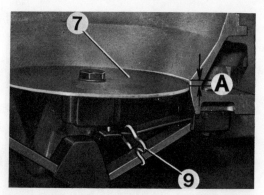

Sensor plate (7) positioning in venturi with adjusting spring (9). "A" is clearance allowable between the top of the venturi and surface of sensor plate

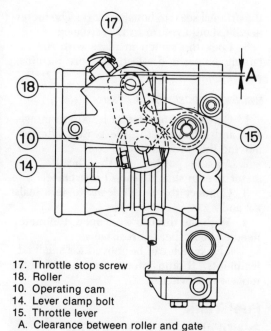

17. Throttle stop screw
18. Roller
10. Operating cam
14. Lever clamp bolt
15. Throttle lever
A. Clearance between roller and gate

Throttle lever adjustment—528i, 530i, 600 series, and 733i

NOTE: *The amount of resistance should be constant when raising the sensor and no resistance should be felt when pushing the sensor plate down quickly.*

3. The sensor plate should be flush or 0.019 in. (0.5mm) below the beginning of the venturi taper. If necessary to adjust, remove the mixture control from the intermediate housing and bend the spring accordingly. Center the sensor plate in the bore by loosening the center plate screw. Tighten when aligned.

NOTE: *With the sensor plate too high, the engine will run on and with the sensor plate too low, poor cold and warm engine start-up will result.*

4. If the sensor plate movement is erratic, the control piston can be sticking. Remove the fuel distributor and inspect the control piston for damage and replace as necessary.

CAUTION: *Do not drop the control valve.*

Throttle Valve

3.0Si

1. Loosen the locknut and loosen the adjusting screw until there is play between the stop and the screw.

2. Tighten the adjusting screw until the stop is just contacted. Operate the throttle lever several times and allow to snap back against the stop by spring pressure.

3. Tighten the adjusting screw one full turn and lock the screw with the locknut.

528i, 530i, 630CSi, 633CSi, 733i

1. Loosen the throttle lever clamp screw and the throttle stop screw.

2. Press the throttle valve closed and tighten the throttle stop screw until the

clearance between the roller and the gate is approximately 0.020–0.040.

3. Tighten the throttle lever clamp screw. Tighten the throttle stop screw one complete turn and lock with the locknut.

4. Adjust the throttle switch and the idle speed.

Throttle Valve Switch

3.0Si

1. Disconnect the electrical terminal plug from the throttle valve switch and loosen the switch retaining screws.

2. Connect the leads of a calibrated ohmmeter to terminals #17 and #45 of the throttle valve switch.

3. Rotate the switch until the meter needle shows infinity. Rotate the switch in the opposite direction until the meter needle moves to 0 resistance.

4. Mark the housing opposite the center indicator on the switch scale.

5. Rotate the switch clockwise 2° as indicated on the scale.

NOTE: *The scale is graduated in ½° increments.*

6. As the switch is rotated, the meter needle should move to infinity as the switch contacts open.

7. Rotate the switch counterclockwise to

the original scale to housing mark. The meter needle should return to O resistance.

8. Lock the switch in place with the retaining screws and attach the wire terminal plug.

528i, 530i, 630CSi, 633CSi, 733i

1. Connect an ohmmeter lead to terminals #18 and #2 of the throttle switch, after removing the terminal plug.

2. At idle position of the throttle, the meter needle should read O resistance.

3. Connect the meter leads to terminals #2 and #3.

4. With the throttle wide open, the meter needle should beat O resistance.

5. The switch can be moved for small adjustments. If adjustments are unattainable, replace the switch.

Fuel Tank

REMOVAL AND INSTALLATION

1600-2, 2002, 2002A

1. Disconnect the negative battery cable.
2. Drain the fuel from the fuel tank.
3. Remove the fiber floor panel from the trunk. Disconnect the positive lead (2), lead (3), and ground wire (1).
4. Disconnect the fuel feed hose from the immersion tube transmitter.
5. Label and disconnect all evaporative control vapor lines.
6. Disconnect the hose clamp from the bottom of the filler neck and push up on the rubber sleeve.
7. Remove the tank retaining bolts and carefully lift out the tank.
8. Reverse the above procedure to install.

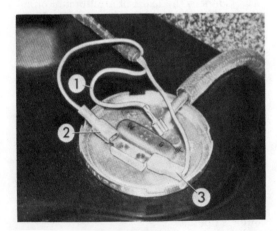

Disconnecting fuel tank leads

2002Tii fuel tank hose connections

2002Tii

1. Disconnect the negative battery cable.
2. Drain the fuel from the tank.
3. Remove the fiber floor panel from the trunk. Disconnect the leads from the fuel gauge sending unit. Disconnect the fuel feed (2) and return (3) lines from the suction unit.
4. Label and disconnect all evaporative control vapor lines.
5. Disconnect the hose clamp from the filler neck.
6. Remove the tank retaining bolts, separate the filler neck sections and carefully lift out the tank.
7. Reverse the above procedure to install.

2800, 3.0 Series

1. Drain the fuel and disconnect the negative battery terminal.
2. Remove the luggage compartment mat and the lining which rests against the right side quarter panel.
3. Remove the fuel hose from the tank sending unit. Pull the three electrical connections off, noting that the ground wire (Brown) goes to the rounded connector, the Brown/Yellow wire to the "G" connector, and the Brown/Black wire to the "W" connector.
4. Remove the filler cap and slip the rubber ring off the filler neck.
5. Detach the tank from the luggage compartment floor, tilt upwards at the front, and remove it.
6. Install in reverse order. Before putting the tank into position, check the foam gasket supporting the tank and replace it if necessary. Make sure to install the sealing ring onto the filler neck before the tank goes into final position.

To remove the 320i fuel tank, disconnect the suction line (1), return line (2), plug (3), and vent line (4)

320i

1. Disconnect the battery negative terminal and drain the fuel.

2. Remove the rear seat. Remove the black guard plate to gain access to fuel lines and the sending unit.

3. Disconnect the electrical connector and the suction and return lines at the sending unit. Disconnect the vent line at the tank.

4. Disconnect the filler neck at the lower end.

5. Remove the mounting screw and remove the guard from behind the connecting hose (which goes to the left side tank).

6. Disconnect the connecting hose. Then, remove the two mounting screws on the inboard side of the tank at the bottom, and lower the tank out of the car.

7. For the tank on the left side, perform Steps 5 and 6 in a similar way, but before lifting the tank out of the car, disconnect the small vent line from the top of the tank. If this line should have to be replaced, limit the length of the replacement hose section to 23.6 in.

8. Install the fuel tanks in reverse order.

530i, 528i

1. Disconnect the battery ground cable. Siphon the fuel out of the tank.

2. Fold the floor mat out of the way for access. Remove the three screws and remove the round black cover which permits access to the sending unit.

3. Disconnect the wires at the sending unit (Brown—ground, Brown/Yellow—G, Brown/Black—W). Detach the (unclamped) vent line.

4. Detach the feed and return lines at the filter and return pipe (both under the car).

5. Detach the front and rear mounting bushings of the rearmost muffler, and then remove the rear bracket from the body.

6. Loosen the tank mounting bolts at the front and right sides, remove the filler cap, and remove the tank.

7. Install in reverse order.

630CSi, 633CSi

1. Disconnect the negative battery cable, and siphon fuel from the tank. Lift the rear compartment rug out of the way. Remove the round access cover.

2. Disconnect the electrical plug and the two fuel lines from the top of the sending unit.

3. Remove the fuel tank filler cap and the rubber seal which surrounds the filler neck. Then, disconnect the four vent hoses.

4. Remove the bushings from the rear muffler at front and rear, and then remove the mounting bracket at the rear.

5. Bend the taps down, remove the mounting bolts, and remove the heat shield. Remove the nut and bolt, and remove the stone guard.

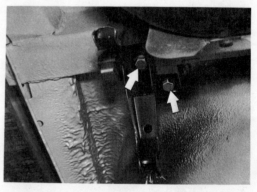

Remove the arrowed bolts and remove the rear mounting bracket—600 series cars

6. Remove the three mounting bolts from the right side panel, and lower the tank, right side first, and then remove it, being careful to avoid pinching any of the hoses.

7. Install in reverse order.

733i

1. Unscrew the filler cap and siphon out the tank.

2. Disconnect the negative battery cable. Fold the rug in the rear compartment out of

the way, and remove the round access panel.

3. Disconnect inlet and outlet hoses at the sending unit.

4. Disconnect the sending unit electrical connector at the plug, located near the wiring harness in the trunk.

5. Remove the mounting bolts from the straps and lower the tank slightly and support it. Pull off the (4) vent hoses. Then, lower the tank out of the car.

6. Install in reverse order, making sure the rubber bumpers against which the tank is held by the mounting straps are in good shape, or replacing them, as necessary.

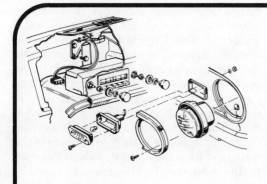

5

Chassis Electrical

UNDERSTANDING BASIC ELECTRICITY

Understanding just a little about the basic theory of electricity will make electrical system troubleshooting much easier. Several gauges are used in electrical troubleshooting to see inside the circuit being tested. Without a basic understanding, it will be difficult to understand testing procedures.

Electricity is defined as the flow of electrons. Electrons are hypothetical particles thought to constitute the basic "stuff" of electricity. In a comparison with water flowing in a pipe, the electrons would be the water. As the flow of water can be measured, the flow of electricity can be measured. The unit of measurement is amperes, frequently abbreviated "amps." An ammeter will measure the actual amount of current flowing in the circuit.

Just as water *pressure* is measured in units such as pounds per square inch, electrical pressure is measured in volts. When a voltmeter's two probes are placed on two "live" portions of an electrical circuit with different electrical pressures, current will flow through the voltmeter and produce a reading which indicates the difference in electrical pressure between the two parts of the circuit.

While increasing the voltage in a circuit will increase the flow of current, the actual flow depends not only on voltage, but on the resistance of the circuit. The standard unit for measuring circuit resistance is an ohm, measured by an ohmmeter. The ohmmeter is somewhat similar to an ammeter, but incorporates its own source of power so that a standard voltage is always present.

An actual electric circuit consists of four basic parts. These are: the power source, such as a generator or battery; a hot wire, which conducts the electricity under a relatively high voltage or pressure to the electrical appliance supplied by the circuit; the load, such as a lamp, motor, resistor, or relay coil; and the ground wire, which carries the current back to the source under very low electrical pressure. In such a circuit, the bulk of the resistance exists between the point where the hot wire is connected to the load, and the point where the load is grounded. In an automobile, the vehicle's frame, which is made of steel, is used as a part of the ground circuit for many of the electrical devices.

Remember that, in electrical testing, the voltmeter is connected in parallel with the circuit being tested (without disconnecting any wires) and measures the difference in voltage between the locations of the two probes; that the ammeter is connected in series with the load (the circuit is separated at one point and the ammeter inserted so it becomes a part of the circuit); and that the ohmmeter is self-powered, so that all the power in the circuit should be off and the portion of the circuit to be measured contacted at either end by one of the probes of the meter.

For any electrical system to operate, it must make a complete circuit. This simply means that the power flow from the battery must make a complete circle. When an electrical component is operating, power flows from the battery to the component, passes through the component causing it to perform its function (lighting a light bulb), and then returns to the battery through the ground of the circuit. This ground is usually (but not always) the metal part of the car on which the electrical component is mounted.

Perhaps the easiest way to visualize this is to think of connecting a light bulb with two wires attached to it to your car battery. The battery in your car has two posts (negative and positive). If one of the two wires attached to the light bulb was attached to the negative post of the battery and the other wire was attached to the positive post of the battery, you would have a complete circuit. Current from the battery would flow out one post, through the wire attached to it and then to the light bulb, where it would pass through causing it to light. It would then leave the light bulb, travel through the other wire, and return to the other post of the battery.

The normal automotive circuit differs from this simple example in two ways. First, instead of having a return wire from the bulb to the battery, the light bulb returns the current to the battery through the chassis of the vehicle. Since the negative battery cable is attached to the chassis and the chassis is made of electrically conductive metal, the chassis of the vehicle can serve as a ground wire to complete the circuit. Secondly, most automotive circuits contain switches to turn components on and off as required.

There are many types of switches, but the most common simply serves to prevent the passage of current when it is turned off. Since the switch is a part of the circle necessary for a complete circuit, it operates to leave an opening in the circuit, and thus an incomplete or open circuit, when it is turned off.

Some electrical components which require a large amount of current to operate also have a relay in their circuit. Since these circuits carry a large amount of current, the thickness of the wire in the circuit (gauge size) is also greater. If this large wire were connected from the component to the control switch on the instrument panel, and then back to the component, a voltage drop would occur in the circuit. To prevent this potential drop in voltage, an electromagnetic switch (relay) is used. The large wires in the circuit are connected from the car battery to one side of the relay, and from the opposite side of the relay to the component. The relay is normally open, preventing current from passing through the circuit. An additional, smaller, wire is connected from the relay to the control switch for the circuit. When the control switch is turned on, it grounds the smaller wire from the relay and completes the circuit. This closes the relay and allows current to flow from the battery to the component. The horn, headlight, and starter circuits are three which use relays.

Your alternator (which supplies the battery) puts out more current at speeds above idle. This is normal. However, it is possible for larger surges of current to pass through the electrical system of your car. If this surge of current were to reach an electrical component, it could burn it out. To prevent this from happening, fuses are connected into the current supply wires of most of the major electrical systems of your car. The fuse serves to head off the surge at the pass. When an electrical current of excessive power passes through the component's fuse, the fuse blows out and breaks the circuit, saving it from destruction.

The fuse also protects the component from damage if the power supply wife to the component is grounded before the current reaches the component.

Let us here interject another rule to the complete circle circuit. *Every complete circuit from a power source must include a component which is using the power from the power source.* If you were to disconnect the light bulb (from the previous example of a lightbulb being connected to the battery by two wires) from the wires and touch the two wires together (please take our word for this; don't try it), the result would be shocking. You probably haven't seen so many sparks since the Fourth of July. A similar thing happens (on a smaller scale) when the power supply wire to a component or the electrical component itself becomes grounded before the normal ground connection for the circuit. To prevent damage to the system, the fuse for the circuit blows to interrupt the circuit—protecting the components from damage. Because grounding a wire from a power source makes a complete circuit—less the required component to use the power—this phenomenon is called a short circuit. The most common causes of short circuits are: the rubber insulation on a wire breaking or rubbing through to expose the current carrying core of the wire to a metal part of the car, or a shorted switch.

Some electrical systems on the car are protected by a circuit breaker which is, basically, a self-repairing fuse. When either of the above-described events takes place in a system which is protected by a circuit breaker, the circuit breaker opens the circuit the same way a fuse does. However, when either the short is removed from the circuit or the surge subsides, the circuit breaker resets itself and does not have to be replaced as a fuse does.

The final protective device in the chassis electrical system is a fuse link. A fuse link is a wire that acts as a fuse. It is connected between the starter relay and the main wiring harness for the car. This connection is under the hood, very near a similar fuse link which protects the engine electrical system. Since the fuse link protects all the chassis electrical components, it is the probable cause of trouble when none of the electrical components function, unless the battery is disconnected or dead.

Electrical problems generally fall into one of three areas:

1. The component that is not functioning is not receiving current.

2. The component itself is not functioning.

3. The component is not properly grounded.

Problems that fall into the first category are by far the most complicated. It is the current supply system to the component which contains all the switches, relays, fuses, etc.

The electrical system can be checked with a test light and a jumper wire. A test light is a device that looks like a pointed screwdriver with a wire attached to it. It has a light bulb in its handle. A jumper wire is a piece of insulated wire with an alligator clip attached to each end.

If a light bulb is not working, you must follow a systematic plan to determine which of the three causes is the villain.

1. Turn on the switch that controls the inoperable bulb.

2. Disconnect the power supply wire from the bulb.

3. Attach the ground wire on the test light to a good metal ground.

4. Touch the probe end of the test light to the end of the power supply wire that was disconnected from the bulb. If the bulb is receiving current, the test light will go on.

NOTE: *If the bulb is one which works only when the ignition key is turned on (turn signal), make sure the key is turned on.*

If the test light does not go on, then the problem is in the circuit between the battery and the bulb. As mentioned before, this includes all the switches, fuses, and relays in the system. Turn to the wiring diagram and find the bulb on the diagram. Follow the wire that runs back to the battery. The problem is an open circuit between the battery and the bulb. If the fuse is blown and, when replaced, immediately blows again, there is a short circuit in the system which must be located and repaired. If there is a switch in the system, bypass it with a jumper wire. This is done by connecting one end of the jumper wire to the power supply wire into the switch and the other end of the jumper wire to the wire coming out of the switch. Again, consult the wiring diagram. If the test light lights with the jumper wire installed, the switch or whatever was bypassed is defective.

NOTE: *Never substitute the jumper wire for the bulb, as the bulb is the component required to use the power from the power source.*

5. If the bulb in the test light goes on, then the current is getting to the bulb that is not working in the car. This eliminates the first of the three possible causes. Connect the power supply wire and connect a jumper wire from the bulb to a good metal ground. Do this with the switch which controls the bulb turned on, and also the ignition switch turned on if it is required for the light to work. If the bulb works with the jumper wire installed, then it has a bad ground. This is usually caused by the metal area on which the bulb mounts to the car being coated with some type of foreign matter.

6. If neither test located the source of the trouble, then the light bulb itself is defective.

The above test procedure can be applied to any of the components of the chassis electrical system by substituting the component that is not working for the light bulb. Remember that for any electrical system to work, all connections must be clean and tight.

HEATER

Blower

REMOVAL AND INSTALLATION

1600-2, 2002 Series, 320i

NOTE: *The entire heater assembly must be removed from the car to replace either the blower motor or the heater core. If the car is air conditioned, the work of discharging the system and removing the evaporator should be left to a trained professional.*

1. Disconnect the negative battery cable.

2. Move the heater control lever on the dash all the way to the "Warm" position. Remove the radiator and engine drain cocks and drain the cooling system.

3. Loosen the hose clamp and disconnect the heater return hose from its fitting on the engine side of the firewall. Also, loosen the clamps and disconnect the heater feed hose (1) from the heater control valve (2) at the firewall. Remove the valve and check that it is not blocked with cooling system deposits. Replace it, as necessary.

4. On 1970 models, remove the retaining screws and pull the storage tray out to the rear. On 1971 and later models, with a full-length console, unscrew the shift knob, pull off the rubber boot, unscrew the phillips head screws for the side and center sections, lift out the center section, disconnect the

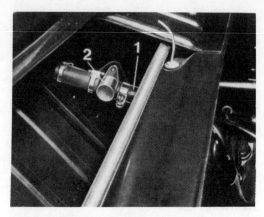

Disconnecting feed hose

electrical connections for the hazard flasher and radio (if so equipped), and lift out the remaining sections of the console.

5. Remove the phillips head retaining screws and remove the following dashboard finish panels: the lower steering column casing, the lower center trim panel, the outer left-hand trim panel, and the bottom half of the upper steering column casing.

6. Pull off the black knobs for the air control and heater temperature controls. On 1970 models, remove the inner knurled nuts and the phillips head screw for the air control outer finish panel and lift off the panel. Then remove the two phillips head screws securing the air controls to the dash. Finally, pull out the ashtray, and remove the two phillips head screws retaining the heater temperature control to the dash. On 1971 and later models, lever out the snap-fit clear plastic covers for both the air control and the heater temperature controls. Then, remove the phillips head screws retaining the controls to the dash (2 each), and pull the levers downward and out.

Disconnecting return hose

Heater assembly removed showing positioning of foam rubber gaskets

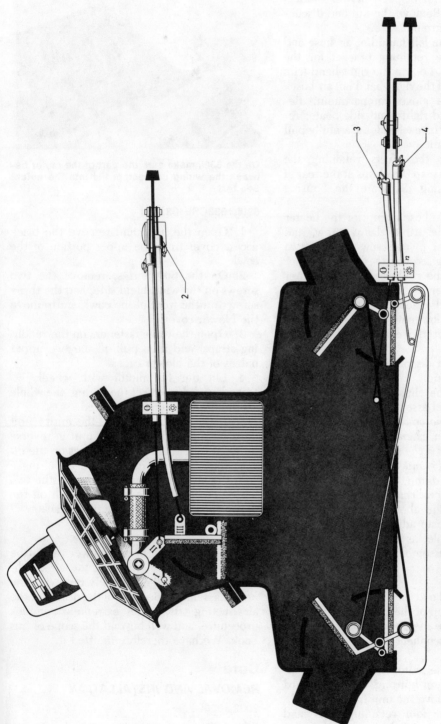

Test: Heater valve at position I = warm.
The mixing flap III must be closed in this position.
Adjustment is effected with the clamp screw (1) at the swinging arm of the heater valve.
Position II = cold.
Adjustment of air mixing, demister and footwell flaps is effected at the Bowden cable retaining screws 2, 3 and 4.
The flaps are lubricated with Ecubsol at the bearing points.

Cross section of heater unit showing proper adjustment procedure for the control cable

7. Label and disconnect the electrical leads for the heater (3 wires for 2-speed blower; 4 wires for 3-speed blower) underneath the dash. Remove the nut and disconnect the heater ground wire.

8. Pull off the left-hand hot air hose and slightly turn the retaining bracket for the steering column. Loosen the right-hand trim panel and pull off the right-hand hot air hose.

9. Open the glove compartment. Remove the left and right-hand side heater retaining nuts (one on each side). Carefully pull out the heater unit.

10. Drill out the rivets retaining the heater cover. Unsnap the clasps at the rear of the heater housing. Separate the housing valves.

11. Loosen the hose clamp for the heater valve. Loosen the cable clamp screw, and remove the lever pivot screw and the two control mounting screws.

12. Remove the rubber sleeves at either side of the blower.

13. Label and disconnect the electrical leads from the blower motor.

14. Disconnect the cable for the heater regulator.

15. Label and disconnect the leads from the heater housing.

16. Unsnap the clips and pull the motor and blower wheel assembly downward.

NOTE: *The motor and blower wheel are balanced as an assembly. If the motor is burned out, or if the blower wheel is damaged, the motor and blower wheel should be replaced as a unit, otherwise the blower will vibrate excessively during operation.*

17. Reverse the above procedure to install, taking care to adjust the operation of the control cable as per the sectioned-through heater assembly illustration.

2800, 3.0

1. Open the hood and remove the cover plate from the top of the cowl.

2. Remove the metal grid from the top of the blower. Disconnect the electrical connectors.

3. Unscrew the motor mount where it attaches to the heater housing, tilt the forward part up, and remove the unit from the cowl.

4. Release the four retaining clips, and then pull the motor off the motor mount.

5. Install in reverse order. Make sure the shorter ends of the retaining clips go over the motor mount.

On the 530i, make sure the part of the motor between the wiring connectors fits into the notch. See text

530i, 630CSi, 633CSi

1. Open the hood and remove the black access cover from the upper portion of the cowl.

2. On the 600 Series, remove the two screws on the windshield side, and the three screws on the front of the cowl, and remove the blower cover.

3. Open the three fasteners on the retaining straps, and then pull off the two upper halves of the blower cages.

4. Lift out the motor with wheels attached, and disconnect the wiring; the whole assembly may then be removed.

5. If the motor is faulty, the entire unit must be replaced. Install the unit in reverse order, positioning the flat surfaces on the intake ducts downward. On the 520i, make sure the area of the motor between the two wiring connectors fits into the notch on the passenger's side of the mounting bracket.

733i

On this model, the heater blower cannot be replaced without discharging the air conditioning system and completely removing the heater assembly. Because of the design of the air ducting, this is an extremely complex procedure, and well beyond the scope of this book. We have therefore omitted it.

Core

REMOVAL AND INSTALLATION

2002, 320i

In order to remove the heater core, it is necessary to first remove the entire heater assembly from the car. See the procedure for removing the blower motor, above. Once the heater is out of the car, the core may be removed by drilling out the rivets and unsnapping the clips which hold the housing halves together.

2800, 3.0 Series

1. Drain the coolant from the system.
2. Disconnect the heater hoses from the heater core, and remove the rubber seal.
3. Remove the fresh air outlet grille cover. Coupe only:
   a. Remove the heater control cover.
   b. Disconnect the air distribution hoses from the discharge nozzles.
   c. Remove the intermediate distribution duct.
4. Remove the buttons from the control levers.
5. Remove the threaded knobs for the left instrument panel trim strip.
6. Remove the rear switch plate.
7. Remove the front switch plate.
8. Remove the heater retaining nuts.
9. Tilt the heater and switch plate inwards, and remove the heater.
10. Detach the cable going to the defroster flap.
11. Pull off the retaining clips, remove the seals, and pull apart the halves of the heater housing (the core will stay in the left side of the housing).
12. Slide the core out of the housing, pulling the outer end toward you to permit the hose connections to clear the housing.
13. To install, reverse the removal procedure, noting the following points:
   A. Slide the air guide baffle in as shown.
   B. First insert the switch plate into the dash and then insert the heater. Tighten attaching nuts firmly. Check the foam rubber seal between the heater and dash panel and replace, if necessary.
   C. When installing the front switch plate, make sure the control levers do not scrape against the trim.
   D. Replace the sealing gasket which goes under the cowl cover.

530i, 528i

1. Remove the center tray.
2. Remove the glove box.
3. Disconnect the battery ground.
4. Push the selector lever to the WARM position.
5. Drain the coolant.
6. Disconnect the heater hoses from the heater core, and remove the rubber seal.
7. Remove the lower instrument panel center trim.
8. Disconnect the heater controls at the instrument panel.
9. Disconnect the control shafts at the joints. To do this, press in locking prongs with needle nose pliers.
10. Disconnect the multiple electrical connector at the heater.
11. Remove the instrument panel center cover.
12. Working from inside the engine compartment, remove the upper section of the fire shield.
13. Disconnect ducts by pulling outward to pull connector pins out of bushings which are in the ducts.
14. Remove clips and remove the outer portion of the lower blower housing. Pull out the motor/blower unit, disconnect wires, and remove it.

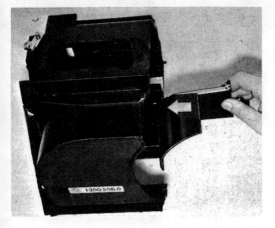

Slide the air guide baffle in as shown (2800, 3.0)

Disconnect the ducts by pulling outward to pull the connector pins out of the bushings. See text

15. Pull the foam rubber seal about half-way off and fold it back.

16. Remove the clamp from the pipe leading to the water valve, disconnect the water valve and remove the valve and pipe as an assembly.

17. Remove clips and detach the right side housing (this housing covers ears which operate the heater damper).

18. Remove the attaching circlip and remove the smaller gear. Then, pull out the shaft to which the smaller gear was mounted.

19. Remove housing clips and separate the housing halves.

20. Press out the grommet and pull wires out from between core pipes and the core. Remove the core from the heater assembly.

21. To install, reverse the above, keeping the following points in mind:

A. Glue new rubber seals onto the outside of the core before installing it into the heater.

B. When reassembling halves of the heater, first position the sleeve on the air flap and position the flap carefully and guide it into the bore on the opposite side of the heater housing.

C. When reinstalling damper gears, mesh the gears so the timing marks line up.

Meshing the damper gears—528i, 530i

D. Replace the water valve seals.

E. When remounting the lower blower motor, make sure the portion of the motor between the two electrical connectors engages with the slot in the heater housing. Then, when reinstalling the blower housing, make sure the flat surface on either side of the intake duct faces down.

F. Secure the cables so that air flaps are closed when the control switch is at "off."

G. Turn the fan swich and water valve and air distribution flaps left to the stop for each when reconnecting the control shafts.

600 and 700 Series

Heater core replacement for these cars requires that the air conditioner unit be discharged and the evaporator assembly removed. These procedures are, therefore, beyond the scope of this book. Such procedures should be left to a trained technician.

Radio

REMOVAL AND INSTALLATION

1600-2, 2002 Series, 320i

1. Disconnect the negative battery cable.

2. Unscrew the shift lever and lift off the boot.

3. Remove the phillips head screws which retain the console to the dash and transmission tunnel.

4. Remove the phillips head screws which retain the left and right-hand side panels of the console to the radio mounting bracket. Remove the side panels, exposing the radio mounting bracket. (The radio mounting bracket houses the speaker.)

5. Disconnect the antenna cable from the radio. Disconnect the radio ground cable (if so equipped) from the left-hand heater mounting bolt. Disconnect the power lead for the radio from the existing plug located inline to the hazard warning switch.

6. Lift the radio mounting bracket forward. The radio may now be disconnected from the speaker by removing the speaker multiple plug from the back of the radio.

7. Pry off the radio control knobs exposing the mounting nuts. Unscrew the mounting nuts and remove the radio from its bracket.

8. Reverse the above procedure to install.

2800, 3.0 Series, 530i, 528i, 630CSi, 633CSi, 733i

1. Remove the four screws from the outside of the underdash console while supporting the radio from underneath. Pull the unit out and lay it on the console.

2. Disconnect the aerial cable (large plug), the negative cable ("B−"), the speaker plugs (from the back of the unit) and the positive cable ("B+"—violet in color).

3. Installation is the reverse of removal.

WINDSHIELD WIPERS

Blade and Arm

Blade and arm removal and installation are described in Chapter 1.

Motor

REMOVAL AND INSTALLATION

1600-2, 2002

NOTE: *The motor is accessible from the engine side of the firewall.*

1. Disconnect the negative battery cable.
2. Remove the nut which retains the drive crank linkage to the motor, and disconnect the drive crank.
3. Remove the 3 mounting bolts for the motor.
4. Label and disconnect the 3 electrical leads from the clear plastic socket connection. Loosen the retaining screw for the ground wire and disconnect the ground wire from the body.
5. Lift out the wiper motor.

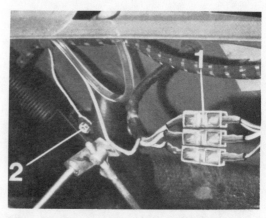

Disconnecting multiple plug (1) and ground (2)

6. Reverse the above procedure to install, taking care to install the drive crank in the end position.

3.0

1. Remove the cover for the heater unit on the cowl panel (except coupes).
2. Remove the crank arm retaining nut and washer.
3. Remove the wiper motor retaining screws, tilt the motor downward and remove.
4. Disconnect the electrical contact plug from the wiper motor.
5. The installation is in the reverse of the removal procedure.

NOTE: *The complete wiper motor, pivot assemblies and linkage can be removed as a unit, if necessary.*

320i, 530i, 630i and 633i

1. Remove the cowl cover to expose the wiper motor (320i and 530i).
2. Disconnect the wiper motor crank arm from the motor output shaft.

Disconnecting wiper drive crank—1600, 2002

Removing motor retaining bolts

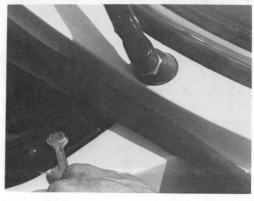

Removing the Cowl cover for access to the wiper motor—320i

3. Remove the motor retaining screws and disconnect the electrical connector.

4. Remove the wiper motor from the vehicle.

5. Reverse the procedure to install the motor.

733i

1. Remove the cowl fresh air intake grill and tilt rearward.

2. Remove the cover from the windshield wiper motor and remove the electrical plugs.

3. Remove the left and right wiper arms. Loosen the left and right pivot bearings.

4. Turn the rubber pad at the motor, counterclockwise and disconnect the right wiper linkage.

5. Remove the motor bracket retaining screws. Separate the spacers and remove the wiper motor assembly.

NOTE: *Do not lose the shims.*

6. The wiper motor can be removed from the bracket after the removal.

7. Reverse the removal procedure to install.

When reinstalling the 733i motor, make sure it is in park position—with the arm positioned as shown (1)

Linkage

REMOVAL AND INSTALLATION

1600, 2002, 2800, 3.0

1. Remove the cover plate from the top of the cowl.

2. Pull off the wiper arms.

3. Loosen the nuts retaining both wiper pivot bearings (the bearings located where the drive passes through the cowl).

4. Swing out the wiper motor complete with linkage.

5. Unplug the multiple connector and remove it with its rubber grommet.

6. Disconnect the connecting link and drive rod by pressing off.

7. Completely unscrew the retaining nuts from the wiper pivot bearings and remove them.

8. Install in reverse order, adjusting the wiper arms so the clearance between blades and the bottom of the windshield is .4–.8 in. Put a new sealing strip between the cowl cover and gutter.

530i, 528i, 630i, 633i

1. Open the hood, loosen the mounting screws, and remove the cover from the top of the firewall.

2. Remove both wiper arms. Press off both the connecting rod and the drive arm at the drive bushings. Disconnect the drive arm and detach the motor crank.

3. Remove the knurled cap from both arm drive shafts, and remove the nut above the cowl. Then, loosen the nut located below the cowl, and remove the assembly.

4. Install in reverse order, making sure to install nuts above and below the cowl on both sides.

733i

1. Remove the wiper motor and linkage assembled as described above.

2. Unscrew the nut on the motor crank, and remove the crank from the motor.

3. Install in reverse order, noting the following points:

A. Make sure to install the unit with the motor in park position. At this position, the crank covers the bolt on the motor side of the crank halfway.

B. Make sure the motor mounting shims fit properly.

C. Turn the rubber mounting pad under the motor to a position which supports the motor securely.

D. Be careful not to pinch vacuum hoses.

INSTRUMENT CLUSTER

REMOVAL AND INSTALLATION

1600-2, 2002 Series

1. Disconnect the negative battery cable.

2. Remove the lower section of the steering column shroud. Remove the lower center instrument panel trim.

3. Disconnect the speedometer cable at the speedometer.

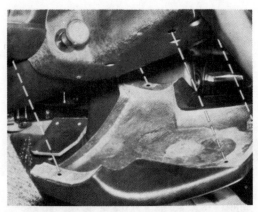

Removing lower section of steering column shroud—1600, 2002

Removing lower center instrument panel trim—1600, 2002

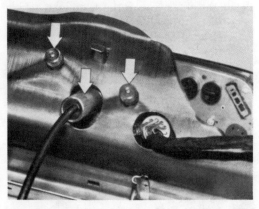

Disconnecting speedometer cable and knurled nuts

4. Unscrew the knurled nuts at the rear of the speedometer housing.

5. On 1970 models, unscrew the cluster hood retaining screws.

6. Push the instrument cluster out the

front of the dash. Disconnect the central plug (12-pronged) at the rear of the cluster.

7. Lift out the instrument cluster, containing the fuel gauge, temperature gauge, warning lights, speedometer, and tachometer or clock.

8. Reverse the above procedure to install.

320i

1. Disconnect the negative battery cable.

2. Remove the steering wheel assembly.

3. Remove the bottom center instrument trim panel.

4. Disconnect the speedometer cable, loosen the knurled nut and pull the instrument assembly outward.

5. Remove the electrical plugs and wires.

6. Remove the instrument cluster from the dash.

2800, 3.0

1. Disconnect the negative battery cable. Remove the two screws attaching the upper instrument panel housing—one at either side, accessible through the hole at the bottom corner of the lower housing.

2. Pull off the upper section of the housing until the speaker wires can be disconnected. Then, disconnect the speaker wires and remove the upper housing.

3. Pull off the two multiple connectors, unscrew the speedometer cable, and remove the cluster.

4. Installation is the reverse of the removal procedure.

NOTE: *This procedure is not included here for the remaining models, as it requires disturbing the collapsible steering column. Improper handling of removal and installation of the steering column can dangerously effect its performance in the event of a crash; therefore, we recommend you leave this work to a competent professional.*

SPEEDOMETER CABLE REPLACEMENT
1600-2, 2002 Series

1. Unscrew the cable fastening bolt on the transmission and pull the cable out.

2. Pull the cable out of the clamp under the car.

3. Remove the cable cover from under the steering column.

4. Reach up behind the instrument cluster and unscrew the cable retaining nut. The

cable may now be pulled from the firewall together with the rubber grommet.

5. Installation is the reverse of the removal procedure.

2800, 3.0

1. Unscrew the retaining bolt, and pull the cable out of the transmission. Pull the cable off the retaining clips under the car.

2. Open the glove compartment on the left side. Reach up behind the instrument cluster and unscrew the cable retaining nut behind the speedometer.

3. Detach the hazard flasher relay, and move it aside. Then, pull the cable and the rubber grommet out of the firewall.

4. Installation is the reverse of the removal procedure.

NOTE: *Cable replacement is not provided for the remaining models as this requires disturbing the collapsible steering column.*

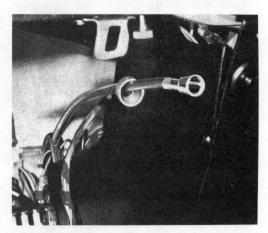

Removing the speedometer cable—2800, 3.0

HEADLIGHTS

Headlight Aiming

Headlights should be precision aimed using special equipment; however, as a temporary measure, you might wish to reaim your lights to an approximately correct position.

Most of the BMW models covered by this book employ large, knurled knobs, located behind the headlights, for aiming purposes. The horizontal adjustment is located on the right side of the light, and the vertical adjustment above the light. Screw the vertical adjustment inward (clockwise) to lower the beam; screw the horizontal adjustment in (clockwise) to turn the beam to left, and vice-versa.

Adjust the headlights at the large knurled knobs. Knobs (1) are for vertical adjustment, knobs (2) for horizontal—320i

The lights may be aimed against a wall. High beams should point just slightly below straight ahead and horizontal. Low beams should point somewhat downward, with the left side beam pointing slightly to the right.

REMOVAL AND INSTALLATION

1600-2, 2002 Series

1. Remove the 4 phillips head screws from the front of the radiator grille.

2. Open the hood. Remove the weatherproof cover, if so equipped. Unscrew the knurled nut which retains the outside edge of the grille to the front panel. Lift off the grille.

3. Disconnect the electrical connector from the back of the sealed beam.

4. Remove the 3 screws which retain the headlight outer ring to the headlight, taking care not to drop the sealed beam.

5. Lift out the headlight.

6. Reverse the above procedure to install. Have the headlights adjusted at a garage with the proper equipment. If this is not possible, park the car on a level surface about 25 feet

Removing outer ring—1600, 2002

1. Vertical adjustment
2. Horizontal adjustment

Headlight adjustment screw locations—2002

from a light colored wall. With the tires properly inflated and a friend sitting in the front seat, adjust the beams to the proper height using the black knurled knobs located inside the fender well. The upper knob controls the vertical setting and the knob at the side controls the horizontal setting.

2800, 3.0 Series

1. Open the hood, and pull the cover off the rear of the headlight. Detach the electrical connector.

2. The bulb is retained by a spring clip—

turn the clip back, and pull the bulb out to the rear.

3. Installation is the reverse of the removal procedure. Make sure to properly align the cutout in the reflector.

320i

1. First, remove the top and bottom screws from the parking light. Pull the parking light lens off. Then, open the hood, disconnect the electrical connector for the parking light, and pull the rubber grommet out of the engine compartment wall. Now pull the entire parking light assembly out of the grill.

2. Remove the attaching screws and remove the grill.

3. Loosen the three screws on the trim ring, remove the trim ring (don't let the headlight fall), and then pull the lamp out. Disconnect the connector and remove the lamp.

4. Install the new lamp in reverse order, making sure the tab on the rear of the lamp is aligned with the notch in the reflector so that the lamp cannot be turned once it is in position.

528i, 530i, 630CSi, 633CSi, 733i

1. On the 733i, disconnect the wiring connector going to the turn indicator light and

Removing parking light assembly—320i

Removing the grill—320i

Removing the trim ring—320i

push the rubber grommet through the engine compartment wall. Then, remove the indicator assembly. Then, on all the models listed, remove the attaching screws and remove the grill.

2. Remove the three screws which fasten the clamping ring to the reflector, pull the lamp out far enough to remove the plug from the back, remove the plug, and remove the lamp.

3. Replace the lamp in reverse order, making sure to fit the tab on the lamp into the notch in the reflector so the lamp cannot be turned once it is in position.

Lightbulb Chart

1600, 2002 Series

Type	Wattage
Headlights	45/40 sealed beam
Side/parking lights	4
Front turn indicators	21
Stoplights	21
Back-up lights	15
Rear turn indicators	21
Rear/parking lights	5
License plate light	5
Interior	10
Instrument illumination	3
Charging system indicator	3
High beam indicator	3
Turn signal indicator	3
Oil pressure indicator	3
Cold start warning light	3
Parking brake warning light	3
Low fuel level warning light	3
Transmission quadrant illumination (2002A)	2
Tachometer illumination (2002Tii)	3
Clock (except 2002Tii)	3
(2002Tii)	2
Hazard warning switch knob	1.2

2800, 3.0 Series, 530i

Type	Designation	Wattage
Instruments	W2 x 4.6d	1.2
Fuel	W2 x 4.6d	1.2
Turn Indicator	W2 x 4.6d	1.2
Brake	W2 x 4.6d	1.2
Alternator	W2 x 9.5d	3
Hi Beam	W2 x 9.5d	1.2
Oil	W2 x 9.5d	1.2

2800, 3.0 Series, 530i (cont.)

Type	Designation	Wattage
Trans Selector	W2 x 9.5d (6)	1.2
Flashers	W2 x 4.6d	1.2
Controls	W2 x 4.6d	1.2
Clock	W2 x 4.6d	1.2
Glovebox	HL 12V 4W	4
Marker (Rear)	HL	4
Marker (Front)	RL	21/5
License	L	4

320i, 528i, 630CSi, 633CSi, 733i

Type	Designation	Wattage
Instrument Cluster	W12V (3)	3
Alternator	W12V	3
Oil	W12V	1.2
Turn Indicator	W12V	1.2
Hi Beam	W12V	1.2
Fog Lamps	W12V	1.2
Brake	W12V	1.2
Fuel	W12V	1.2
Coolant	W12V	1.2
Trans Selector	W12V	1.2
EGR Warning	W12V	1.2
Thermal Reactor	W12V	1.2
Clock	W12V	1.2
Ash Tray	W12V	1.2
Oxygen Sensor (528)	W12V	1.2
Clock	W12V	1.2
Ash Tray	W12V	1.2
Glove Box	1HL12V	5
Push Button Switches	W12V	1.2
Control Lighting	W12V	1.2
Side Marker (Front)	RL	21/5
Side Marker (Rear)	RL	4
Rear/Parking	G	10
Turn	—	21
Stop Lamp	—	21
Back-Up	—	21

FUSES AND FLASHERS

FLASHER REMOVAL AND INSTALLATION

528i, 530i, 630CSi, 633i, 733i

1. Remove the screws and remove the bottom center instrument panel trim. Disconnect the battery negative terminal.
2. Detach the flasher from the mounting bracket. Unplug the electrical connector and remove the flasher.
3. Install in reverse order.

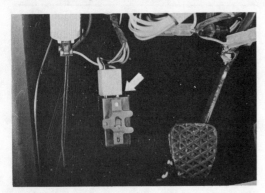

Removing the hazard flasher—733i

2800, 3.0 Series

1. Open the glovebox at the left side. Pull the relay hanger off the panel on which it is hung.
2. Disconnect the electrical connector. Install in reverse order.

FUSES

The fuse box is located under the hood on the right or left fender well, except on the 3.0 Series; on that series, it is behind the left glove box door.

The transparent cover lists accessories

Typical late model fusebox. Circuits are labeled on the cover

served by each circuit, except on the 1600 and 2002 Series, which are simply coded. Codes are explained for this model in the chart below.

Fuse Specifications— 1600, 2002

		1970
Fuse Location	Capacity (amps)	Circuits Protected
1	8	Front parking lights (right and left)
2	8	Right taillight and license plate lights
3	8	Left taillight and instrument illumination
4	8	Interior light, clock, cigar lighter and buzzer
5	8	Stop and turn lights, back-up lights
6	16	Heater blower, horn, windshield wiper and washer, fuel and temperature gauges, oil pressure and brake warning lights

		1971 and Later
Fuse Location	Capacity (amps)	Circuits Protected
1	5	Taillights and left parking light
2	5	Taillights, right parking light, license plate and instrument illum., side marker lights, fog light relay
3	8	Left low beam
4	8	Right low beam
5	5	Left turn signal
6	5	Right turn signal
7	16	Cigar lighter
8	8	Clock, interior light, ignition buzzer, hazard warning flashers, trailer flashers system
9	16	Heater blower
10	16	Rear window defroster
11	8	Automatic choke, electric fuel pump, oil pressure warning, fuel and temperature indicators, brake fluid warning, and tachometer
12	16	Stoplights, turn signals, horn, windshield wiper/washer, back-up lights

WIRING DIAGRAMS

Wiring diagrams have been left out of this book. As cars have become more complex, and available with more and more electrical accessories, wiring diagrams have become more complex also. It has become virtually impossible to provide a readable reproduction in a reasonable number of pages. Furthermore, this increased complexity has made it increasingly difficult for the layman to read and interpret the diagram and troubleshoot the very complex circuitry. Several diagrams of the simpler accessories are included in the owner's manuals.

6

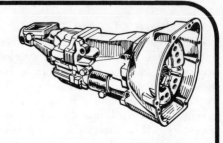

Clutch and Transmission

MANUAL TRANSMISSION

Identification

Gearboxes are used on various vehicles as listed below:
1600—Universal 232/6
2002—242/6
2800, 3.0—Getrag 262/8[1]
       ZF—S4/18/3[1]
320i—Getrag 242/9
528i, 530i—Getrag 262/8
630i, 633i—Getrag 262/9
733—Getrag 262/9.10 (49 States)
      Getrag 262/9.3 (California and High Altitude)
See the nameplate on the vertical surface, left/rear.

REMOVAL AND INSTALLATION

1600-2, 2002

1. From inside the car, lift up the rubber boot to the shift lever. Raise the foam rubber ring and unsnap the circlip (1). Then, pull out the shifter from its socket. Take care not to lose the shims which take up the clearance in the shifter socket under the circlip.

2. Raise the hood. Remove all of the transmission-to-engine retaining bolts within reach.

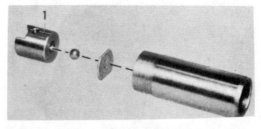

Tensioning piston disassembled

3. Jack up the front of the car and place jackstands beneath the front jacking points or beneath the lower suspensions arms. Place blocks behind the rear wheels and make sure that the parking brake is firmly applied.

CAUTION: *Test the stability of the sup-*

Using screwdriver to bleed tensioner

*ports by rocking the car sideways and for-
ward and backward. Before climbing
under the car, make sure that it will stay
up there.*

4. Remove the drain plug from the transmission and drain the contents into a drain
pan for inspection. Check the fluid for metal
particles. Clean and replace the drain plug.

5. Disconnect the exhaust pipe bracket
from the back of the transmission. Disconnect the head pipe from the exhaust manifold.

6. Disconnect the driveshaft from the
transmission at the flexible coupling (dough-
nut) leaving the coupling attached to the
driveshaft. Discard the old locknuts.

Removing flexible coupling from transmission

7. Remove the two bolts which retain the
driveshaft center support bearing housing to
the underbody. Push the driveshaft downward and away from the centering pin.

8. Using an allen wrench, loosen the set
screw (2) and drive out the retaining pin (1)
from the shift linkage.

Disconnecting shifter linkage

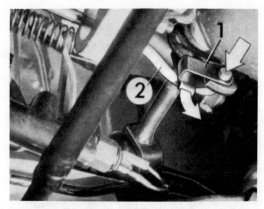

Disconnecting 1600-2 clutch linkage

9. On 1600-2 models, detach the clutch
linkage return spring. Push the retainer
downward and remove the pushrod (2) to the
front.

10. On 2002 and 2002Tii models, disconnect the slave cylinder from the throwout
lever by lifting out the retaining ring (1),
slipping off the rubber collar (2), unsnapping
the circlip (3), and withdrawing the cylinder
forward.

NOTE: *Mark the position of the torsional
retainer.*

Disconnecting 2002 series slave cylinder

11. Loosen the bolts for the transmission
support bracket. Remove the bolts which retain the flywheel inspection cover to the
transmission and remove the cover.

12. Place a wooden block beneath the oil
pan between the pan and front crossmember
to support the engine. Support the weight of
the transmission with a hydraulic floor jack.

13. Loosen the speedometer cable set bolt
(1) and disconnect the speedometer. Disconnect the back-up light leads (2). Remove the
transmission support crossmember.

14. Turn the front wheels to the full right-

hand lock position. The transmission may now be removed by pulling it out straight to the rear. When the transmission is clear of the pressure plate, carefully lower the jack and transmission to the ground.

15. Reverse the above procedure to install, using the following installation notes:

a. When hooking up the clutch linkage on 1600-2 models, adjust the linkage as outlined under "Clutch Linkage Adjustment."

b. When hooking up the shift linkage, first drive in the retaining pin and then secure it with the allen head setscrew.

c. When hooking up the driveshaft, check the freeness of the centering bearing and pack it with chassis grease, as necessary. Use new locknuts for the flexible coupling.

d. When installing the center support for the driveshaft, preload the bearing housing 0.08 in. (distance A) to the front. The bolts are tightened after the transmission is installed.

e. When connecting the exhaust pipe support bracket (2), the bracket must lie tension-free against the head pipe (3), or severe engine vibration may result.

f. When installing the shift lever, fill the ball socket with chassis grease. Use shims beneath the circlip to obtain a tight fit.

g. The transmission-to-engine bolts are torqued to 18.1 ft lbs (small bolts) and 34.0 ft lbs (large bolts).

h. Remember to fill the transmission to the bottom of the filler plug hole with SAE 80 gearbox oil before road testing.

320i

1. Drain the transmission. Unscrew all transmission mounting bolts (4) accessible from above. Swing up the bracket mounted to the top/left bolt.

2. Disconnect the exhaust system support at the rear of the transmission.

3. Detach the exhaust pipe at the manifold.

4. Detach the driveshaft at the transmission by pulling out bolts from the rear of the coupling (the coupling remains attached to the driveshaft).

5. Remove the heat shield. Remove the bolts for the center bearing bracket, and pull the bracket downward. Bend the driveshaft downward and pull it out of the bearing journal.

6. Remove the bolt and disconnect the

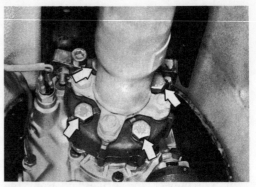

Remove the arrowed bolts from the driveshaft coupling—320i

speedometer drive cable. Disconnect the backup light switch wire, and pull the wire out of the clips on the transmission.

7. Remove the two allen bolts at the top and pull the console off the transmission.

8. Disconnect the gearshift selector rod by pulling off the circlip, removing the washer and pulling the rod off the pin.

9. Detach the clutch slave cylinder line bracket at the front of the transmission, remove the mounting bolts from the slave cylinder mounting, and remove the slave cylinder.

10. Remove the flywheel housing cover.

11. Support the transmission securely at the center with a floor jack and wooden block.

12. Detach the crossmember by removing the nuts attaching it to the body at either end. Remove the three remaining front mounting bolts and pull the transmission out toward the rear.

13. Reverse the removal procedure to install. Bear the following points in mind:

A. Front mounting bolts are torqued to 18–19 ft-lbs on the M8 transmissions;

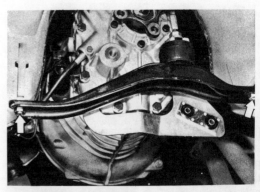

Detach the crossmember at the body by removing the two arrowed nuts

Install the clutch slave cylinder in the position shown

34–37 on the M10 transmissions. Torque the crossmember rubber mounts to 31–35 ft-lbs.

B. When reinstalling the clutch slave cylinder, make sure the bleeder screw faces downward.

C. When installing the driveshaft center support bearing, preload it forward .078 in.

D. Replace the locknuts on the driveshaft coupling and tighten the nuts only— not the bolts.

E. Inspect the gasket at the joint between the exhaust manifold and pipe and replace it if necessary.

F. When reattaching exhaust system support at the rear, leave the attaching nut/bolt slightly loose; loosen the two nuts/bolts attaching the support via slots to the transmission; push the support toward the exhaust pipe until all tension is removed and then secure nuts and bolts.

2800, 3.0, 528i, 530i, 830CSi, 633CSi

1. Remove the exhaust system. Drain the transmission.

2. Remove the circlip and washer at the selector rod and disengage the rod at the transmission.

3. Unzip the leather boot surrounding the gearshift lever. With a pointed object such as an ice pick, release the circlip at the bottom of the gearshift lever and then pull the lever upward and out of the transmission. Lubricate the nylon bushings at the bottom of the lever mechanism with a permanent lubricant for reassembly.

4. Remove the three bolts from the coupling at the front of the driveshaft out through the rear of the coupling, leaving the nuts/bolts attaching the driveshaft to the coupling in place.

5. Remove the heat shield. Remove the mounting bolts and remove the center bearing support bracket. Bend the driveshaft downward at the front and slide the spline out of the center bearing.

6. Support the transmission securely between the front axle carrier and oil pan with a floorjack and wooden block.

7. Remove the attaching bolt and pull out the speedometer cable. Disconnect the backup light wiring electrical connectors and pull the wire out of the clips on the transmission.

8. On all models *except* the 2800 and 3.0 Series, loosen the connection to the rubber bushing at the transmission, remove the mounting nuts at either end, and remove the crossmember. On the 630CSi and 633CSi, lower the transmission to the front axle carrier.

9. On the 630CSi and 633CSi, disconnect the mount for the clutch hydraulic line at the front of the transmission. Then, on all models, unscrew the mounting nuts and detach the clutch slave cylinder (with the line connected).

10. Remove the mounting nuts at the clutch housing and separate the transmission and clutch housing. On the 2800 and 3.0 Series models, now perform Step 8 to remove the crossmember.

11. On all models but the 2800 and 3.0, pull the gearbox to the rear and out of the car. On the 2800 and 3.0, pull the box out slightly and then lift both sides of the spring at the pivot point of the clutch throwout arm over the spherical collar to prevent breaking it. Then, remove the transmission from the car.

On the 2800 and 3.0, lift both sides of the spring at the pivot point of the throwout arm over the collar (1) to prevent breaking it

12. Install the transmission in reverse order, keeping the following points in mind:

A. Use the slave cylinder to move the clutch throwout arm to the correct position. Align the throwout bearing. Grease the guide sleeve and groove in the throwout bearing with a permanent lubricant.

B. Put the transmission into gear before installation.

C. On 2800 and 3.0 models, make sure the seal is situated between the collar and the throwout arm.

D. Make sure, when installing the clutch slave cylinder, that the hose connection faces downward.

E. Preload the center bearing .08 in. toward the front.

Preload the bearing .08 in. (A) in the forward direction

F. When tightening the coupling, hold the bolt heads and torque only the nuts only to 74 ft-lbs. Use new nuts. Torque the transmission-to-engine bolts to 16–17 ft-lbs (M8 transmission) or 31–35 ft lbs (M10) transmission); torque the bolt for the rubber bushing on the crossmember to 18 ft lbs.

733i

NOTE: *This procedure requires a special tool for clamping the flexible drive coupling.*

1. Remove the circlip and washer from the front end of the selector rod, and disconnect it from the lower end of the shift lever.

2. Push up the dust cover, and with needle nose pliers, remove the circlip which holds the gearshift lever in place. Lubricate the nylon bushings surrounding the socket with a permanent lubricant for reassembly.

Using special tool 26 1 011 to aid removal of coupling bolts—733i

3. Disconnect the back-up light plug near the gearshift lever.. Remove the large cirlip which surrounds the gearshift mount.

4. Drain the transmission. Raise the car and support it. Install the special tool (BMW 26 1 011 or equivalent) which clamps around the flexible coupling. Then, unscrew the three nuts on the forward side of the coupling, withdraw the bolts out the rear. This requires tightening the clamping tool until the bolts can be pulled out by hand.

5. Remove the web type crossmember located under the driveshaft. Then, loosen the mounting nuts for the center bearing bracket and detach it. Bend the driveshaft downward and pull it off the centering pin.

6. Support the transmission securely with a floor jack working through a wooden block. Then, remove the mounting nut from the crossmember rubber bushing, the nuts and bolts from either end of the crossmember where it bolts to the body, and remove the crossmember.

7. Detach the exhaust system bracket both at the transmission and at the exhaust pipes and remove it.

8. Detach the mounting bracket for the clutch slave cylinder hydraulic line at the transmission and then remove the two mounting bolts and remove the slave cylinder. Detach the fourth gear switch wires, if so equipped.

9. Detach the transmission at the clutch housing and remove it toward the rear.

10. Install the transmission in reverse order, keeping the following points in mind:

A. Use the clutch slave cylinder to put the release lever in position for transmission installation. Align the clutch bearing and lubricate the lubrication groove inside it with Molykote BR2-750 or its equivalent.

B. Put the transmission into gear prior to installation.

C. Install the guide sleeve of the transmission into the bearing carefully, then turn the output flange until the drive shaft slides into the drive plate. Then, remove the slave cylinder while mounting the transmission. Torque transmission-to-clutch housing bolts to 54–59 ft lbs.

D. When installing the clutch slave cylinder, make sure the bleeder screw faces downward.

E. When remounting the exhaust system bracket, make sure there is no torquional strain on the system.

F. Preload the center driveshaft bearing toward the front of the car .08 in.

G. When reassembling the flexible drive coupling, use new self-locking nuts Leave the special tool in compression while installing the bolts, and then install the nuts, holding the bolts in position and turning only the nuts.

H. Torque the transmission mount-to-crossmember bolt to 36–40 ft lbs, and the crossmember-to-body nuts to 16–17 ft lbs.

I. When installing the shift lever, note that the tab on the damper plate nuts engage in the opening in the shift arm.

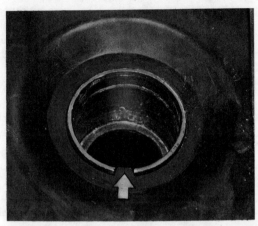

The opening in the shift arm is arrowed

Troubleshooting Clutch and Manual Transmission Problems

Problem	Cause(s)
Excessive clutch noise	Throwout bearing noises are more audible at the lower end of pedal travel. The usual causes are: • Riding the clutch • Too little pedal free-play • Lack of bearing lubrication A bad clutch shaft pilot bearing will make a high pitched squeal, when the clutch is disengaged and the transmission is in gear or within the first 2″ of pedal travel. The bearing must be replaced. Noise from the clutch linkage is a clicking or snapping that can be heard or felt as the pedal is moved completely up or down. This usually requires lubrication. Transmitted engine noises are amplified by the clutch housing and heard in the passenger compartment. They are usually the result of insufficient pedal free-play and can be changed by manipulating the clutch pedal.
Clutch slips (the car does not move as it should when the clutch is engaged)	This is usually most noticeable when pulling away from a standing start. A severe test is to start the engine, apply the brakes, shift into high gear and SLOWLY release the clutch pedal. A healthy clutch will stall the engine. If it slips it may be due to: • A worn pressure plate or clutch plate • Oil soaked clutch plate • Insufficient pedal free-play

Troubleshooting Clutch and Manual Transmission Problems (cont.)

Problem	Cause(s)
Clutch drags or fails to release	The clutch disc and some transmission gears spin briefly after clutch disengagement. Under normal conditions in average temperatures, 3 seconds is maximum spin-time. Failure to release properly can be caused by: • Too light transmission lubricant or low lubricant level • Improperly adjusted clutch linkage
Low clutch life	Low clutch life is usually a result of poor driving habits or heavy duty use. Riding the clutch, pulling heavy loads, holding the car on a grade with the clutch instead of the brakes and rapid clutch engagement all contribute to low clutch life.
Transmission shifts hard	Common causes of hard shifting are: • Improper lubricant viscosity or lubricant level • Clutch linkage needs adjustment/lubrication
Transmission leaks lubricant	The general location of a leak can be found by putting a clean newspaper under the transmission overnight. • Lubricant level too high • Loose or missing bolts • Cracks in the transmission case • Drain or fill plug loose or missing • Vent hole plugged
Transmission is noisy in gear	Most problems such as this require the services of a mechanic. Causes include: • Insufficient lubricant • Worn bearings • Chipped gear teeth • Worn gears (excessive end-play) • Damaged synchronizers
Transmission is noisy in Neutral	Noises in Neutral are usually caused by: • Insufficient/incorrect lubricant • Worn bearings or gear teeth • Worn reverse idler gear

CLUTCH

PEDAL HEIGHT AND OVERCENTER SPRING ADJUSTMENTS

2800, 3.0 Series, 528i, 530i, 630i, 633i, 733i

Measure the length of the overcenter spring (Dimension "A") and, if necessary, loosen the locknut and rotate the shaft as necessary to get the proper clearance. Measure the distance (Dimension "B") from the firewall to the tip of the clutch pedal and move the pedal in or out, if necessary, by loosening the locknut and rotating the shaft. Specifications for the various models are shown below.

	Dimension "A"	Dimension "B"
733i	1.338 in.	10.472–10.787 in.
630CSi, 633CSi	1.138–1.358 in.	9.644–9.960 in.
528i, 530i	1.283–1.302 in.	10.078–9.764 in.
2800, 3.0	1.34–1.36	10.35–10.63 in.

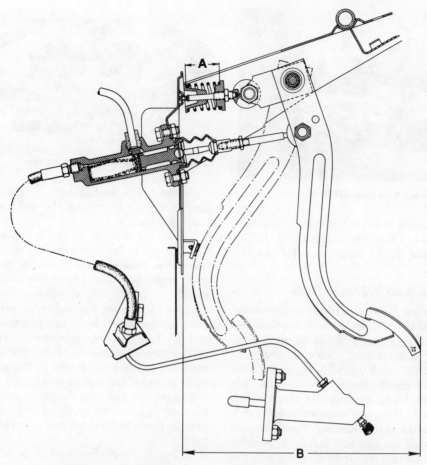

Adjusting pedal height and overcenter spring—six cylinder models

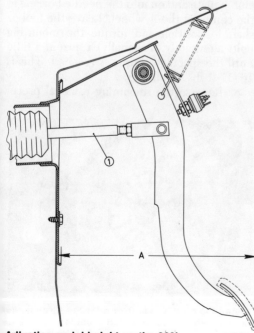

Adjusting pedal height on the 320i

PEDAL HEIGHT ADJUSTMENT

320i

Measure the distance between the bottom edge of the clutch pedal and the firewall (**A**). It should be 9.920–10.197 in. If out of specification, loosen the locknut and rotate the piston rod (1) to correct it.

1600-2, 2002

Measure the length of the clutch tension spring (hook-to-hook). Specified length is 3.622 in. If the dimension is incorrect, unlock the two nuts, rotate them together as necessary to get the right dimension, and then relock them.

FREE PLAY ADJUSTMENT

1600-2

On 1600-2 models, the free-play of the thrust rod at the release lever is adjusted at 8,000 mile intervals. Loosen the locknut (1) and

Adjusting clutch free-play—1600-2

Checking pressure plate for warpage

turn the nut (2) until 0.12–0.14 in. clearance exists between the release lever and the adjustment nut on the thrust rod. Tighten the locknut.

REMOVAL AND INSTALLATION

1. Remove the transmission as described above. On six cylinder models, remove the clutch housing as described in the next step. On four cylinder models, proceed to Step 3.

2. On 2800 and 3.0 models equipped with an external clutch throwout arm, pull back the rubber boot, remove the circlip with needle nose pliers, and remove the slave cylinder from the clutch housing. On all six cylinder models but the 528i and 530i, remove the black cover plate from the front of the housing. Then, unscrew the mounting bolts and remove the clutch housing.

3. On 1600-2 and 2002 models, mark the relationship between the clutch and flywheel for reinstallation in the same position. On all models block the flywheel from turning using a screwdriver bearing against a bolt screwed in where the clutch housing attaches.

4. Loosen the clutch mounting screws about one turn at a time going diagonally

from one to the next. When all spring pressure is released, remove the bolts and remove the clutch.

5. Even if the disc is being replaced for what seems to be normal wear, you should check the flywheel and pressure plate for what might be signs of excessive heat—blue metal, or a warped condition. Check for warping by running a straightedge across the working surface of both the pressure plate and flywheel. If either is warped, it requires replacement if adequate clutch life is to be expected. Also loose rivets in the pressure plate is reason for replacement.

6. Position the clutch plate inside the pressure plate, and position the pressure plate against the flywheel and over the dowel pins.

7. Insert a centering tool or an old input shaft from the type of transmission the car uses through the splines at the center of the clutch plate and on into the needle bearing at the center of the flywheel. Leave the tool or shaft in position and torque the mounting bolts alternately (diagonally) a turn at a time until the specified torque is reached. This is 16–17 ft lbs on all cars.

8. Reverse the remaining removal proce

On some six cylinder models, remove the black cover plate from the front of the clutch housing

Install the clutch assembly over the three dowel pins, as shown. Then, insert a centering tool, as shown

dures to install. Grease the input shaft of the transmission.

Clutch Master Cylinder

REMOVAL AND INSTALLATION

1. Remove the necessary trim panel or carpet.

2. On model 320i, disconnect the accelerator cable and pull it forward out of the engine firewall.

3. Disconnect the push rod at the clutch pedal.

4. Remove enough brake fluid from the tank until the level drops below the refill line.

5. Disconnect the windshield washer fluid tank without removing the hoses on model 733i.

6. Disconnect the lines and retaining bolts and remove the master cylinder from the firewall.

7. Installation is the reverse of removal. Bleed the system as described below and adjust the pedal travel with the push rod to 6 in.

Clutch Slave Cylinder

REMOVAL AND INSTALLATION

1. Remove enough brake fluid from the reservoir until the level drops below the refill line connection.

2. Remove the circlip or retaining bolts depending on the model.

3. Disconnect the line and remove the slave cylinder.

4. Installation is the reverse of removal. Bleed the system as described below.

Bleeding the Clutch Hydraulic System

1. Fill a glass bottle with an approved brake fluid; also, make sure the clutch or brake/clutch reservoir is full.

2. Run a small plastic hose down into the fluid and force the other end tightly over the bleeder screw on the slave cylinder. Have someone depress the clutch pedal 10 times and hold it floored.

3. Open the bleeder screw and keep it open until the bleeding fluid has no bubbles in it. Then, tighten the screw again.

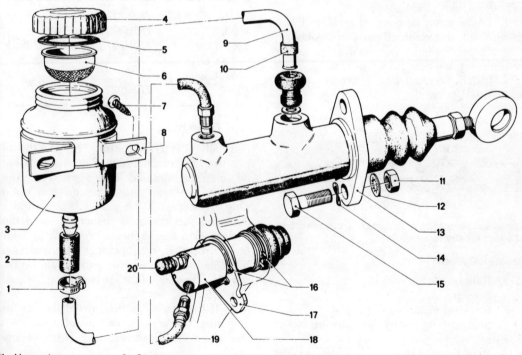

1. Hose clamp	6. Strainer	11. Hex nut	16. Lockring
2. Connection hose	7. Sheet metal screw	12. Internal star washer	17. Support plate
3. Brake fluid tank	8. Support	13. Transmitting cylinder	18. Transmitting cylinder
4. Filler cap	9. Tube	14. Lockwasher	19. Hose line
5. Gasket	10. Rubber sleeve	15. Screw	20. Dust cap

Clutch hydraulic system components—2002 series

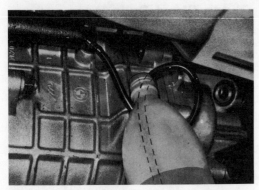

Bleeding the clutch hydraulic system with a special bleeder. To bleed using ordinary equipment, simply force the upper end of a hose tightly over the end of the bleeder screw, rigging the lower end as shown here. See text

4. Refill the fluid reservoir, and then repeat the pumping procedure. Repeat Step 3.

5. Repeat Steps 2–4 until no more bubbles emerge. Refill the reservoir and remove the bleed tube and bottle.

Clutch Master and Slave Cylinder Overhaul

1. Remove the master cylinder and slave cylinder as described above.

2. Remove rubber boots or seals, pull the pistons out, and clean all parts in alcohol.

3. Inspect cylinder bores for corrosion or scoring; replace parts as necessary.

4. Install overhaul kits, consisting of the parts listed below:

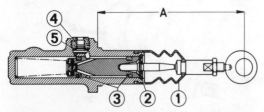

Cross section of the clutch master cylinder. See the text for key to numbers

Master Cylinder—

1. Rubber boot
2. Circlip
3. Grooved piston ring seals
4. Sealing plug (which fits into the top of the unit)
5. Washer (situated under the sealing plug)

Slave Cylinder—

1. Ring type retainer (retains the part below)

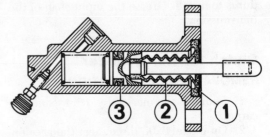

Cross section of the clutch slave cylinder. See the text for key to numbers

2. Rubber boot (goes in bore and around the piston rod)

3. Grooved sleeve type piston seal.

4. Install the master and slave cylinders in reverse of the procedures above and bleed the system.

AUTOMATIC TRANSMISSION

Identification

Vehicle	Transmission	Cover Designation
2002A, 320i	ZF3HP12	028
2800, 3.0	ZF3HP20	1019
528i, 530i, 630CSi, 633CSi	ZF3HP22	Silver/Black
733i	ZF3HP22	J

PAN REMOVAL

Normally, it is not required to remove the oil pan from the transmission. The transmission oil may be drained and refilled at the required intervals using the oil pan drain plug. However, if the pan is leaking and a damaged pan gasket is suspected, or if the transmission fluid appears brownish in color on the dipstick, or if a clogged transmission oil filter is suspected, the pan should be removed. The procedure for removing the pan is as follows:

1. If the car is running, drive the car for 3–5 miles to warm up the transmission. Park the car on a level surface. Shut off the engine.

2. Place a drip pan (minimum 2 quart capacity) beneath the oil pan. Unscrew and remove the transmission oil drain plug, taking care not to get scalded by the hot fluid.

3. Inspect the drained oil. If the oil has a

"burned" smell or is dark brown in color, the transmission should be disassembled and rebuilt. Also, if the oil contains tiny iron or aluminum particles (fluid is grey in color), the transmission will be needing service.

4. On the ZF 22 type transmissions, disconnect the oil filler neck at the oil pan. On ZF 12 and ZF 20 transmissions, remove the pan mounting bolts, noting the location of the two clips on one side, and remove the pan and gasket. On ZF 22 transmissions, remove the retaining bolt and bracket at each corner and remove the pan and gasket.

5. If desired, service the strainer, as described below.

6. Clean the gasket surfaces. Replacing the gasket, reinstall the pan. On ZF 22 transmissions, place the magnetic disc next to the oil filter screen in the oil pan, and make sure the retaining brackets are installed with the shorter leg going inside the groove on the pan. Torque the bolts alternately and in small steps to the following values:

Removing the transmission oil strainer—(2800, 3.0)

on all 22 type transmissions except those designated "J" (733i). On "J" type transmissions, the figure is 4.3–5.0 ft lbs.

4. Replace the oil pan as described above.

NEUTRAL SAFETY SWITCH ADJUSTMENT

2002A

The neutral safety switch (starter lock switch) used in the ZF automatic transmission is combined with the back-up light switch. Therefore, if you are having problems with the back-up lights going on or staying on when they are not supposed to, chances are that you might have difficulty starting the car with the selector lever in Park or Neutral.

1. Check the operation of the switch by disconnecting the two leads at terminals 50. Ground one terminal tag. Connect a 12 volt test lamp to the positive terminal and the

Transmission	Oil Pan	Filler Neck
ZF3HP12	7 ft. lbs.	—
ZF3HP20	7.2 ft. lbs.	—
ZF3HP22	6–6.5 ft. lbs.	74–84 ft. lbs.

7. With the car parked on a level surface, and the selector lever in Park, fill the transmission slowly until the fluid level is ¼ in. above the minimum mark on the dipstick. Consult Chapter 1 for the type of fluid to use and approximate quantities.

8. Start the engine and let it warm up to normal operating temperature. Recheck the fluid level with the selector lever in park. If the level is not between the two marks on the dipstick (slightly more than a pint from one to the other), or drain fluid as required.

FILTER SERVICE

1. Drain and remove the oil pan as described above.

2. Remove the bolts retaining the strainer to the valve body, remove the strainer, and clean it in trichloroethylene. Allow it to dry.

3. Install the strainer and gently retighten the mounting bolts or screws alternately and evenly. On the 22 type transmissions, the valve body to transmission bolts should be torqued to 7–8 ft lbs (some of these retain the strainer); the phillips screws which retain the strainer should be torqued to 3.6–4.3 ft-lbs

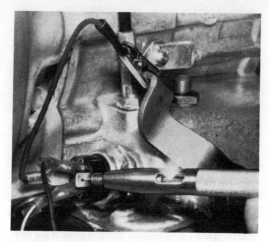

Hooking up test light

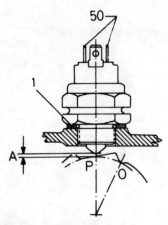

Cross-section of neutral start safety switch showing terminals 50 and shims (1). Distance "A" inside the transmission is .02 in.

Loosen the locknut (1) and adjust via the bolt (2)

second terminal tag. The test lamp should light when the selector lever is placed in P (Park) or O (Neutral), if the switch is properly adjusted.

2. If the switch is in need of adjustment, unscrew the switch and place correspondingly thicker seals (shims) behind the switch and the transmission housing.

ADJUSTMENT OF BRAKE BANDS

2800, 3.0

These adjustments are made externally. Each is made at a square headed bolt retained by a hex type locknut. Adjustment is required after 600 miles and every 15,000 miles thereafter.

1. Loosen the locknut (1) about 1 turn (an offset hex wrench will be helpful). Tighten the adjusting (square) bolt (2) to 50.61 ft lbs.

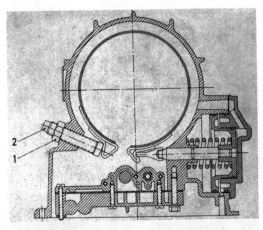

Adjusting the transmission band. See text for key to numbers

2. Note the exact position of the adjusting bolt, and loosen it exactly ¾ of a turn. Then, tighten the locknut.

SHIFT LINKAGE ADJUSTMENT

All Models

1. Detach the selector rod (1) at the selector lever lower section (2).

2. Move the selector lever (3) on the transmission to position 0.

3. Press the selector lever (4) against the stop (5) on the shift gate.

4. Adjust the length of the selector rod (1) until the pin (6) aligns with the bore in the selector lever lower section (2). Shorten the selector rod length by: 1 turn–320i, 630CSi, 733i; 2–2½ turns–528i, 530i; 3 turns–2002, 3.0.

NOTE: *If equipped with air conditioning on the 4 cylinder models, plates (7) must be installed between the bearing bracket and float plate and selector rod (1) must be attached in bore K of selector lever (3).*

ACCELERATOR LINKAGE ADJUSTMENT

2002A

1. Remove the air cleaner.

2. Remove the accelerator cable.

3. Press the accelerator pedal down to the kick down stop into the full acceleration position. In this position the throttle valve must be fully open and not extend beyond the vertical position. When adjusting, bend the stop.

4. Adjust the length of the accelerator linkage using the eye bolt.

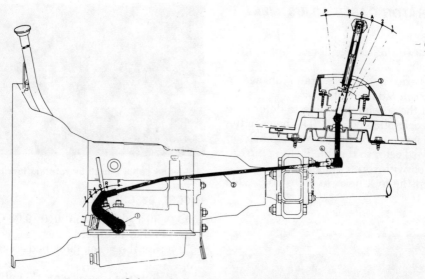

Selector lever adjustment—typical

3.0, 528i, 530i

1. Synchronize the idle speed with the engine at operating temperature.

2. Detach linkage (1).

3. Detach the accelerator cable at the operating lever (2).

4. Adjust linkage (1) so that the operating lever (2) rests on stop (3).

NOTE: *Make sure that linkage (1) is not pulled down into the kickdown position.*

5. The swivel joint (5) must align with the hole in the operating lever (2) leaving a play (0.009–0.019 in.) between nipple (4) and the end of the cable sleeve.

6. The acclerator must not sag. Press lever (6) against the acceleration stop (7) and adjust linkage (8) until the distance between nipple (4) and the end of the cable sleeve is 1.456 in. When in kickdown, the nipple (4) must be at least 1.69 in. from the end of the cable sleeve.

NOTE: *If the idle speed is altered, repeat the above procedure.*

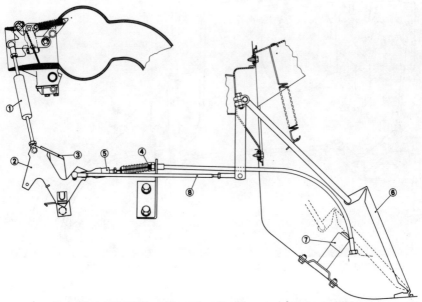

Accelerator linkage and cable adjustment—528i, 530i, 2800, 3.0

ACCELERATOR CABLE ADJUSTMENT

2002A

1. Remove the accelerator cable from the rotary shaft.

2. Press down the accelerator linkage to the full acceleration position.

3. Pull the accelerator cable to determine the full acceleration postion. The holes in the fork head must now coincide with the hole on the rotary selector so that the bearing pin can be inserted with correct alignment.

4. Turn the fork head to adjust the cable length.

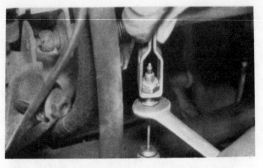

Adjusting cable length by rotating fork head

630CSi, 633CSi, 733i

1. Adjust play (S) to 0.010–0.030 in. with nuts when in neutral.

2. Press the accelerator pedal against the stop.

3. Adjust the pressure rod (7) until the distance from the seal (3) to the end of the cable (4) is 630i—(1.732–2.008 in.), (4) is 630i—(1.732–2.057 in.)

320i

1. Adjust the accelerator cable at nuts (1) until the accelerator cable eye (2) has a play of 0.008 in.–0.012 in.

2. Depress the accelerator pedal (3) to the full throttle stop screw (4).

3. There must be 0.020 in. play between the operating lever (5) and stop nut (6).

Inserting bearing pin for accelerator cable— 2002A

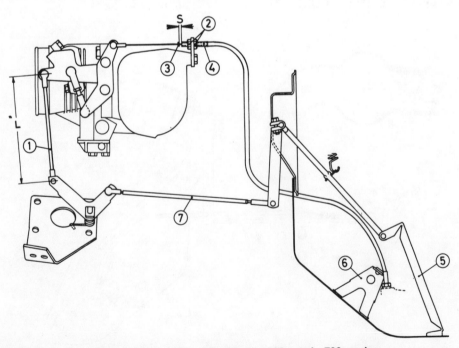

Accelerator cable adjustment—600 and 700 series

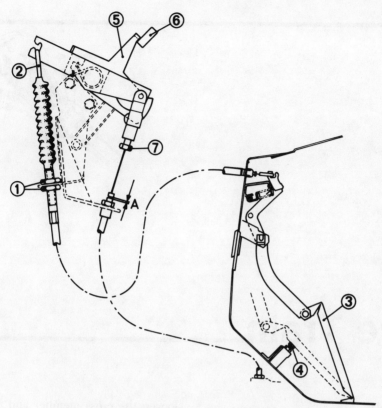

Accelerator and transmission cable adjustments—320i

4. Adjust by the full throttle stop screw 4).

TRANSMISSION CABLE ADJUSTMENT
320i

NOTE: *The accelerator cable must be correctly adjusted.*

1. With the transmission in the neutral position, adjust play (A) to 0.010–0.030 in. with the screw (7).

2. Depress the accelerator pedal (3) to kickdown stop; play (A) must now be 1.712–2.027″. Make corrections with screw (4).

7

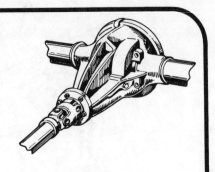

Drive Train

DRIVELINE

Driveshaft and U-Joints

NOTE: *BMW U-joints are not serviced. If U-joint bearings are worn or defective, the entire driveshaft must be replaced.*

REMOVAL AND INSTALLATION

All Models

1. On 530i, 630i, remove the entire exhaust system.

2. On 1600 and 2002 remove the primary muffler from the exhaust pipe.

3. On 3.0 and 2800 remove the primary and main mufflers.

4. On 320i, detach the outer pipe at the manifold and support it at the transmission.

5. Remove the heat shield if so equipped.

6. On the 733i, install a special clamping tool (BMW 261011 or the equivalent) around the flexible coupling and tighten it. Then, on all models, remove the three through bolts which pass through the coupling from the rear (nuts on the front).

7. Remove the attaching nuts from the center bearing bracket.

8. On 733i, with manual transmissions, loosen the cross member and push the left end forward.

9. Bend the propeller shaft down and pull out.

10. Installation is the reverse of removal.

11. The propellershaft is balanced in line and must only be renewed as a complete assembly.

12. Align the driveshaft with a gauge (BMW-26-1-000) or equivalent by moving the center bearing sideways or by placing washers underneath the center bearing.

13. On 733i, remove the special coupling tool only after the nuts have been tightened to prevent stress on the coupling. On other

Checking driveshaft alignment

Troubleshooting the Driveline

The Problem	Is Caused By	What to Do
Shudder as car accelerates from stop or low speed	• Loose U-joint • Defective center bearing	• Tighten U-joint or have it replaced • Have center bearing replaced
Loud clunk in driveshaft when shifting gears	• Worn U-joints	• Have U-joints replaced
Roughness or vibration at any speed	• Out-of-balance, bent or dented driveshaft • Worn U-joints • U-joint clamp bolts loose	• Have driveshaft serviced • Have U-joints serviced • Tighten U-joint clamp bolts
Squeaking noise at low speeds	• Lack of U-joint lubrication	• Lubricate U-joint; if problem persists, have U-joint serviced
Knock or clicking noise	• U-joint or driveshaft hitting frame tunnel	• Correct overloaded condition

models, pry rearward (against the rear transmission crossmember) on the flexible coupling to install the bolts. Torque the nuts while holding the bolts stationary to avoid pre-stressing the coupling.

14. Preload the center bearing by 0.078 in. in the forward direction.

Center Driveshaft Bearing
REMOVAL AND INSTALLATION
2800, 3.0, 528i, 630CSi, 633CSi, 733i

1. Bend down the driveshaft and pull it out of the centering pin on the transmission (Refer to DriveShaft Removal and Installation).
2. Loosen the threaded bushing.
3. Mark the drive shaft position on slide with a punch mark and pull the front half of the propeller shaft out of the slide.
4. Remove the circlip and dust guard.
5. Using a standard puller remove the center bearing without the dust guard.
6. Use a puller and remove the grooved ball bearing in the center bearing.
7. Installation is the reverse of removal. Drive the center bearing onto the grooved ball bearing with Tool (BMW-24-1-050) or equivalent.

Remove the circlip and dust cap—six cylinder models

320i

1. With the propeller shaft removed, mark the shafts location of the coupling.
2. Remove the circlip and pull out the propeller shaft.
3. Using a standard puller remove the center bearing without its dust cover.
4. Drive the grooved ball bearing out of the center bearing.
5. Installation is the reverse of removal.

1600, 2002, 320

1. With the propeller shaft removed, remove the coupling nut.

2. Using a standard puller, pull off the center bearing without the dust guard plate.

3. Remove the grooved ball bearing with a puller.

4. Installation is the reverse of removal.

Centering ring components: spring (1); washer (2); centering ring (3); ball socket (4); retaining ring (5); and sealing cap (6)

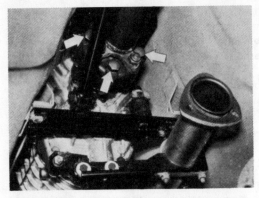

Disconnecting front rubber coupling from transmission flange

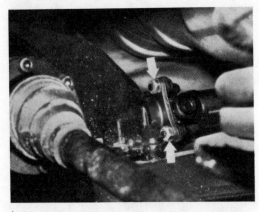

Disconnecting driveshaft from differential flange

Flexible Coupling Centering Ring

REMOVAL AND INSTALLATION

1600, 2002, 2800, 3.0

1. Press off the sealing cap.

2. Lift out the circlip.

3. Take out the ball cup, centering ring, disc and spring.

4. Installation is the reverse of removal. Fill the centering assembly with approximately 6g (0.2 oz.) of grease.

All Other Models

1. Fill the center with grease and using a 14mm (0.551") dia. mandrel, drive out the ring.

2. Installation is the reverse of removal. NOTE: *The shaft ring faces out.*

REAR AXLE

Identification

Generally, BMW axle ratios do not vary with options (such as automatic transmission), but only with engine size. The axle ratio, as well as an alpha-numerical identification code required in ordering parts, are displayed on the outside of the housing as indicated in the chart below.

Rear Axle Identification Code Locations

1600, 2002	One side of the housing
320i	Rear case cover
2800, 3.0, 528i, 530i, 630CSi, 633CSi	Under oil filler plug
733i	Below drive flange on case

Output Shaft

REMOVAL AND INSTALLATION

Constant Velocity Type

1. Detach the output shaft at the final drive and drive flange.

2. On 733i, support the control arm if the spring strut and shock absorber are detached.

Troubleshooting the Rear Axle

BASIC REAR AXLE PROBLEMS

First determine when the noise is most noticeable.

Drive Noise: Produced under vehicle acceleration.

Coast Noise: Produced while the car coasts with a closed throttle.

Float Noise: Occurs while maintaining constant car speed (just enough to keep speed constant) on a level road.

Road Noise

Brick or rough surfaced concrete roads produce noise that seem to come from the rear axle. Road noise is usually identical in Drive or Coast and driving on a different type of road will tell whether the road is the problem.

Tire Noise

Tire noises are often mistaken for rear axle problems. Snow treads or unevenly worn tires produce vibrations seeming to originate elsewhere. Temporarily inflating the tires to 40 lbs will significantly alter tire noise, but will have no effect on rear axle noises (which normally cease below about 30 mph).

Engine/Transmission Noise

Determine at what speed the noise is most pronounced, then stop the car in a quiet place. With the transmission in Neutral, run the engine through speeds corresponding to road speeds where the noise was noticed. Noises produced with the car standing still are coming from the engine or transmission.

Front Wheel Bearings

While holding the car speed steady, lightly apply the footbrake; this will often decrease bearing noise, as some of the load is taken from the bearing.

Rear Axle Noises

Eliminating other possible sources can narrow the cause to the rear axle, which normally produces noise from worn gears or bearings. Gear noises tend to peak in a narrow speed range, while bearing noises will usually vary in pitch with engine speeds.

NOISE DIAGNOSIS

The Noise Is	Most Probably Produced By
1. Identical under Drive or Coast	Road surface, tires or front wheel bearings
2. Different depending on road surface	Road surface or tires
3. Lower as the car speed is lowered	Tires
4. Similar with car standing or moving	Engine or transmission
5. A vibration	Unbalanced tires, rear wheel bearing, unbalanced driveshaft or worn U-joint
6. A knock or click about every 2 tire revolutions	Rear wheel bearing
7. Most pronounced on turns	Damaged differential gears
8. A steady low-pitched whirring or scraping, starting at low speeds	Damaged or worn pinion bearing
9. A chattering vibration on turns	Wrong differential lubricant or worn clutch plates (limited slip rear axle)
10. Noticed only in Drive, Coast or Float conditions	Worn ring gear and/or pinion gear

3. On 630i, the spring strut serves as a retaining strap and the trailing arm must be supported if the spring strut is detached.

4. Replace the bellows as follows:
   a. Take off the sealing cover.
   b. Remove the circlip.
   c. Remove the clamp.

d. Press the output shaft out of the joint then slide off the bellows.

5. Installation is the reverse of removal.

Sliding Type (1600, 2002)

1. Remove the output shaft from the final drive and half-shaft.

Constant velocity type output shaft

Check the spacer (arrowed) and radial oil seals, and replace the drive flange and seals, as necessary

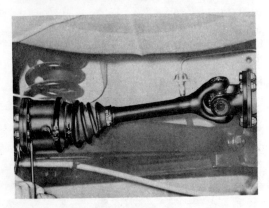

Sliding joint type output shaft

2. Replace the bellows as follows:
   a. Drain the oil.
   b. Remove the hose clamps.
   c. Pull off the sliding joint housing.
   d. Remove the mushroom head caps.

NOTE: *Be careful not to lose the lower needle bearing pin and lift over the upper needle bearing pin.*

3. To install, reverse the above.

NOTE: *If the bore in the joint yoke is distorted, the complete output shaft must be replaced.*

Rear Axle Shaft, Wheel Bearings, and Seals

REMOVAL AND INSTALLATION

Six Cylinder Models

1. Remove the wheel.
2. Loosen the brake caliper attaching bolts, leaving the brake line connected.
3. Remove the brake rotor.
4. Remove the driving flange as follows:
   A. Disconnect the output shaft at the flange.

Lock the collared nut in the drive flange groove (arrowed)

    B. Remove the lockplate.
    C. Loosen the collared nut and, with a puller, pull the flange off.

5. Then, reinstall and tighten the collared nut and drive the rear axle shaft out, using a soft hammer against the collared nut.

6. Drive off the wheel bearings and seals toward the outside.

7. Inspect the spacer and radial seals on the axle shaft and replace if necessary. BMW recommends replacing the rear wheel bearings at 60,000 miles.

8. Install in reverse order, making sure to lock the collared nut with the lockplate in the groove in the driving flange.

Four Cylinder Models

1. Remove the wheel.
2. Remove the cotter pin from the castellated nut.
3. Apply the handbrake.
4. Loosen the castellated nut.
5. Release the handbrake.

Axle bearing components—four cylinder models

10. Drive out the bearing and sealing ring.

11. Take out the spacer sleeve and shim.

12. Check the condition of the axle bearings, (2) sealing rings, (1) spacer sleeve (4) and shims (3). The sealing ring should be flat and undamaged. The ball bearings should rotate easily and not be scored or galled. The axle bearing play is adjusted by the insertion of shims behind (inside) the outer axle bearing. To determine the necessary shim thickness, measure the length of the spacer sleeve (A). With the inner ball bearing installed, measure the distance (B) from the contact surface of the outer ball bearing in the hub to the outer race of the inner ball bearing. Proper end-play for the bearing is 0.0039 in. Therefore, A–B–end-play equals the necessary shim thickness (C). Normal shim thickness is 0.1142 in.

6. Remove the brake drum.

7. Pull off the drive flange with a puller.

8. Disconnect the output shaft and tie it up.

9. Drive out the half shaft with a plastic hammer using the castellated nut to protect the end of the shaft.

13. Reverse the above procedure to install, taking care to pack the shaft hub with wheel bearing grease.

Determine installation play:

$$
\begin{array}{ll}
A = 64.0 \text{ mm } (2.5197'') \\
-B = 61.0 \text{ mm } (2.4016'') \\
\hline
3.0 \text{ mm } (0.1181'') \\
-0.1 \text{ mm } (0.0039'') \text{ play} \\
\hline
C\ 2.9 \text{ mm } (0.1142'') \\
\text{shim thickness}
\end{array}
$$

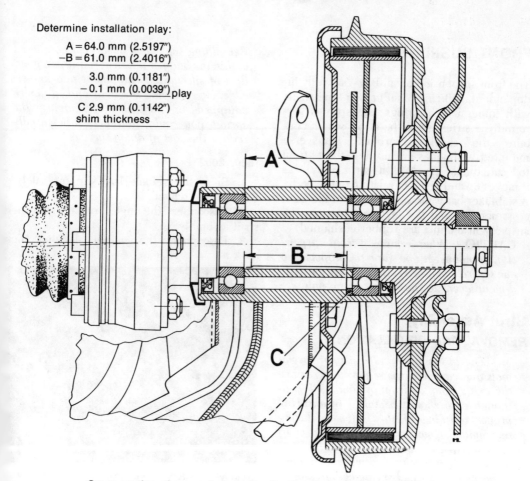

Cross-section of rear axle hub showing bearing adjustment lengths

8

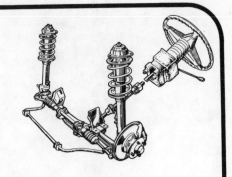

Suspension and Steering

FRONT SUSPENSION

The front suspension on all BMWs is fully independent, utilizing MacPherson type struts with integral coil springs (the springs surround the structure of the strut, which contains the shock absorber). Transverse mounted wishbones are used at the bottom to locate the lower end of the strut laterally as it moves up and down in relation to the body. A stabilizer bar is mounted between the front crossmember and the lower wishbones. All suspension mounts are rubber cushioned.

CAUTION: *When removing front suspension components, be sure to support the car securely via the reinforced box-member area adjacent to the front jacking points.*

Strut Assembly

REMOVAL AND INSTALLATION

NOTE: *Not too much in the way of special tools and equipment is required to remove the struts from the front of your BMW, although care should be taken in ensuring proper torquing of the fasteners during reassembly. However, once the strut is off the car, special equipment is required to disassemble it safely. You will either have to purchase a special spring compressor or take the strut to a qualified repair shop.*

Rebuilding the shock absorbers contained within the body of the strut requires a good deal of specialized equipment and knowledge. By removing the strut and, if you're equipped to handle it, removing the spring, you could, however, substantially reduce the cost of doing the work.

1600, 2002

1. Raise the vehicle and support safely. Remove the wheel.

2. Disconnect the angle bracket from the strut assembly.

3. Disconnect the caliper, leaving the

Removing safety wiring from strut assembly– 1600, 2002

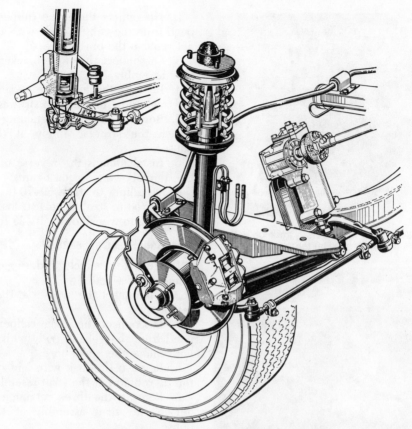

Front suspension and steering system—2002

brake line attached. Tie the caliper to the vehicle body so that the weight is not supported by the brake hose.

4. Disconnect the lower arm from the axle beam.

5. Remove the lockwire and disconnect the track rod arm from the strut assembly.

6. Remove the three retaining nuts and detach the strut assembly at the wheelhouse.

7. Installation is the reverse of the removal procedure. When reattaching the wishbone at the front axle beam, use a new self-locking nut and make sure the spacer touches the axle beam. Torque specifications are as follows: Strut thrust bearing at wheelhouse: 16–17.4 ft lbs. Lower arm to axle: 123–137 ft. lb—this should be finalized after the vehicle has been lowered to the ground. Track rod arm from strut: 18–24 ft lb. Caliper to strut: 58–69 ft. lb.

320i

1. Raise the vehicle and support safely. Remove the wheel.

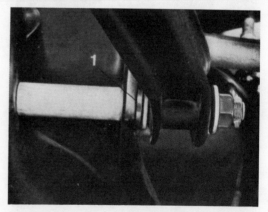

Proper installation of wishbone to front axle carrier with spacer ring (1) facing carrier

2. Detach the bracket at the strut assembly.

3. Disconnect and suspend the brake caliper with a wire from the vehicle body. Do not disconnect the brake line.

4. Remove the cotter pin and castle nut. Press the tie rod off the steering knuckle.

5. Remove the cotter pin and castellated

Press the tie rod off the steering knuckle with a tool such as the BMW special tool pictured

Remove the three retaining nuts from the top of the strut housing—320i

nut and press the control arm off the steering knuckle with an appropriate tool.

6. Remove the three retaining nuts and detach the strut assembly at the wheel house.

7. Installation is the reverse of removal. When installing the castellated nut which attaches the control arm to the steering knuckle, apply a coat of nitro lacquer to the nut and stud, diluted with 50% water. Torque specifications are as follows:

  Brake caliper to backing plate: 58–69 ft. lbs.
  Tie rod to steering knuckle: 25–29 ft. lbs.
  Control arm to steering knuckle: 44–50 ft. lbs.
  Strut to wheelhouse: 16–17 ft. lbs.

3.0

1. Raise the vehicle and support safely. Remove the wheel.

2. Disconnect the brake caliper and suspend from the vehicle body with a wire. Do not remove the brake hose.

3. Disconnect the angle bracket from the strut assembly.

4. Remove the lock wire and disconnect the track rod arm from the strut assembly.

5. Remove the three retaining nuts and detach the strut assembly at the wheel house.

6. Installation is the reverse of removal. Use the following torque figures:

  Brake caliper to strut: 59–70 ft. lbs.
  Track rod to strut: 33–44 ft. lbs.
  Bearing to wheelhouse: 16–18 ft. lb.

528i, 530i, 630CSi, 633CSi

1. Raise the vehicle and support safely. Remove the wheel.

2. Disconnect the bracket at the strut assembly.

3. Disconnect the brake caliper and suspend from the vehicle body with wire. Do not remove the brake hose.

4. Remove the lock wire and disconnect the tie rod arm at the strut assembly.

5. Remove the three retaining nuts and detach the strut assembly at the wheel house.

The wheelhouse strut mounting nuts on 500 and 600 series cars

6. Installation is the reverse of removal. Use the following torque figures:

  Caliper to strut: 58–69 ft. lb.
  Strut bearing to wheelhouse: 16–18 ft. lb.
  Tie-rod to Strut: 32.5–43 ft. lb.

733i

1. Raise the vehicle and support safely. Remove the wheel.

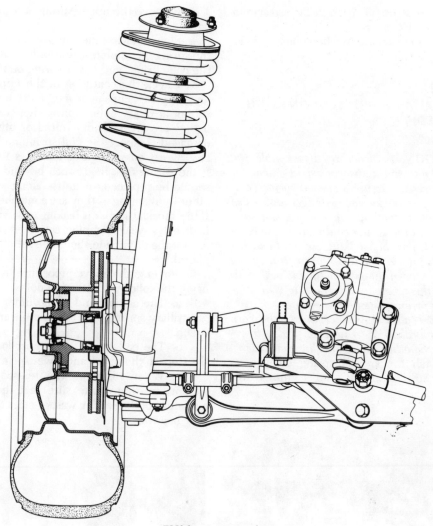

733i front suspension

2. Disconnect the vibration strut from the control arm.

3. Disconnect the bracket and clamps from the strut assembly.

4. Disconnect the wire connection and press out the wire from the clamp on the spring strut tube.

5. Remove the brake caliper and suspend it from the vehicle body with a wire. Do not remove the brake hose.

6. Disconnect the tie rod from the shock absorber.

7. Remove the three retaining nuts and disconnect the strut assembly from the wheel house.

8. Installation is the reverse of removal. In installing the bolts attaching the tie rod arm to the lower strut, both male and female threads must be clean and a locking com-

Tie rod arm-to-shock absorber retaining bolts— 733i

pound such as green Loctite No. 270 must be used on the bolts. Observe the following torque specifications:

Vibration strut to control arm: 18–20 ft lbs

Caliper to strut: 59–70 ft. lb Tie rod arm to strut: 96–107 ft. lb.

Strut upper bearing to wheelhouse: 16–17 ft. lb.

Spring

REMOVAL AND INSTALLATION (STRUT REMOVED)

1600, 2002

CAUTION: *In order to disassemble the spring and shock absorber strut assembly, it is necessary to use a special spring compressor. It is extremely dangerous to use any other method of compressing the spring, as the spring could slip while compressed, possibly striking you and causing serious injury. For this reason, if a spring compressor of the proper type is not available, this procedure is best left to your dealer or a qualified repair shop.*

NOTE: *If a spring is determined to be worn out or broken, it is necessary also to replace the other spring on the same axle.*

1. Install the special spring compressor on the strut assembly and compress the spring.

Strut assembly mounted in spring compressor tool BMW 6035—1600, 2002

2. Lift off the plastic sealing cap from the top of the strut. Unscrew the elastic locknut (1), while holding the shock absorber piston rod (2) steady. Lift out the telescopic leg support bearing assembly from the top of the strut.

Removing telescopic leg support bearing assembly

3. Remove the upper spring cup and support.

4. Slowly release the compressor tool until the spring is completely tensionfree. Remove the coil spring, and lower spring cup.

5. Check the condition of the upper and lower spring cups (collars), and the inner rubber auxiliary buffer spring. Replace them if they are cracked, dry-rotted or otherwise damaged. Inspect the coil spring and shock absorber. Coil spring free length is 13.12 in. If the spring is sagged much beyond this, it should be replaced, of course along with the other front spring as they are a matched pair. If the shock absorber is leaking excessively or it displays weak damping action, it and the one on the other side should be rebuilt or replaced.

6. Reverse the above procedure to install, using the following assembly notes:

    a. The conical end of the inner rubber auxiliary spring must face the lower spring cup.

    b. The coil spring ends must locate on the stops in the upper and lower spring cups.

    c. When installing the telescopic leg support bearing, make sure that the inner curvature of the sealing washer faces the support bearing.

Proper order of assembly of telescopic leg support bearing components

    d. Tighten the locknut for the strut assembly to 52 ft lbs. Only after the locknut is tightened to its final figure should you release the spring compressor, and then, very slowly.

320i

1. Compress the spring coil with a special tool such as BMW 31 3 110. Lift off the rubber cap.

2. Hold the piston rod with one wrench while removing the self-locking nut with another.

3. Release the spring and remove the strut support bearing.

4. To install, reverse the removal procedure, keeping the following points in mind:

A. A tapered special tool is available to facilitate installation of the support bearing over the shock absorber piston rod.

B. Check mounting rings for the spring, auxiliary spring (which fits over the piston rod) and outer tube, and replace any which are faulty.

C. Make sure the spring ends rest on the locating shoulders in both upper and lower spring retainers before compressing the spring and support bearing.

D. Replace the self locking nut which goes on the piston rod, and torque to 57–62 ft lbs.

E. Sequence of installation above spring itself is: large washer (1) sealing washer (2), support bearing (3), concave washer (4), self locking nut (5).

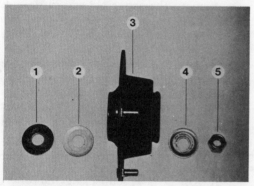

Sequence of installation of parts at the top of the strut—320i

2800, 3.0

1. Compress the coil spring with a spring compressor.

2. Remove the rubber cap, lock the piston rod with one wrench, and use another wrench to remove the locknut.

3. Remove the strut thrust bearing from the top of the strut.

4. Gradually loosen the spring compressors and remove the spring plate and spring.

5. Check the rubber bushings above and below the spring and replace if necessary.

6. Wind the spring into the spring plates so spring ends rest against stops, and then reverse the remaining procedures to install, keeping the following points in mind:

A. The internal dish of the sealing washer (1) that goes right above the thrust bearing should face the spring. Another washer (2) goes on top of that.

The internal dish of the sealing washer should face toward the thrust bearing—2800, 3.0

B. Torque the retaining nut to 53–59 ft lbs.

528i, 530i, 630CSi, 633CSi, 733i

1. Compress the coil spring with a tool such as BMW 31 3 100 (on 733i use a tool which works on the strut and support bearing, surrounding the whole assembly, such as BMW 31 1 111).

2. Lift off the rubber cap. Holding the piston rod with one wrench, use another to remove the locknut.

3. Then, release the spring and remove the mount, washers, and spring.

4. Check the rubber damper rings at either end of the spring and at the ends of the auxiliary spring (which surrounds the piston rod) and the outer tube below it, and replace any which are defective.

5. Align the spring before starting the compression process, winding it against the stops on the strut and upper retainer.

6. A special tool (such as BMW 31 3 113) may be screwed onto the top of the piston

A special tool such as BMW 31 3 113 may ease the insertion of the piston rod into the strut mount. Make sure to install the disc (1) on the 733i

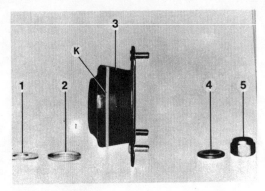

Order of installation of upper strut mounting parts—see text

rod to ease inserting it into the thrust bearing. Pull the piston rod all the way up. Install parts above the spring upper retainer as follows:

    A. Large diameter washer (1)
    B. Seal (2)
    C. Thrust bearing (3)
    D. Small diameter washer (4)
    E. Self locking nut (5) (use a new nut only!)

    7. Torque the self locking nut to 52—58 ft lbs except on 733i; on the 733i, the torque is 57–63 ft lbs.

Shock Absorbers

TESTING

The basic test for shock absorber performance is the vehicle's behavior on the road. Shock absorbers have the job of eliminating spring bounce shortly after the car hits a bump. If the car tends to lose control over washboard surfaces or if there is any sign of fluid leakage, shock absorber work is required.

If you're uncertain about shock performance, you can jounce test the car. To do this, rest your weight on the front bumper or hood and release it repeatedly, in sympathy with the natural rythm of the springs until the car is bouncing up and down as fast as you can make it. Then release it, and carefully observe its behavior. The car should move upward, and then return to its normal riding height and virtually stop. Several bounces after release indicates worn shock absorbers.

REMOVAL AND INSTALLATION

With the MacPherson strut type front suspension used on BMWs, the shock absorber is an integral part of the strut. Since the strut and associated parts are a very expensive as-

sembly, the shock absorbers in front are rebuilt. This is an extremely difficult job requiring a good deal of specialized mechanical skill and a number of special tools. The work is best left up to a qualified repair shop, but you can reduce the cost by removing the strut and, if you're equipped, removing the spring from it, and taking the strut to the shop to be rebuilt.

Control Arm (Wishbone)
REMOVAL AND INSTALLATION
1600, 2002

    1. Raise the vehicle and support safely. Remove the wheel.
    2. Disconnect the trailing link at the lower arm.
    3. Disconnect the lower arm from the front axle beam and push off at the trailing link.
    4. Remove the cotter pin and castle nut. Press off the track rod at the track rod arm with a special tool such as BMW 00-7-500 or equivalent.
    5. Remove the lockwire and nuts. Remove the track rod arm with the lower arm.
    6. Remove the cotter pin and nut. Press off the track rod arm from the guide joint with a special tool such as BMW 00-7-500 or equivalent.
    7. Installation is the reverse of removal. Note the following points:

    A. Use a new self-locking nut where the trailing link connects to the wishbone, and torque to 51–65 ft lbs. Also, make sure the convex faces of both washers face the wishbone.
    B. Use a new self-locking nut where the wishbone attaches to the front axle

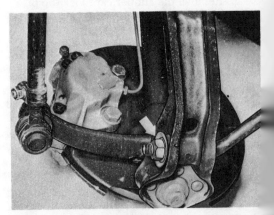

Make sure the convex faces of both washers face the wishbone—1600, 2002

Proper installation of wishbone to front axle carrier with spacer ring (1) facing carrier—1600, 2002

beam. Also make sure the spacer is on the axle beam side and that you install washers on either side of the wishbone.

C. Torque the track rod to track arm castellated nut to 25–29 ft lbs.

D. Torque the nuts attaching the track rod arm and wishbone to the bottom of the strut to 18–24 ft lbs. Replace the lockwire.

E. Torque the castellated nut attaching the track rod arm to the wishbone to 43–50 ft lbs.

F. Check the guide joint end play and if it exceeds .094 in., replace the guide joint.

2800, 3.0

1. Raise the vehicle and support safely. Remove the wheel.

2. Remove the lock wire and disconnect the track rod arm from the strut assembly.

3. Press the guide joint out of the track rod arm with an extractor.

4. Disconnect the lower arm from the axle carrier.

5. Disconnect the trailing link from the lower arm.

6. Installation is the reverse of removal. Note the following points:

A. Torque bolts fastening track rod arm to the strut to 33–44 ft lbs. Use new lockwire.

B. When attaching the wishbone to the front axle carrier, tighten it snugly, complete assembly of the front suspension, and then lower the vehicle and allow it to sit at its normal ride height. Torque the stop nut to 60–66 ft lbs.

C. Make sure, when reattaching the trailing link to the wishbone that the convex faces of the washers are outward. Check the play of the guide joint and replace it if the play is greater than .0945 in.

D. Some wishbones and some track rods have metal stops cast integrally into the structure. A wishbone with a stop may be used in conjunction with a track rod arm without a stop, but if the track rod arm has a stop, the wishbone must also have a stop. Torque the nut attaching the trailing link to the wishbone to 52–66 ft lbs.

Control Arm

REMOVAL AND INSTALLATION

320i

1. Disconnect the stabilizer bar at the control arm.

2. Disconnect the control arm at the front axle support.

3. Remove the cotter pin and castle nut.

4. Press the control arm off the steering knuckle with special tool BMW 31-1-100 or equivalent.

5. Installation is the reverse of removal. Note the following points:

A. When attaching the stabilizer bar to the control arm, use new self locking nuts and torque to 50–65 ft lbs.

B. When installing the control arm to the axle support, insert the bolt back-to-front, install a new self locking nut, and torque to 58–65 ft lbs.

C. When installing the guide joint stud, coat it with a 50–50 solution of lacquer and torque to 44–50 ft lbs. Also, replace the seal on the joint if necessary. Check the axial play of the joint—it should be no more than .055 in. Also, there should be resistance in turning the joint stud, or replacement is required.

528i, 530i, 630CSi, 633CSi

1. Raise the vehicle and support safely. Remove the wheel.

2. Disconnect the stabilizer at the control arm.

3. Remove the tension strut nut on the control arm.

4. Disconnect the control arm at the front axle support and remove it from the tension strut.

5. Remove the lock wire, remove the bolts and take the control arm off the spring strut.

6. Remove the cotter pin and nut.

7. Using special tool BMW 007-500 or equivalent, pull the guide joint from the tie rod arm.

8. Installation is the reverse of removal. Note the following points:

A. Replace all self locking nuts. Where tension strut connects to the control arm, install the washers with the convex side toward the rubber bushing.

B. Replace the lockwire where the control arm attaches to the strut.

C. If axial play in the control arm guide joint exceeds .094 in., replace the joint.

D. Torque the control arm to the front axle carrier with the vehicle sitting on its wheels and normally loaded.

E. Torque figures are:
Stabilizer at control arm—16–17 ft lb
Control arm at front axle carrier—58–65 ft lb
Control arm at bottom of strut—32.5–43 ft lb
Control arm to stub axle—16–17 ft lb.

733i

1. Raise the vehicle and support safely. Remove the wheel.

2. Disconnect the vibration strut from the control arm.

3. Disconnect the control arm from the axle carrier.

4. Disconnect the tie rod arm from the shock absorber.

5. Remove the cotter pin and castle nut. Press off the control arm with special tool BMW 31-1-110 or equivalent.

6. Installation is the reverse of removal. Keep the following points in mind:

A. Replace all self locking nuts.

B. Tie-rod-to-strut bolts and the female threads in the bottom of the strut must be perfectly clean. A locking compound such as Loctite® 270 must be used.

C. Make sure you install a control arm marked "L" or "R" for the proper side of the car.

D. Check the axial play of the ball joint. It must not exceed .055 in. Also, there must be friction when turning the stud, or the unit is worn and must be replaced.

E. Applicable torque figures are: vibration strut to control arm—18–20 ft lb control arm to axle carrier—59–66 ft lb. Final torquing of the control arm-to-axle-carrier bolts must be done with the car resting on the wheels and normally loaded.

Guide Joint (Ball Joint)
REMOVAL AND INSTALLATION

NOTE: *These joints are replaceable only on the 1600 and 2002 Series. On other models, the entire control arm must be replaced if the joint is defective.*

Drilling out guide joint attaching rivets—1600, 2002

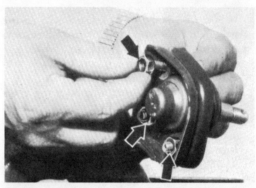

Attaching guide joint to wishbone with nuts and bolts

1600, 2002, Series

1. Remove the lower wishbone from the car as outlined under "Lower Wishbone Removal and Installation".

2. Clamp the wishbone in a vise.

3. Drill out the rivets which retain the guide joint to the wishbone.

4. Install a new guide joint using M8x20 hex bolts and M8 hex nuts. Use Loctite® on the threads.

5. Install the lower wishbone as outlined under "Lower Wishbone Removal and Installation".

Front End Alignment
CASTER AND CAMBER

Caster and camber are not adjustable, except for replacement of bent or worn parts.

TOE-IN-ADJUSTMENT

Toe-in is adjusted by changing the length of the tie rod and tie rod end assembly. When adjusting the tie rod ends, adjust each by equal amounts (in the opposite direction) to increase or decrease the toe-in measurement.

Wheel Alignment

Year	Model	Caster (deg)	Front Suspension		Steering Axis Inclination (deg)	Rear Suspension	
			Camber (deg)	Toe-In (in.)		Camber (deg)	Toe-In (in.)
1970–76	1600, 2002	4P	$\frac{1}{2}$P	.07	$8\frac{1}{2}$P	2N	.06
1977–79	320i	$8\frac{1}{3}$P	0	.07	$10\frac{1}{2}$P	2N	.04
1977–79	530i	$7\frac{2}{3}$P	$\frac{1}{2}$P	.07	$8P\frac{1}{2}$	2N	.04
1978–79	733i	9P	0	.03	$11\frac{1}{2}$P	$1\frac{1}{2}$N	.08
1973–76	2800, 3.0	$9\frac{2}{3}$P	$\frac{1}{2}$P	.07	$8P\frac{1}{2}$	2N	.04

N Negative
P Positive

REAR SUSPENSION

BMW rear suspension incorporates semi trailing arms pivoting on maintenance-free rubber bushings. Springs are coil type, and the spring strut incorporates the double acting shock absorber on later models. Some models include a rear stabilizer bar. All are fully independent for maximum ride comfort and control.

Springs

REMOVAL AND INSTALLATION

All Models Except 2002, 1600

1. On the 733i, remove the rear seat and backrest.
2. Raise the car and support the body. Then, *support the lower control arm securely*.
3. Then, remove the nut and pull out the

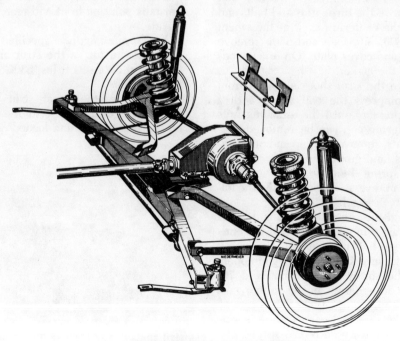

Rear suspension system—2002

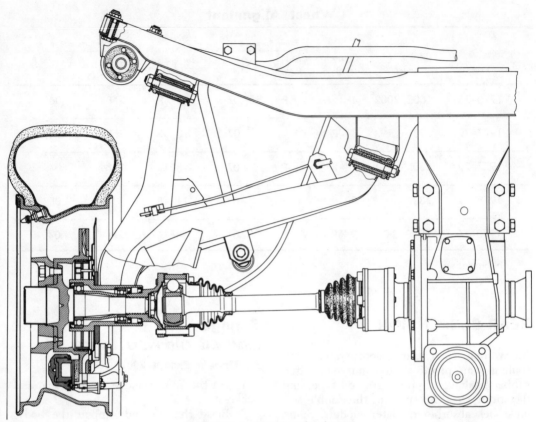

600 series rear suspension layout

bolt which attaches the spring strut at the control arm.

4. On the 733i, remove the hatrack and covers. Remove the three nuts and bolts and disconnect the centering shell at the wheel well. On 2800, 3.0, 528i and 530i, remove the damper and cover plate. On other models, remove the gasket.

5. Remove the strut/shock absorber from the car. Compress the coil string with a spring compressor, until the attaching nuts for the centering cup can be removed. Remove the nuts, remove the cup and other retaining parts, and gradually release the tension on the spring. Remove the spring.

6. Install in reverse order, bearing the following points in mind:

A. Wind the centering shell and lower spring retainer in such a way that the ends of the spring butt up against their stops.

B. Make sure knurled bolts go in openings of the spring liner on 600 and 700 Series, or in openings in the rubber boot on top of the spring on 500 Series cars.

C. Make sure that color coding, spring length, and the gauge of the spring wire are the same on both sides.

D. On the 2800, 3.0 and 530i, put spacers over the knurled bolts and make sure the damper ring is installed with the rubber tabs pointing front and rear, not side-to-side.

E. Torque figures specified for the nut(s) at the top of the strut are: 320i—7–9 ft lbs; 530i—21 ft lbs; 630CSi, 633CSi 18–22 ft lbs.

F. Torque the lower strut mounting bolt (at the control arm) with the car sitting on the rear wheels and loaded normally.

Install spacers and position the damper ring (3) with the tabs front and rear—2800, 3.0, 530i

2002, 1600

CAUTION: *Make sure that the car is firmly supported with jackstands.*

1. Remove the shock absorber as outlined under "Shock Absorber Removal and Installation". Make sure that the trailing arm is *securely* supported with a jack.

2. Remove the rear wheel and tire assembly.

Disconnecting and hanging up the output shaft—1600, 2002

3. On 2002 series models, disconnect the stabilizer bar from its mount on the trailing arm.

4. Disconnect the output shaft at the half-shaft flange and tie the output shaft up to an underbody component so that it does not hang down.

5. Safety wire or chain the bottom coil of the spring to an underbody component to protect yourself from injury should the spring slip off its lower mount during removal.

6. Slowly lower the jack supporting the trailing arm and carefully release the spring.

Locating recess in lower damping ring into projection on lower mounting plate

7. Inspect the condition of the rubber damping rings. Replace them if they are damaged or dry-rotted. Make suer that the lower ring's locating recess fits into the projection on the lower mounting plate. If the spring is broken, it is recommended that both springs be removed and replaced with new ones of the same wire diameter, free length, and color coding (spring rate).

8. Reverse the above procedure to install, taking care to rotate the coil spring so that the spring ends locate on the stop (projection) of the upper and lower damping rings.

Shock Absorbers
TESTING

The basic test for shock absorber performance is the vehicle's behavior on the road. Shock absorbers have the job of eliminating spring bounce shortly after the car hits a bump. If the car tends to lose control over washboard surfaces or if there is any sign of fluid leakage, shock absorber work is required.

If you're uncertain about shock performance, you can jounce test the car. To do this, rest your weight on the rear bumper or hood and release it repeatedly, in sympathy with the natural rhythm of the springs until the car is bouncing up and down as fast as you can make it. Then release it, carefully observe its behavior. The car should move upward, and then return to its normal riding height and virtually stop. Several bounces after release indicates worn shock absorbers.

REMOVAL AND INSTALLATION
All Models Except 2002, 1600

1. Remove the 2800 and 3.0, remove the sleeve which surrounds the shock absorber and the auxiliary spring as well as: the rubber washer; large metal washer; spacer tube; and the fastening plate.

3. On the other models (except 2002, 1600) remove the support disc, auxiliary spring (which fits around the shock absorber piston rod), and the outer tube. Remove both upper and lower liners, and inspect them, replacing if necessary.

4. Install in reverse order. In case you are replacing a shock absorber which has failed prematurely (especially due to leakage), it may be possible to avoid the cost of replacing the unit located on the opposite side. BMW dealers and some other shots are equipped

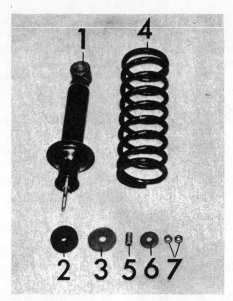

1. Shock absorber
2. Rubber washer
3. Large metal washer
4. Spring
5. Spacer tube
6. Fastening plate
7. Mounting nuts

Identification of shock absorber mounting parts for the 2800 and 3.0

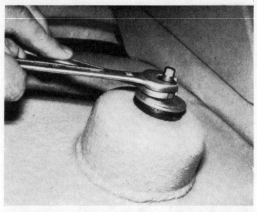

Disconnecting upper shock absorber mount —1600, 2002

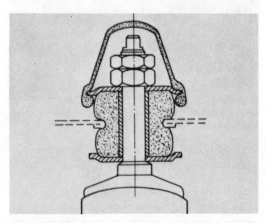

Cross section of shock absorber upper mount—2002

with a machine designed for testing the shocks. You might be able to remove both shocks and have the performance of a new shock compared with that of the apparently effective old shock. If machine testing proves the performance of a new shock and slightly used shock to be sufficiently similar, re-use is possible. However, it is dangerous to risk replacing only one rear shock without machine testing!

2002, 1600

CAUTION: *Make sure that the car is firmly supported with jackstands before climbing under it. Never rely on the car jack alone.*

1. Place blocks in front of the front wheels. Jack up the rear of the car and place jackstands beneath the reinforced box-member area adjacent to the rear jacking points.

2. Support the trailing arm with a jack. The shock absorber is used to limit the downward travel of the suspension. If the trailing arm is not supported, the output shafts may swivel downward beyond their design limit when the shock absorber lower mount is released, possibly damaging the output shaft joints.

3. Open the trunk and remove the protec-

tive cap covering the shock absorber upper mount. Disconnect the shock absorber upper mount from the body.

4. Disconnect the shock absorber from its lower mount at the brake backing plate. Fully compress the shock absorber and remove it from the vehicle.

5. Inspect the condition of the bushing at the upper mount. Replace it if it is damaged or dry-rotted, by pressing it out of the body cavity. When replacing the mount, insert the small end facing down and replace the spacing sleeve. If the damping action of the shock absorber is insufficient, replace both rear shock absorbers as a matched pair.

6. Reverse the above procedure to install.

Rear Suspension Alignment

The rear suspension of the BMW is not adjustable. However, the rear wheel alignment can be checked using the figures in the

Wheel Alignment Specifications Chart to check for bent components. The trailing arm, if, suspected of causing improper rear wheel alignment, can be checked with a special jig. If bent but not cracked or dented, it may be possible to straighten it with special equipment.

STEERING

Steering Wheel

REMOVAL AND INSTALLATION

1. Turn the wheel to exactly the straight ahead position for reinstallation at the same angle.

2. Remove the steering wheel pad.

3. Remove the retaining nut and remove the wheel.

4. Install in reverse order, torquing the wheel attaching nut precisely. On the 1600 and 2002 Series, torque the 12 mm nut to 40 ft lbs, the 14 mm nut to 61 ft lbs. On the 2800, 3.0 Series, and 733i, torque to 63–70 ft lbs; on all other models, torque to 62–69 ft lbs.

Turn Signal Switch

REMOVAL AND INSTALLATION

1600, 2002

1. Remove the steering wheel. Unscrew and remove the padded trim surrounding the column.

2. Unscrew the choke knob, and the retaining nut behind it. Unscrew the mounting screws and remove the steering column lower surround.

3. Mark the position of the turn signal switch; then, remove the attaching screws and remove the switch.

4. In installation, note that the switch is mounted via slots and, before tightening the mounting screws, slide switch back and forth until the gap between the cancelling cam and the actuating dog on the switch is .0118 in.

5. Connect wiring to the switch as follows:
Gray—P
Green/Yellow—54
Blue/Black—R
Blue/Red—L
Brown/Black—H
Gray/Green—PR
Gray/Black—Pl

2800, 3.0

1. Put the steering wheel in the straight ahead position. Remove the lower steering column housing and the lower center instrument panel trim on the left side.

2. Remove the steering wheel.

3. Remove the attaching screws and remove the turn signal switch.

4. Extract the cable harness from the retaining clips. Pull out the control lever light, detach the plug, and separate the cable connector.

5. Pull off the black multiple connector and the gray/blue cable.

6. Install in reverse order with the switch in the center position, the actuating peg pointing toward the center of the cancelling cam, and the clearance between the cancelling cam and switch cam follower ("A") at .012 in. The switch is slotted at the mounting points to allow for this adjustment before the mounting screws receive final tightening.

1600, 2002 turn signal switch (right side of the steering column). Dimension "A" is the gap between the canceling cam and the actuating dog (see text)

"A" represents the gap between the cancelling cam and the switch cam follower. The mounting screws are arrowed

320i

1. Turn the steering wheel to the straight ahead position. Remove the steering wheel and the lower steering column cover.

2. Disconnect the (−) cable from the battery. Disconnect the direction signal switch multiple connector from under the dash by squeezing in the locks on either side and pulling it off.

3. Remove the cable straps from the column.

4. Loosen the mounting screws and remove the switch and harness.

5. Install in reverse order, noting the following points:

A. Make sure to mount the ground wire.

B. Make sure the switch is in the middle position and that the follower faces the center of the cancelling cam on the steering column shaft. Then, before finally tightening the switch mounting screws, adjust the switch on slotted mounting holes so the gap between the cam and follower is .118 in.

530i, 528i

1. Turn the steering wheel to the straight ahead position. Remove the steering wheel and the lower column cover.

2. Disconnect the battery (−) cable. Disconnect the parking light cable connector near the column.

3. Disconnect the supply plug at the center of the connector panel on the cowl. Then, loosen the clips from the harness going from the cowl up to the switch.

4. Loosen the mounting screws and remove the switch.

On the 500 series, disconnect the parking light connector near the column

Disconnect the main supply plug (arrowed)

5. Install in reverse order. Before final tightening of the switch mounting screws, slide the switch on its slots to adjust the gap between the cancelling cam and cam follower as follows:

A. Make sure the switch is in its middle position and that it points to the middle of the cancelling cam.

B. Adjust the gap to .012 in.

630CSi, 633CSi

1. Follow the procedure above exactly; when adjusting the gap between the cancelling cam and the switch follower, use the dimension .118 in.

733i

1. Remove the steering wheel and disconnect the battery ground cable.

2. Remove the trim from below the steering column. Remove the mounting screws and detach the switch from the switch plate.

3. Loosen the straps holding the switch cable to the steering column. Pull the center plug out of the panel on the cowl and remove the switch.

4. Install in reverse order.

Ignition Switch

REMOVAL AND INSTALLATION

All Models

1. Disconnect negative battery terminal.

2. Remove lower steering column casing.

3. On models 2800 and 3.0, remove lower center left instrument panel trim.

4. Unscrew set screw and remove switch.

5. Disconnect central fuse/relay plate plug.

6. Installation is the reverse of removal.

NOTE: *Turn ignition key all the way back*

On the 2800 and 3.0, also remove screws numbered 2, 3, and 4 to remove the lower center, left section of the instrument panel

On the 2800 and 3.0, remove the screw shown (1) to remove the lower, center left section of the instrument panel housing

and set the switch at the "O" position before installing. Marks on the switch must be opposite each other.

Tie Rod Ends

REMOVAL AND INSTALLATION

All Models

1. Remove the cotter pin and then the castellated nut which retains the outer tie rod to the spindle lever.

2. Using a ball joint puller, press the outer end of the rod from the lever.

3. If it is necessary to replace the inner tie rod end repeat the procedure where the rod is linked to the center tie rod.

Disconnecting outer tie-rod from spindle lever

4. Loosen the mounting bolt(s) retaining the end or ends to the tie rod, and then unscrew the end(s) from the rod.

5. Reverse the removal procedure to install. Have the toe in set on an alignment machine.

6. Use the following torques:

A. On four cylinder models, torque the clamp bolts to 8.7 ft lbs. On six cylinder models, torque them to 9–11 ft lbs.

B. Torque the castellated nuts fastening the tie rod to the steering knuckle or center tie rod to:

1600, 2002—18 ft lbs.
320i—25–29 ft lbs.
2800, 3.0—26–29 ft lbs.
528i, 530i—26–29 ft lbs.
630CSi, 633CSi—33–40 ft lbs.
733i—26–30 ft lbs.

9

Brakes

BRAKE SYSTEM

Rear Drum Brake/Handbrake Adjustment

1600, 2002, 320i

Common adjustment of these two items is recommended at every major service (8,000 miles until 1974, 12,500 miles thereafter). In addition, if the handbrake can be pulled up more than four notches on 1970–74 cars, or five notches on later model years, adjutment should be performed.

1. Support the rear of the car securely on axle stands. Release the handbrake fully.

2. The brake adjusting bolt is located at the rear of the backing plate, right behind the drive axle. It is turned counterclockwise on the left side and clockwise on the right side to tighten. Spin the wheel and gradually tighten up on the adjustment until the wheel just stops and cannot be readily turned. Then, loosen exactly ⅛th turn—*just* to the point where there is no drag felt. Repeat on the other side.

3. Pull the handbrake lever up five notches (1975 and later vehicles) or four notches (earlier vehicles). Measure the distance between the middle of the handbrake lever and the driveshaft tunnel. It should be 4.3–4.7 in.; otherwise, reset the handbrake

Location of brake adjusting bolt. A special tool is shown here, but a socket wrench with extension could also be used

Adjusting the handbrake at the adjusting nuts

Brake System Troubleshooting

The Problem	Is Caused By	What to Do
The brake pedal goes to the floor	• Leak somewhere in the system • Brakes out of adjustment	• Check/correct fluid level; have system checked • Check automatic brake adjusters
Spongy brake pedal	• Air in brake system • Brake fluid contaminated	• Have brake system bled • Have system drained, refilled and bled
The brake pedal is hard	• Improperly adjusted brakes • Worn pads or linings • Kinked brake lines • Defective power brake booster • Low engine vacuum (power brakes)	• Have brakes adjusted • Check lining/pad wear • Have defective brake line replaced • Have booster checked • Check engine vacuum (see Section 6, Engine)
The brake pedal "fades" under pressure (repeated hard stops will cause brake fade; brakes will return to normal when they cool down)	• Air in system • Incorrect brake fluid • Leaking master cylinder or wheel cylinders • Leaking hoses/lines	• Have brakes bled • Check fluid • Check master cylinder and wheel cylinders for leaks • Check lines for leaks
The car pulls to one side or brakes grab	• Incorrect tire pressure • Contaminated brake linings or pads • Worn brake linings • Loose or misaligned calipers • Defective proportioning valve • Front end out of alignment	• Check/correct tire pressure • Check linings for grease; if greasy, replace • Have linings replaced • Check caliper mountings • Have proportioning valve checked • Have wheel alignment checked
Brakes chatter or shudder	• Worn linings • Drums out-of-round • Wobbly rotor • Heat checked drums	• Check lining thickness • Have drums and linings ground • Have rotor checked for excessive wobble • Check drums for heat checking; if necessary, replace drums
Brakes produce noise (squealing, scraping, clicking)	• Worn linings • Loose calipers • Caliper anti-rattle springs missing • Scored or glazed drums or rotors	• Check pad and lining wear • Check caliper mountings • Check calipers for missing parts • Check for glazing (light glazing can be removed with sandpaper)

Brake System Troubleshooting (cont.)

The Problem	Is Caused By	What to Do
Brakes drag (will not release)	• Incorrect brake adjustment • Parking brake stuck or adjusted too tight • Caliper pistons seized • Defective metering valve or master cylinder • Broken brake return springs	• Have brakes checked • Check cable where it enters the brake backing plate. In winter, water frequently freezes here • Have calipers checked • Have system checked • Check brake return springs, replace if necessary
Brake system warning light stays lit	• One part of dual circuit inoperative, defective warning light switch, differential pressure valve not centered	• Have brake system checked

into another notch until the dimension is correct.

4. Then, pull up the rubber boot, loosen the locknut on one side and tighten the adjusting nut until the wheel on that side is locked. Repeat for the other side. Tighten both locknuts.

5. Check to make sure the adjustment is correct by checking that the wheels are released completely when the brake is released and that both wheels are slowed at the same point as the lever is raised. Repeat the adjustments if necessary.

Hydraulic System

MASTER CYLINDER

Removal and Installation

1600, 2002, 528i, 530i, 630CSi, 633CSi, 2800, 3.0

1. Remove the air cleaner if necessary.

2. Drain and disconnect the brake fluid reservoir from the master cylinder. The brake fluid reservoir will be mounted in one of two ways: (1) assembled directly on top of the master cylinder; it is removed by tilting the reservoir to one side and lifting it off of the master cylinder, or (2) the reservoir is mounted in the engine compartment where it is attached to the inner fender sheet metal by means of attaching bolts; carefully disconnect hoses leading to the master cylinder and allow the reservoir to drain.

1. O-ring   2. Pushrod

Removing master cylinder from vacuum unit —2002

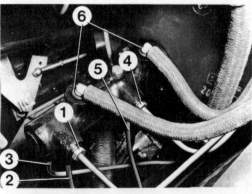

1. Right brake line—front
2. Left brake line—front
3. Brake line to rear wheel brakes
4. Right brake line—front (2nd circuit)
5. Left brake line—front (2nd circuit)

Removing the 600 series master cylinder

CAUTION: *Exercise extreme care in handling brake fluid near painted surface of vehicle as fluid will destroy the paint finish if allowed to come into contact with it.*

3. Disconnect all brake lines from the master cylinder.

4. Remove the master cylinder to power booster attaching nuts, and remove the master cylinder.

NOTE: *Observe the correct seating of the master cylinder-to-power booster seals (1).*

5. Bench-bleed the master cylinder.

NOTE: *Check for proper seating of master cylinder to power booster O-ring. Check clearance between the master cylinder piston and push rod with plastic gauge, and, if necessary, adjust to 0.002 inch by placing shims behind the head of the push rod.*

6. Position master cylinder onto studs protruding from the power booster; install and tighten the attaching nuts.

7. Connect all brake lines.

8. Install the brake fluid reservoir and fill with brake fluid.

NOTE: *An alternate method to bench bleeding the master cylinder is to bleed the master cylinder in the vehicle by opening (only slightly) the brake line fitting at the master cylinder, and allowing the fluid to flow from the master cylinder into a container. However, this method should be considered as an ALTERNATE METHOD ONLY as it is more difficult to control the fluid leaving the master cylinder during bleeding, thereby increasing the chance of accidentally splashing brake fluid onto the painted surface of the vehicle.*

5. Bleed the brake system.

320i

1. Remove the fuel mixture control unit.

2. Disconnect the hose at the clutch connection.

3. Drain and disconnect the brake fluid reservoir.

4. Disconnect the brake lines from the master cylinder.

5. Working from the underside of the left-side inner fender panel (wheel opening area) remove the two master cylinder support bracket attaching nuts.

6. Remove the master cylinder to power booster attaching nuts, and remove the master cylinder.

7. Install in the reverse order of removal.

NOTE: *Bench bleed the master cylinder prior to installation. Refer to the aforementioned note concerning an ALTERNATE bleeding procedure.*

8. Bleed the brake system.

733i

1. Drain and disconnect the fluid reservoir.

2. Disconnect the brake lines at the master cylinder.

3. Remove the master cylinder to hydraulic booster attaching bolts, and remove the master cylinder.

4. Install in the reverse order of removal.

NOTE: *Bench bleed the master cylinder prior to installation. Refer to the aforementioned note concerning an ALTERNATE bleeding procedure.*

OVERHAUL

1600, 2002

1. Remove the master cylinder as outlined under "Tandem Master Cylinder Removal and Installation".

2. Press in lightly on piston (1) and remove stop screw (2).

3. Remove the circlip (3) and withdraw the piston (1) from its bore. Then, pull off the stop washer (4), secondary sleeve (5), spacer ring (6), secondary sleeve (7), and stop washer (8).

4. Unscrew the retaining screw (9), and pull off the spring cap (10), spring (11), spring cap (12), pressure cup (13), and O-ring (14). Remove and discard the primary sleeve (8).

5. Using low pressure compressed air, push out the piston (15). Then, pull off the spring (16), spring cap (17), pressure-cap (18), primary sleeve (19), and the O-ring (20). Lift out the secondary sleeve (21), and primary sleeve (22).

6. Clean all parts in methylated alcohol or clean brake fluid. Check the cylinder bore for

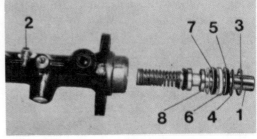

Removing master cylinder components—1600, 2002: piston (1), stop screw (2), circlip (3), stop washer (4), secondary sleeve (5), spacer ring (6), secondary sleeve (7), and stop washer (8)

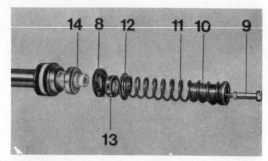

Disassembling master cylinder components: primary sleeve (8), retaining screw (9), spring cap (10), spring (11), spring cap (12), pressure cap (13), and O-ring (14)

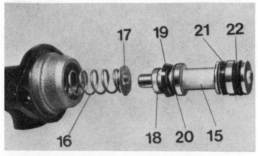

Removing master cylinder components: piston (15), spring (16), spring cap (17), pressure cap (18), primary sleeve (19), O-ring (20), secondary sleeve (21), primary sleeve (22)

Proper assembly sequence for sleeves 5 and 7

surface defects. Replace any cylinder in questionable condition. Prior to assembly, thinly coat all parts with clean brake fluid.

7. Reverse the above procedure to assemble. Clamp the master cylinder vertically in a vise to prevent the pressure cap from slipping off during assembly. When assembling sleeves 5 and 7, make sure that they point in one direction. Coat the space between the secondary sleeve and spacer ring with silicone grease. Also, coat the piston shank with silicone grease. When installing the piston shanks in the bore, take care not to

damage the rubber sleeves. Finally, push the piston assemblies into the bore, place a new copper washer under the stop screw, then screw in the stop screw, completing the assembly.

2800, 3.0

1. Apply slight pressure to the piston. Remove the stop screw.

2. Remove the circlip, and then extract the piston.

3. Pull off the stop washer, secondary sleeve, intermediate ring, second secondary sleeve, and stop washer.

4. Remove the screw from the end of the spring cap, and then remove the spring cap, spring, spring cup, pressure plate, and spacer.

5. Build up air pressure carefully until the piston comes out of the bore.

6. Pull off the spring, spring cup, pressure plate, primary sleeve, and spacer.

7. Clean all parts in alcohol. Inspect the master cylinder bore for scratches or pits and replace if necessary.

8. Clamp the master cylinder vertically into a vise to prevent the pressure plate from slipping during reassembly. Apply silicone grease to the new components, and to the piston rod.

9. Assemble in reverse order, noting the following points:

A. A special tapered sleeve (such as BMW 6063) is available for installation of the piston back into the bore without damaging seals. Use some sort of sleeve or at least exercise extreme caution in reinstalling the piston so that seal lips do not fold back double.

B. Use a new copper gasket under the stop screw.

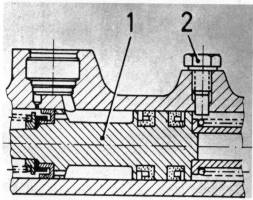

Note the positions of the piston (1) and the stop screw (2)—2800, 3.0

C. Note that the piston must be inserted far enough into the bore to fully pass the stop screw before the screw in inserted.

The 320i master cylinder

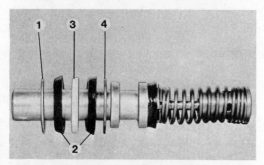

Disassembly of 320i master cylinder

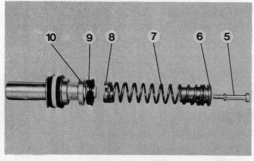

Further disassembly of the 320i master cylinder

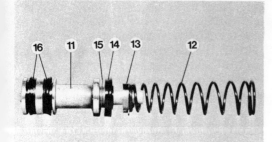

Disassembly of master cylinder intermediate piston—320i

320i

1. Push the piston (1) into the bore slightly and then remove the stop screw (2).

2. Remove the circlip (3) and pull out the piston.

3. Remove the bearing ring (1), secondary cups (2), intermediate ring (3) and the second bearing ring (4).

4. Loosen the connecting bolt (5), and pull off the spring retainer (6), spring (7), support ring (8), primary cup (9), and filler disc (10).

5. Then, remove the intermediate piston (11) by knocking the housing lightly against a block of wood. Pull off the spring (12), support ring (13), primary cup (14), the filler disc (15). Remove the separating cups (16).

6. Clean all parts in alcohol. Inspect the master cylinder bore and replace the unit if it is scored or pitted.

7. Reassemble in reverse order noting the following:

A. Apply a very light coating of silicone lubricant or cylinder paste to new parts.

B. The separating cups are marked with a ring of paint. Install them so their lips are opposite each other.

C. Make sure both support rings (13) and (8) are positioned properly on the primary cups.

D. When assembling parts to the primary piston (the piston with the rod which protrudes from the master cylinder after assembly), note the following sequence of installation: bearing ring (1); secondary cups (2) (both pointing in the same direction); intermediate ring (3); and bearing ring (4). Coat the space between the secondary cups and intermediate ring with silicone grease.

E. When inserting pistons into the bore, use a tapered special tool such as

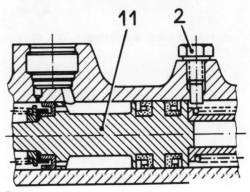

Cross section of master cylinder on 320i showing the intermediate piston and stop screw

BMW 343000, or be very careful to ensure that seal lips do not fold over.

F. Coat the primary piston skirt with silicone grease. Put light pressure on the piston and then install the stop screw with a new copper seal. Make sure the intermediate piston (11) is beyond the stop screw (2).

528i, 530i, 630CSi, 633CSi, 733i

1. Push the piston (1) inward using light pressure, and then remove the stop screw (7). Then remove the circlip (2) and pull out the piston. Remove the stop washer (3), secondary cup (5), intermediate ring (4) and bearing ring (6).

2. Loosen the connecting screw (9), and pull off the spring washer (10), spring (11), support (12), primary cup (8), and filler disc (13).

3. Remove the intermediate piston by knocking the housing against a wooden block lightly. Then, remove the spring (15), support (16), primary cup (17), and filler disc (18) and separating cups (19).

4. Clean all parts in alcohol and inspect the bore of the master cylinder carefully for scoring or pitting. Replace if damaged.

5. To reassemble, first mount the cylinder in a vise with the bore facing downward at an angle, to prevent the support ring from slipping during assembly. If possible, use a ta-

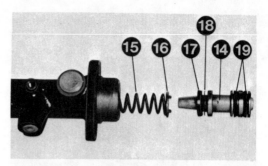

Disassembly of the intermediate piston and associated parts—500, 600, and 700 series master cylinders

pered sleeve such as BMW part No. 34 3 000 to install the pistons. Otherwise, take care to ensure the seal lips do not double over during installation. Coat all parts with ATE Brake Cylinder paste or a similar silicone lubricant designed for this purpose. Also, keep the following points in mind:

A. The separating cups are marked with a colored ring and must be installed with their lips opposite each other.

B. Make sure both primary cup supports (12 and 16) are located in the primary cups correctly.

C. Install both secondary cups in the same direction. Coat the space between the secondary cups and intermediate ring with silicone lubricant.

D. When installing the piston, apply silicone lubricant to the piston rod and apply light pressure to the rod of the primary piston to push the intermediate piston past the location of the stop screw. Then, install the stop screw with a new copper washer.

Brake Pressure Control Regulator

REMOVAL AND INSTALLATION

320i

1. Syphon brake fluid out of the reservoir. If the fluid is to be reused, make sure the hose and container are clean and have not been used to contain other fluids.

2. Disconnect the four union nuts and pull the lines off the regulator.

3. Remove the two mounting bolts from inside the wheel well.

4. When replacing the unit, make sure the unit is marked "25/8".

5. Install in reverse of the removal procedure, torquing hydraulic connections to 9–11 ft lbs. Bleed the system.

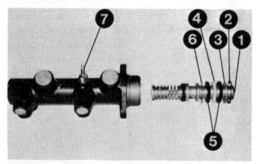

Disassembling the master cylinder—500, 600 and 700 series cars

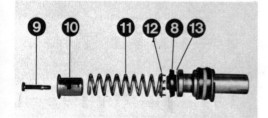

Further disassembly of 500, 600, and 700 series master cylinders

1. Front wheel brakes inlet
2. Front wheel brakes outlet
3. Rear wheel brakes inlet
4. Rear wheel brakes outlet

The 320i brake pressure regulator

2800, 3.0

1. Syphon brake fluid out of the reservoir. If the fluid is to be reused, make sure the hose and container are clean and have not been used to contain other fluids.

2. Unscrew the left/rear brake hose at the control arm and brake pressure regulator. Unscrew the brake lines at the pressure regulator limiter.

3. Remove the regulator mounting bolts at the underside of the body and remove the regulator.

4. Install in reverse order and bleed the system.

528i, 530i, 630CSi, 633CSi

1. Syphon brake fluid from the reservoir using a clean hose and container not used for other fluids.

2. The unit is located near the steering shaft coupling. Remove the two lines and remove the unit.

3. Install in reverse order and bleed the system. Torque connections to 10–11 ft lbs.

Bleeding

1600, 2002

Whenever a spongy brake pedal indicates that there is air in the system, or when any part of the hydraulic system has been removed for service, the system must be bled. In addition, if there are any fluid leaks, or if the level of fluid in the master cylinder reservoir is allowed to go below the minimum mark, air may enter the system, necessitating bleeding.

Be careful not to spill any brake fluid onto the discs, pads, drums or linings. If any brake fluid spills onto the paintwork, wipe it off immediately, as it will dissolve the finish. Always use brake fluid bearing the designation SAE 70R3 (SAE 1703), DOT 3 or DOT 4. Never reuse old brake fluid.

1. Fill the master cylinder reservoir to the maximum level with the proper brake fluid.

2. Remove all dirt and foreign material from around the 3 bleed screws on each front caliper and the one on each rear wheel cylinder. Remove the protective caps from the bleed screws.

3. The proper bleeding sequence always starts with the brake unit farthest from the master cylinder and always ends with the brake unit closest to the master cylinder. Therefore, the sequence for your car will be; right rear, left rear, right front and then left front. Start out by inserting a tight fitting plastic tube over the bleed nipple for the right rear wheel (located on the backing plate), and inserting the other end of the tube in a transparent container partially filled with clean brake fluid.

4. Have a friend apply pressure to the brake pedal. Open the bleeder screw while observing the bottle of brake fluid. If bubbles appear in the container, there is air in the system. When your friend has pushed the pedal to the floor, have him hold it there, and immediately close the bleeder screw before he releases the pedal. Otherwise, air or the brake fluid you just removed from the system, will be sucked back in. Repeat this procedure until no more bubbles appear in the jar. Periodically check the level of fluid in the reservoir to keep it at the maximum mark.

5. Repeat Step 4 for the left rear brake unit.

6. Jack up the front of the car and install jackstands beneath the reinforced box-member area adjacent to the front jacking points. Remove the front wheel and tire assemblies. Each front caliper must be bled in a specified sequence. Starting with the right front caliper, attach the tube and bottle containing clean brake fluid to bleed nipple "A" (see the illustration). Have your friend press down the pedal, and open the bleed screw. When the pedal hits the floor, close the bleed screw immediately. Once the brake fluid is free of bubbles, proceed to nipple "B", and finally nipple "C". It is imperative that this sequence (A, then B, then C) be used.

7. Recheck the level of fluid in the reser-

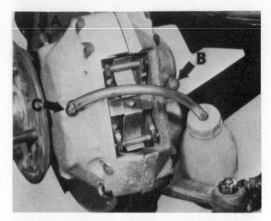

Bleeding sequence for front caliper—1600, 2002

voir. Repeat Step 6 for the left front caliper.

8. Install the front wheels, remove the jackstands, and lower the car. The system should now be free of air bubbles. Road test the car and check brake operation.

320i

Follow the procedure for the 1600 and 2002 models described above. However, note that the 320i has only one bleed point on each wheel cylinder and one on each caliper. The calipers may be bled without removing the wheels.

2800, 3.0, 528i, 530i, 630CSi, 633CSi

Follow the procedure for the 1600 and 2002 models described above. Note that these models have disc brakes at the rear. Bleed points for these calipers are at the top on the inside. When bleeding front calipers, follow the sequence (A,B,C) shown in the illustration.

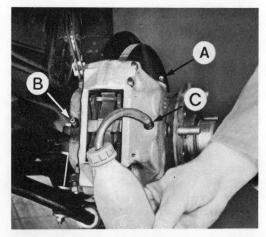

Bleeding sequence for the 500 and 600 series cars. Bleed A, then B. C is bleed port

Bleed the 733i brake calipers in the sequence shown (A, then B)

733i

Follow the procedure for the 1600 and 2002 models described above. Note that these models have disc brakes at the rear. Bleed points for these calipers are located at the top on the inside. When bleeding front calipers, follow the sequence (A,B) shown in the illustration.

Disc Brake Pads
INSPECTION

Measure the thickness of the entire pad assembly or the lining itself as specified below and replace a pad which is at or near the wear limit. In case local inspection law specifies more lining material as a minimum requirement, the local law should take precedence.

BMW standards are as follows:
1600, 2002—.275 in. (entire pad)
320i—.301 in. (entire pad)
2800, 3.0—.276 in. (entire pad)
528i, 530i—.275 in. (entire pad)
630CSi, 633CSi, 733i—.080 in. (liner only)

REMOVAL AND INSTALLATION
1600, 2002, 320i, 528i, 530i, 2800, 3.0

1. Support the front of the vehicle in a raised position.

2. Remove the front wheels.

3. Drive the support pins out of the calipers.

4. Remove the cross-springs (anti-rattle spreader springs). Note the correct position of the cross-spring prior to removal. Replace if necessary.

5. Attach a BMW special hook tool 34-1-010 or an equivalent pad removal tool to the brake pad, and pull the pad out and away from the caliper.

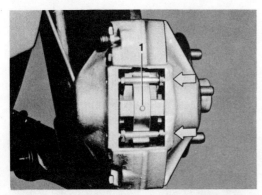

Driving the support pins out of the calipers

Remove the retaining pins (arrowed) and the cross spring (1)—600 and 700 series

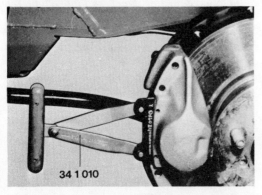

34 1 010

Removing the pads with BMW special tool

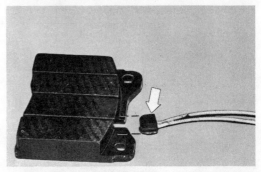

Installing a new pad wear indicator—600 and 700 series

6. Using a cylindrical brush, clean the pad guide surface of the caliper assembly.

7. Press the caliper piston into the caliper up to the stop with a BMW special tool 34-1-050 or an equivalent tool.

630i, 633i, and 733i

1. Support the front of the vehicle in a raised position.

2. Remove the front wheels.

3. Disconnect the electrical connector for the pad wear indicator, and pull the wires out of the clamp.

4. Drive the support pins out of the calipers.

5. Remove the cross-springs (anti-rattle spreader springs). Note the correct position of the cross-spring prior to removal. Replace if necessary.

6. Attach a BMW special hook tool 34-1-010 or an equivalent pad removal tool to the brake pad, and pull the pad out and away from the caliper.

7. Using a cylindrical brush, clean the pad guide surface of the caliper assembly.

8. Press the caliper piston into the caliper

up to the stop with a BMW special tool 34-1-050 or an equivalent tool.

9. Install in the reverse order of removal. NOTE: *When replacing the front brake pads, be sure to install a new wear indicator in the front left side of the right brake pad.*

Front Brake Caliper

REMOVAL AND INSTALLATION

All Models

1. Support the front of the vehicle in a raised position, and remove the front wheels.

2. Remove the brake pads.

3. Disconnect the brake lines at the caliper, and cap the lines to prevent brake fluid from escaping.

CAUTION: *If fluid appears to be contaminated, discolored, or otherwise unusual in appearance, viscosity, or smell, then allow the fluid to drain from the uncapped brake lines, and flush the system.*

4. Remove the caliper to steering knuckle attaching bolts, and remove the caliper.

5. Install in the reverse order of removal.

6. Torque the caliper to steering knuckle attaching bolts to 58–70 ft lbs.

OVERHAUL

2002Tii, 530i, 630i, 633i, 3.0S, and 3.0Si (Four Piston Caliper)

1. Remove the protective-dust-boot snap ring, and remove the dust boot.

2. Using a BMW special tool 34-1-050 or an equivalent piston pressing device, press one piston into the caliper cylinder to the fully retracted position, and lock into place.

3. Insert a piece of hardwood, plastic, or any material of similar consistency, approximately 0.31 inch thick, between the secured piston and the opposing piston.

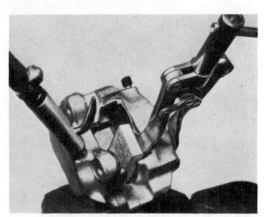

Removing pistons from their bores using compressed air and a wooden block

4. Apply compressed air through the threaded brake line port and into the circuit which controls the locked piston, thereby forcing the opposed piston out of the cylinder.

5. Remove the piston pressing tool, and plug the open cylinder bore with an Ate sealing plate and clamp or any similar sealing device.

6. Insert the protective block of wood between the remaining piston and the caliper housing, and, again, apply compressed air through the threaded brake line port and into the circuit which controls the remaining piston, thereby forcing the piston out of the cylinder.

CAUTION: *Apply compressed air through the circuit which corresponds with the piston to be removed. DO NOT apply compressed air to the other circuit unless the corresponding pistons are protected with the piece of wood previously mentioned.*

7. Repeat steps 2 through 6 for the remaining pistons.

8. Carefully remove the piston O-ring.

9. Examine the pistons and cylinder bores for a scoring or binding condition. Replace if necessary.

NOTE: *The manufacturer specifically advises against machining either the piston or the cylinder bore. The recommended extent of overhaul should include only the examination of parts and/or the replacement of the dust boot and piston O-ring.*

The caliper halves should not be separated. An exception to this would be a problem involving a piston which is jammed in the cylinder bore. In this case it may be necessary to separate the cylinder halves in order to free the piston from the cylinder bore.

10. Lubricate the piston, cylinder wall, and piston O-ring with brake fluid prior to assembly.

11. Assemble in the reverse order of disassembly.

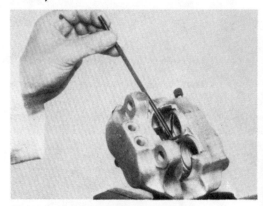

Removing piston sealing rings

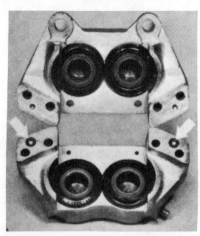

Separated caliper halves—typical. Arrows indicate fluid passages

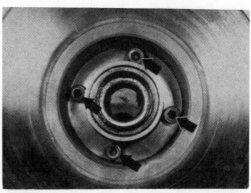

Removing allen bolts retaining disc to hub assembly

iston dust boot (2) and snap ring (1) emoved—733i

33i

The procedure for overhauling the four piston caliper on the 733 model is the same in all respects as the procedure for overhauling the four piston caliper on the 2002, 2002 i, etc., models with one major distinction. There is only one brake line to the caliper which attaches to a single line port as opposed to two brake lines with two brake line ports on the 2002 models. Because of the dual circuit arrangement on the 2002 models it is possible to isolate two of the four pistons, thus facilitating piston removal. The circuits to the pistons on the 733 model can not be isolated, and it is for this reason that it is easier to remove two pistons at a time.

Instead of locking only one piston, two pistons (side by side) are locked into position in the cylinder bores, while the two opposed pistons are removed. A special sealing plate will be needed to seal the two open cylinder bores. Proceed as though overhauling a model 2002 four piston caliper.

20i

The caliper used on the Model 320i is similar in construction to the standard four piston caliper, however, it is comprised of only two pistons. Proceed as though overhauling a four piston caliper.

Brake Disc

REMOVAL AND INSTALLATION AND INSPECTION

600, 2002, 280, 3.0, 528i, 530i

1. Remove the hub cap and loosen the lug nuts a few turns. Jack up the front of the car and place jackstands beneath the reinforced box-member area adjacent to the front jacking points.

2. Remove the wheel and tire assembly.

3. Remove the two bolts which retain the caliper to the spindle and slide it off the discs. Wire the caliper up out of the way so that the flexible brake hose is not strained.

4. Remove the grease cap from the hub. Remove the cotter pin, castellated nut, and washer retaining the disc and hub assembly to the spindle. Pull off the wheel and hub assembly together with the wheel bearings and grease seal.

5. Remove the 4 or 5 allen head bolts which retain the disc to the hub and lift off the disc. If the disc is rusted or otherwise fused to the hub, loosely bolt the wheel and tire back to the hub. Then, (no greasy fingers please) grasp the disc firmly and twist the disc back and forth briskly, while pulling up on the disc simultaneously. This should jerk the disc loose from the hub. A little penetrating fluid on the lug nut studs will help also.

6. Check the disc for scoring or excessive corrosion. If the pads were ever allowed to run down to the bare metal, the disc will have to be refinished or replaced. Minimum disc thickness is .354 in. on the 1600 and 2002, .460 in. on 500 series cars, .461 in. on the 2800, and .827 in. on the 3.0. If the refinishing operation cuts the disc to less than the minimum thickness, the disc must be replaced. Also, the thickness of the disc must not vary more than .0008 in. measured at 8 points on the contact surface with a micrometer. The contact surfaces of the disc should be absolutely clean of dirt, grease, or brake fluid.

7. At this time, it is good practice to remove, clean, repack and install the wheel

bearings into the hub as outlined under "Wheel Bearings Removal and Installation".

8. Install the disc onto the hub. Tighten the allen bolts to 43 ft lbs (44–48 on 528 and 530i).

9. Install the disc and hub assembly onto the spindle. Adjust the wheel bearings as outlined under "Wheel Bearing Adjustment". Once the wheel bearings are properly adjusted, check disc run-out with a dial gauge. Maximum permissible run-out is .008 in.

Checking the disc runout with dial gauge

10. Install the caliper, tightening the retaining bolts to 58 ft lbs.

11. Install the wheel and tire assembly. Lower the car and perform a road test.

320i, 630CSi, 633CSi, 733i

1. Remove the lug bolts and remove the front wheel.

2. Detach the bracket and, on the 733i, the clamp, at the spring strut.

3. Remove the caliper mounting bolts, and tie the caliper up out of the way (brake line still connected).

4. With an allen wrench, remove the bolt retaining the disc to the hub. Then, remove the disc.

NOTE: *These discs are balanced. Be careful not to disturb the weights.*

5. To inspect the disc, reposition it on the hub, install the retaining bolt, and torque it to 3–3.5 ft lbs (733i—23–24 ft lbs).

6. Adjust the wheel bearings as described below.

7. Use a dial indicator mounted at a point on the front suspension to measure the total runout of the disc. Runout maximum is .008 in. except on the 733i; on that model, it is .006 in. Also, use a micrometer and measure the total variation in the thickness of the disc

Note the balance weights (arrowed) and do not disturb their locations

Measuring total variation in disc thickness with a micrometer

where the pads have worn it at 8 evenly spaced points around the disc. The allowance is .0008 on all models. If tolerances are greater than this, the disc must be machined.

8. Install the wheel.

Wheel Bearings
ADJUSTMENT
1600, 2002, 320i, 630CSi, 633CSi, 733i

1. Raise the vehicle and support it and remove the front wheel.

2. Remove the end cap, and then straighten the cotter pin and remove it. Loosen the castellated nut.

3. While continuously spinning the brake disc, torque the castellated nut down to 22–24 ft lbs. Keep turning the disc throughout this and make sure it turns at least two turns after the nut is torqued and held.

4. Loosen the nut until there is end play and the hub rotates with the nut.

5. Torque the nut to no more than 2 ft-lbs. Finally, loosen slowly just until castellations and the nearest cotter pin hole line up and insert a new cotter pin.

6. Make sure the slotted washer is free to turn without noticeable resistance; otherwise, there is no end play and the bearings will wear excessively.

2800, 3.0, 528i, 530i

1. Remove the wheel. Remove the locking cap from the hub by gripping it carefully on both sides with a pair of pliers.

2. Remove the cotter pin from the castellated nut, and loosen the nut.

3. Spin the disc constantly while torquing the nut to 7 ft lbs. Continue spinning the disc a couple of turns after the nut is torqued and held.

4. Loosen the castellated nut ¼–⅓ turn—until the slotted washer can be turned readily.

Assembly sequence for wheel bearing components

Make sure the slotted washer can be turned freely, using a screwdriver, as shown

5. Fasten a dial indicator to the front suspension and rest the pin against the wheel hub. Preload the meter about .039 in. to remove any play.

6. Adjust the position of the castellated nut while reading the play on the indicator. Make the play as small as possible while backing off the castellated nut just until a new cotter pin can be inserted. The permissible range is .0008–.0024 in.

7. Install the new cotter pin, locking cap, and the wheel.

REMOVAL AND INSTALLATION (PACKING)

1. Remove the wheel and the brake disc, as described above. On models with separate disc, remove the locking cap by gripping carefully on both sides with a pair of pliers, remove the cotter pin from the castellated nut, and remove the nut and, where

Force the outer bearing through the recesses (arrowed) in the wheel hub

equipped, the slotted washer. Then, remove the entire hub and bearings.

2. Remove the shaft sealing ring and take out the roller bearing.

3. On most models, the outer bearing race may be forced out through the recesses in the wheel hub. A BMW puller 00 8 550 or equivalent may also be used. On the 733i the recesses are not provided and a puller is necessary.

4. Clean all bearings and races and the interior of the hub with alcohol, and allow to air dry.

Do not dry with compressed air as this can damage the bearings by rolling them over one another unlubricated or force one loose from the cage and injure you.

5. Replace *all* bearings and races if there is any sign of scoring or galling.

6. Press in the outer races with a suitable sleeve. Pack a new shaft seal with graphite grease and refill the hub with fresh grease.

7. Assemble in this order: outer race; inner race; outer race; inner race; shaft seal.

8. Adjust wheel bearing play as described above.

REAR DISC BRAKES

Disc Brake Pads

REMOVAL AND INSTALLATION

NOTE: *The position of the caliper piston must be checked with a special BMW gauge (or equivalent) 34 1 000 series (order by the model of your car) and, if necessary, aligned with a special tool such as 34 1 060 or equivalent. It would be best to price these tools and weigh their cost against the cost of having the repairs performed before proceeding. Do not attempt to perform the job without the special tools.*

2800, 3.0, 528i, 530i

1. Support the rear of the vehicle in a raised pisition, and remove the rear wheels.
2. Drive out the retaining pins.
3. Remove the cross springs (anti-rattle clips).
4. Using a BMW special hook tool 34–1–010 or an equivalent tool, pull the pads out and away from the caliper.
5. Using a BMW special tool 34–1–050, press the piston into the caliper to the fully retracted position. You may wish to dra.n fluid from the master cylinder first as doing this will displace fluid and raise the level there.
6. Check the 20 degree position of the caliper piston with a BMW special gauge 34–1–000 or an equivalent gauge. The 20 degree step must face the inlet or the brake disc.

Checking the 20 degree position of the caliper piston—528i, 530i

Correcting the angle of the caliper piston to 20 degrees with a special pair of pliers—528i, 530i

7. Install the new brake pads in the reverse order of removal.

630CSi, 633CSi, 733i

NOTE: *The position of the caliper piston must be checked with a special BMW gauge (or equivalent) 34 1 000 series (order by the model of your car) and, if necessary, aligned with a special tool such as 34 1 060 or equivalent. It would be best to price these tools and weigh their cost against the cost of having the repairs performed before proceeding. Do not attempt to perform the job without the special tools.*

1. Remove the rear wheel. Disconnect the right rear plug for the pad wear indicator. Take the wires out of the clamp.
2. Drive out the retaining pins and remove the cross spring.
3. Pull the pads straight out with a tool which will grab them via backing plate holes. If the pads are to be reused, make sure not to mix them up—they must be reinstalled in the same place.
4. When ordering new pads, note both the color code and make. Replace all four pads on rear axle together if any pads are excessively worn.
5. Install a new wear sensor on the right side of the left brake pad (thicker side toward disc).
6. Use a brush and alcohol to clean the guide surface of the housing opening.
7. Force the pistons back into the caliper with an appropriate special tool (for example BMW 34 1 050). Forcing the pistons back will displace the fluid in the caliper and raise the level in the master cylinder. Drain some fluid out of the master cylinder reservoir before proceeding.

Use an alcohol soaked brush to clean the guide surface of the housing opening

8. The step on the piston must face the side of the caliper where the disc enters the caliper when the vehicle is moving forward. If necessary, correct the angle of the piston with a special tool such as BMW 34 1 060. Measure the angle with BMW gauge 34 1 100 or equivalent.

9. Reinstall pads in reverse order. Check the cross spring and retaining pins and replace if necessary. Pump the brake pedal until all motion has been taken out of the pads and they rest at the calipers. Keep the master cylinder fluid reservoir full while doing this.

Disc Brake Calipers

REMOVAL

2800, 3.0, 528i, 530i, 630CSi, 633CSi, 733i

1. On the 2800 and 3.0, disconnect the fluid line at the reservoir and plug the two openings with pointed sticks. On later models, remove fluid from the master cylinder.

2. On 600 and 700 Series, disconnect the plug for the brake sensor. Detach the brake

line, unscrew the two mounting bolts, and remove the caliper.

3. To install, reverse the removal procedure, and bleed the system. Torque caliper mounting bolts to 44–48 ft lbs.

OVERHAUL

2800, 3.0, 528i, 530i, 630CSi, 633CSi, 733i

1. Remove the caliper as described above. Remove the brake pads.

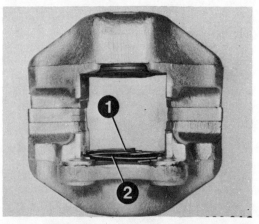

Remove the clamp (1) and rubber piston seal (2) on both sides

2. Remove the clamp and rubber piston seal on both sides.

3. Place a felt pad or hardwood block in the caliper jaws and between the pistons.

4. On the 2800 and 3.0, plug the brake line connecting hole and retain the piston on the connecting hole side with brake pliers. On other models, hold the piston opposite the brake line connecting hole with brake pliers and apply the compressed air to the connecting hole. Apply air pressure gradu-

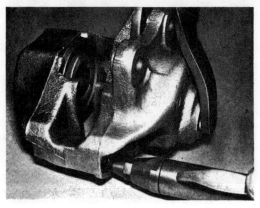

Disconnecting and plugging fluid reservoir connections on the 2800 and 3.0

Plugging the brake line connecting hole in the caliper—2800, 3.0

ally to reduce the chance of personal injury, just until the first piston pops out.

5. Plug the open piston bore with some sort of sealing plate. On the 500, 600, and 700 series, also plug the connecting hole and switch the air pressure hose to the bleed hole. Then, force out the second piston in the same manner.

6. Lift out seals with a soft (plastic) probe.

7. Clean all parts in alcohol and dry with clean compressed air. Replace calipers with damaged bores and pistons with scored or pitted surfaces.

8. Reassemble in reverse order, using all new seals from an overhaul kit. Be careful not to cock pistons in the bores when reinstalling, and coat all parts with silicone lubricant.

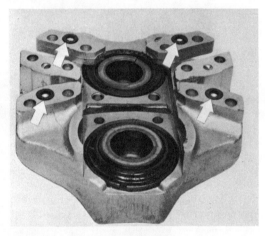

Locations of the four ring seals

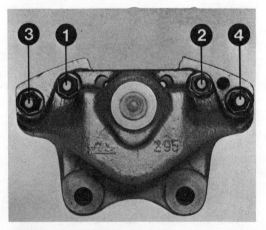

Tighten new stretch bolts in the numbered sequence

9. Check the 20 degree position of the pistons, install the capipers and pads, and bleed the system, as described above.

10. On the 2800, 3.0 and 528i and 530i, the calipers can be split for replacement of seals inside. Split the calipers and replace these four ring seals only if absolutely necessary. When reassembling, make sure to torque the bolts to 16–19 ft lbs in the numbered order shown, only. Use new bolts only.

Brake Discs

REMOVAL AND INSTALLATION

2800, 3.0, 528i, 530i, 630CSi, 633CSi, 733i

1. Remove the rear wheel, and, if necessary, unclamp the brake line from the rear suspension. Remove the caliper as described above.

2. On the 2800, 3.0, 528i and 530i, simply pull the disc off the axle shaft. Note position of holes in the disc and axle shaft flange (on 500 Series models, the large hole in the disc aligns with the large hole in the axle shaft flange.

3. On the 600 and 700 Series, remove the allen bolt and remove the disc.

4. Reverse the removal procedure to install. Torque allen bolts retaining the disc to 22–24 ft lbs.

INSPECTION

1. Mount a dial indicator on the rear caliper with the pin against the disc. It may be convenient to pull the rear brake pads out and measure between the jaws of the caliper.

2. Measure the thickness of the disc at eight points around the diameter on the worn surfaces with a micrometer. Compare the thickness readings and subtract the lowest from the highest. If this figure is greater than the maximum specification described below, the disc must be machined. Note also the minimum thickness figures and the fact that, if the disc requires machining and cannot be cleaned up before the thickness drops below the minimum figure, it must be replaced.

3. Preload the dial indicator a small amount and measure the total runout of the disc as it rotates. Compare with specifications and if runout is excessive, have the disc machined (note that wheel bearing problems, if they exist, can show up as excessive runout).

4. Specifications (in inches) are:

Model	Minimum Thickness	Thickness Tolerance	Runout (installed)
2800	.335	.0008	.008
3.0	.709	.0008	.008
528,			
530	.334	.0008	.008
630,			
633	.827	.0008	.008
733	.827	.0008	.006

Note that if one disc is either replaced or machined, the other disc on the rear axle must receive the same treatment.

Rear Drum Brakes
BRAKE DRUMS

REMOVAL AND INSTALLATION

1. Support the rear of the car securely and remove the rear wheel. On the 320i, remove the allen bolt from the brake drum.

2. If the drum will not pull off, severe wear may have grooved it, causing the brake linings to prevent it from coming off. See the brake adjustment procedure at the front of this chapter, and loosen both the brake adjuster and the hand brake adjustment; then, pull the drum off the axle flange.

3. Check the contact surface of the drum for scoring and measure the inside diameter to check for ovality. Ovality must not exceed .02 in. The drum may be machined .02 in. at a time to a maximum oversize of .04 in. Always cut the drums in pairs.

4. To check the drum for cracks, hang the

drum by a piece of wood and tap with a small metal object. A cracked drum will sound flat.

5. Reverse the above procedure to install and adjust the brakes.

Brake Shoes
REMOVAL AND INSTALLATION
1600, 2002

1. Remove the hub cap and loosen the lug nuts a few turns. Jack up the rear of the car and install jackstands beneath the reinforced box-member area adjacent to the rear jacking points. Make sure that the parking brake is released.

2. Remove the wheel and tire assembly.

3. Pull off the brake drum.

4. Loosen the brake shoes by turning the brake adjustment screw at each backing plate clockwise (left-hand side) or counterclockwise (right-hand side).

5. Remove the cotter pin and castellated nut from the axle shaft. Using a hub puller, pull off the axle shaft drive flange.

Pulling off axle shaft drive flange—1600, 2002

Remove the allen bolt from the brake drum—320i

Disconnecting brake show spring

6. Disconnect the brake shoe spring at the bottom of the shoes. Lever the shoes together at the bottom end and remove the upper ends from the wheel cylinder.

7. Disconnect the thrust rod and parking brake cable. Lift off the brake shoes, noting their placement.

8. If the shoe linings are worn down to less than 0.12 in., the shoes must be replaced or new linings riveted on. All 4 linings for the rear brakes must be replaced at the same time to provide even braking action. If the linings wore down to the point where the rivets made metal-to-metal contact with the brake drum, have the brake drum turned to remove the score marks. If the drums are cut, purchase new shoes to match the drum oversize. Also, at this time, check the wheel cylinder for leakage. If any trace of brake fluid is found, remove and overhaul the brake cylinders as outlined under "Wheel Cylinder Overhaul".

9. Reverse the above procedure to install, using the following installation notes:

a. Take care not to contaminate the brake linings with dirt, grease, or brake fluid.

b. When installing the shoes on the backing plate, insert the long end of the spring between the parking brake lever and the brake shoe (see the illustration).

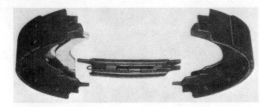

Inserting long end of spring between parking brake lever and brake shoe

c. When installing the nut for the axle shaft drive flange, adjust the nut as outlined under step 8 and 9 of "Half-shaft Removal and Installation" in Chapter 7.

d. Adjust the brakes as outlined under "Drum Brake Adjustment".

320i

1. Remove the brake drum as described above.

2. Turn the retainers 90 degrees and remove the retaining springs at the center of both shoes.

3. Disconnect the return springs at the

Turn the retainers (arrowed) 90 degrees to release the retaining springs

Disconnecting the parking brake cable—320i

bottom with a return spring tool, noting their exact locations. Disconnect the bottoms of the shoes from the retainer.

4. Pull the tops of the shoes out of the brake cylinder piston rods, and pull slightly away from their mountings for clearance. Then, disconnect the parking brake cable from the actuating hook, and remove the shoes.

5. Measure brake linings—minimum thickness is .118 in. Also check the return spring for signs of heat damage and replace, if necessary.

6. Install in reverse order, making sure you connect the long end of the return spring between the parking brake lever and brake shoe.

Wheel Cylinders
REMOVAL AND INSTALLATION

1. Remove the brake drum as outlined under "Brake Drum Removal and Installation".

2. Loosen the brake shoes by rotating the adjustment screw at each backing plate. To loosen, turn the left-hand screw clockwise and the right-hand screw counterclockwise.

3. Disconnect and plug the brake line to the wheel cylinder. Remove the bleed screw and mounting screws for the wheel cylinder from behind the backing plate.

4. Push the wheel cylinder to the right and lift out forward.

5. Reverse the above procedure to install, taking care to adjust the brakes as outlined under "Drum Brake Adjustment", and bleed the brakes as outlined under "Bleeding the Hydraulic System".

OVERHAUL

1. Remove the wheel cylinder as outlined under "Wheel Cylinder Removal and Installation".

2. Remove the protective rubber end caps (5) from the cylinder (1) and withdraw the pistons (4), sleeves (3), and compression spring (2).

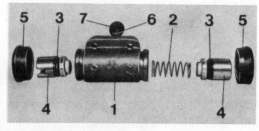

Wheel cylinder components—see text

3. Clean all parts in clean brake fluid or methylated alcohol. Inspect the compression spring, pistons and cylinder bore. Replace the spring if it is distorted. Replace the pistons and cylinder if either is corroded or scored. Always use new rubber sleeves and protective end caps to assemble. Also, make sure that the grooves at the ends of the cylinder for the rubber caps are not damaged.

4. Dip the cylinder bore, pistons, and the new seals in clean brake fluid or Ate cylinder paste. Insert the piston and seal assemblies together with the compression spring into the bore. Install the new rubber end caps on the cylinder, making sure that the lips on the end caps seat fully in the cylinder grooves.

5. Install the wheel cylinder as outlined under "Wheel Cylinder Removal and Installation". Remember to adjust the brakes and bleed the hydraulic system.

Gaining access to the rear brake shoe adjusting starwheel—733i

PARKING BRAKE

Cable

ADJUSTMENT

For vehicles equipped with rear wheel drum brakes, see the "Brake Adjustment" procedure at the front of this chapter.

For vehicles equipped with disc brakes on the rear, also follow that procedure; however, note that the adjuster is a star wheel, accessible with a screwdriver via a .6 inch hole in the backing plate at the rear. Turn the star wheel until the disc and rear wheel cannot be turned, just as the conventional adjuster is turned in the procedure for drum brakes.

REMOVAL AND INSTALLATION
2002

1. Pull off the parking brake lever boot. Unscrew the locknut (1) and nut (2) from the parking brake cable (3).

2. Loosen the brake shoes by rotating the adjustment screw at each rear wheel backing plate. To loosen, turn the left-hand screw

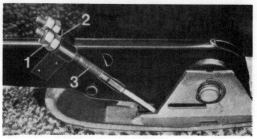

Parking brake lever components—1600, 2002

clockwise and the right-hand screw counterclockwise.

3. Remove the brake drums as outlined under "Brake Drum Removal and Installation".

4. Remove the cotter pin and castellated nut from the axle shafts. Using a hub puller, pull off the axle shaft drive flanges.

5. Remove each parking brake cable from its guide at the rear trailing arm. Disconnect each brake shoe spring at the bottom.

6. Disconnect the parking brake cables from each cable lever, and remove the cables.

7. Reverse the above procedure to install, taking care to adjust the parking brake as outlined under "Parking Brake Adjustment". Also, follow the installation notes for Step 9 under "Brake Shoe Replacement".

320i

1. Remove the brake drum as described above. Pull off the rubber boot at the handbrake lever, loosen and remove the locknuts on the appropriate side, and disconnect the cable at the handbrake lever.

2. Proceed with Steps 1–4 of the "Brake Shoe Removal and Installation Procedure" above.

3. Then, pull the cable out of the holder toward the rear of the car.

4. Install in reverse order, making sure the cable holders are both located properly— one in the protective tube, and the other in the backing plate. Adjust the brakes as described at the front of this chapter.

2800, 3.0, 528i, 530i, 630CSi, 633CSi, 733i

1. Remove the parking brake shoes as described below.

2. See the illustration, and pull out "A" to the right. Then, press out the pin "B". Finally, pull "C" to the left, and remove the expander.

3. On the 733i only, disconnect the bat-

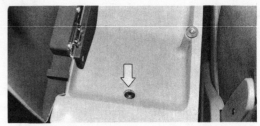

Loosening the footwell nozzle mounting screw (arrowed) on the 733i

tery (−) cable, loosen the mounting screw and pull off the footwell nozzle.

4. Unscrew mounting bolts, and pull the tray at the front of the footwell out far enough to disconnect the wires. Then, remove the tray.

5. Remove the rubber boot from the handbrake lever. Unscrew the locknuts and remove them and pull the cable out of the brake lever.

6. Working under the car, detach the brake cable at the suspension arm. Remove the two mounting nuts at the brake backing plate, and then pull the cable out of the protective tube.

7. Reverse the removal procedure to install.

Parking Brake Shoes (Rear Disc Brakes Only)

REPLACEMENT

1. Remove the rear caliper.

2. Remove the rear brake disc.

3. Remove the bottom return spring.

4. Using a tool such as BMW special tool 34-4-000, turn the retaining springs 90 degrees, and remove the springs.

5. Pull the brake shoes apart at the bottom, and lift them out.

6. Install the new brakes shoes in the reverse order of removal.

Turning the retaining springs with a special tool to remove rear parking brake shoes—typical

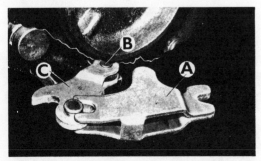

Removing the brake shoe expander—2800, 3.0

Brake Specifications

All measurements given are (in.) unless noted

Model	Lug Nut Torque (ft/lb)	Master Cylinder Bore	Brake Disc		Brake Drum		Minimum Lining Thickness	
			Minimum ° Thickness	Maximum Run-Out	Diam-eter	Max Machine O/S	Front	Rear
1600-2	53–65	.8100	.354	.008	7.87	7.91	.275	.079
2002	53–65	.8100	.354	.008	9.06	9.10	.275	.079
2002Ti	53–65	.9375	.459	.008	9.06	9.10	.275	.079
2002Tii	53–65	.9375	.459	.008	9.06	9.10	.275	.079
320i	59–65	.812	.827	.008	9.84	9.89	.301	.118
2800, 3.0	60–66	.874	.827F/.709R	.008	—	—	.276	.276
528i, 530, 630CSi, 633CSi	59–65	.936	.460F/.334R	.008	—	—	.080①	.080①
733i	60–66	.874	.827	.006	—	—	.080	.080

* F—Front
  R—Rear
① 528i and 530i—.275 minimum pad thickness front and rear

10

Body

The list of tools and equipment you may need to fix minor body damage ranges from very basic hand tools to a wide assortment of specialized body tools. Most minor scratches, dings and rust holes can be fixed using an electric drill, wire wheel or grinder attachment, half-round plastic file, sanding block, various grades of sandpaper (#120, which is coarse through #600, which is fine, in both wet and dry types), auto body plastic, primer, touch-up paint, spreaders, newspaper and masking tape. If you intend to try straightening any dents, you'll probably also need a slide hammer (dent puller).

Most auto body repair kits contain all the materials you need to do the job right in the kit. So, if you have a small rust spot or dent you want to fix, check the contents of the kit before you run out and buy any additional tools.

ALIGNING BODY PANELS

Doors

There are several methods of adjusting doors. Your vehicle will probably use one of those illustrated.

Whenever a door is removed and is to be reinstalled, you should matchmark the posi-

tion of the hinges on the door pillars. The holes of the hinges and/or the hinge attaching points are usually oversize to permit alignment of doors. The striker plate is also moveable, through oversize holes, permitting up-and-down, in-and-out and fore-and-aft movement. Fore-and-aft movement is made by adding or subtracting shims from behind the striker and pillar post. The striker should be adjusted so that the door closes fully and remains closed, yet enters the lock freely.

DOOR HINGES

Don't try to cover up poor door adjustment with a striker plate adjustment. The gap on each side of the door should be equal and uniform and there should be no metal-to-metal contact as the door is opened or closed.

1. Determine which hinge bolts must be loosened to move the door in the desired direction.

2. Loosen the hinge bolt(s) just enough to allow the door to be moved with a padded pry bar.

3. Move the door a small amount and check the fit, after tightening the bolts. Be sure that there is no bind or interference with adjacent panels.

4. Repeat this until the door is properly positioned, and tighten all the bolts securely.

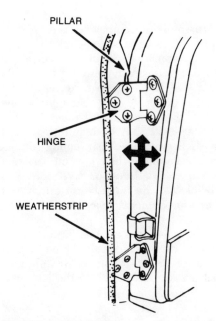

Door hinge adjustment

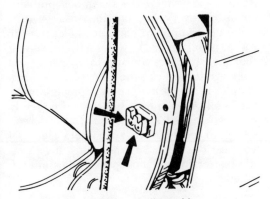

Move the door striker as indicated by arrows

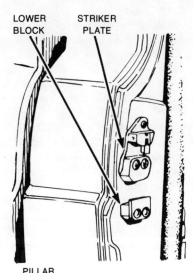

Striker plate and lower block

Hood, Trunk or Tailgate

As with doors, the outline of hinges should be scribed before removal. The hood and trunk can be aligned by loosening the hinge bolts in their slotted mounting holes and moving the hood or trunk lid as necessary. The hood and trunk have adjustable catch locations to regulate lock engagement bumpers at the front and/or rear of the hood provide a vertical adjustment and the hood lockpin can be adjusted for proper engagement.

The tailgate on the station wagon can be adjusted by loosening the hinge bolts in their slotted mounting holes and moving the tailgate on its hinges. The latchplate and

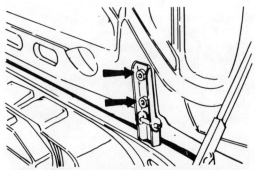

Loosen the hinge boots to permit fore-and-aft and horizontal adjustment

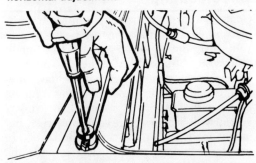

The hood is adjusted vertically by stop-screws at the front and/or rear

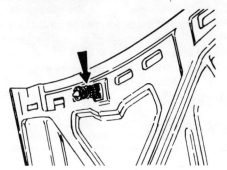

The hood pin can be adjusted for proper lock engagement

latch striker at the bottom of the tailgate opening can be adjusted to stop rattle. An adjustable bumper is located on each side.

RUST, UNDERCOATING, AND RUSTPROOFING

Rust

About the only technical information the average backyard mechanic needs to know about rust is that it is an electro-chemical process that works from **the inside out** on unprotected ferrous metals such as steel and iron. Salt, pollution, humidity—these things and more create and promote the formation of rust. You can't stop rust once it starts. Once rust has started on a fender or a body panel, the only sure way to stop it is to replace the part.

It's a lot easier to prevent rust than to remove it, especially if you have a new car and most late model cars are pretty well rustproofed when the leave the factory. In the early seventies, it seemed like cars were rusting out faster than you could pay them off and Detroit (and the imports) realized that this is not exactly the way you build customer loyalty.

Undercoating

Contrary to what most people think, the primary purpose of undercoating is not to prevent rust, but to deaden noise that might otherwise be transmitted to the car's interior. Since cars are pretty quiet these days anyway, dealers are only too willing to promote undercoating as a rust preventative. Undercoating will of course, prevent some rust, but only if applied when the car is brand- new. In any case, undercoating doesn't provide the protection that a good rustproofing does. If you do decide to undercoat your car and it's not brand-new, you have a big clean-up job ahead of you. It's a good idea to have the underside of the car professionally steam-cleaned and save yourself a lot of work. Spraying undercoat on dirty or rusty parts is only going to make things worse, since the undercoat will trap any rust causing agents.

Rustproofing

The best thing you can do for a new or nearly new car is to have it properly rust-proofed. There are two ways you can go about this. You can do it yourself, or you can have one of the big rustproofing companies do it for you. Naturally, it's going to cost you a lot more to have a big company do it, but it's worth it if your car is new or nearly new. If you own an older car that you plan to hang onto for a while, then doing it yourself might be the best idea. Professional rust-proofing isn't cheap ($100–$250), but it's definitely worth it if your car is new. The rustproofing companies won't guarantee their jobs on cars that are over three months old or have more than about 3000 miles on them because they feel the corrosion process may have already begun.

If you have an older car that hasn't started to rust yet, the best idea might be to purchase one of the do-it-yourself rustproofing kits that are available, and do the job yourself.

Drain Holes

Rusty rocker panels are a common problem on nearly every car, but they can be prevented by simply drilling some holes in your rocker panels to let the water out, or keeping the ones that are already there clean and unclogged. Most cars these days have a series of holes in the rocker panels to prevent moisture collection there, but they frequently become clogged up. Just use a small screwdriver or penknife to keep them clean. If your car doesn't have drain holes, it's a simple matter to drill a couple of holes in each panel.

Repairing Minor Body Damage

Unless your car just rolled off the showroom floor, chances are it has a few minor scratches or dings in it somewhere, or a small rust spot you've been meaning to fix. You just haven't been able to decide whether or not you can really do the job. Well, if the damage is anything like that presented here, there are a number of auto body repair kits that contain everything you need to repair minor scratches, dents, and rust spots. Even rust holes can be repaired if you use the correct kit. If you're unsure of your ability, start out with a small scratch. Once you've mastered small scratches and dings, you can work your way up to the more complicated repairs. When doing rust repairs, remember that unless all the rust is removed, it's going to come back in a year or less. Just sanding the rust down and applying some paint won't work.

Repairing Minor Surface Rust and Scratches

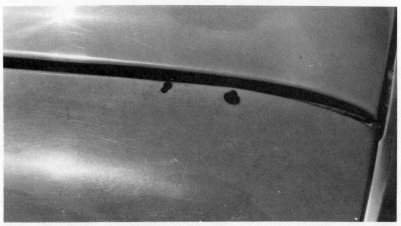

1. Just about everybody has a minor rust spot or scratches on their car. Spots such as these can be easily repaired in an hour or two. You'll need some sandpaper, masking tape, primer, and a can of touch-up paint.

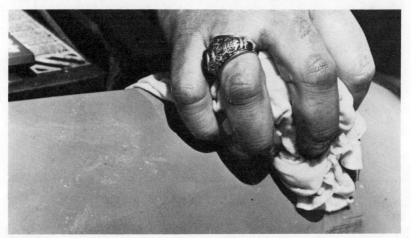

2. The first step is to wash the area down to remove all traces of dirt and road grime. If the car has been frequently waxed, you should wipe it with thinner or some other wax remover so that the paint will stick.

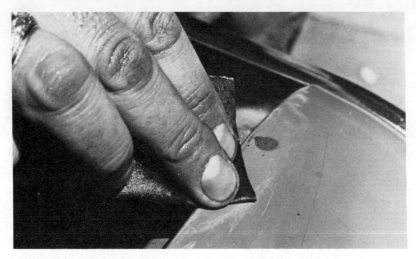

3. Small rust spots and scratches like these will only require light hand sanding. For a job like this, you can start with about grade 320 sandpaper and then use a 400 grit for the final sanding.

4. Once you've sanded the area with 320 paper, wet a piece of 400 paper and sand it lightly. Wet sanding will feather the edges of the surrounding paint into the area to be painted. For large areas, you could use a sanding block, but it's not really necessary for a small job like this.

5. The area should look like this once you're finished sanding. Wipe off any water and run the palm of your hand over the sanded area with your eyes closed. You shouldn't be able to feel any bumps or ridges anywhere. Make sure you have sanded a couple of inches back in each direction so you'll get good paint adhesion.

6. Once you have the area sanded to your satisfaction, mask the surrounding area with masking tape and newspaper. Be sure to cover any chrome or trim that might get sprayed. You'll have to mask far enough back from the damaged area to allow for overspray. If you mask right around the sanded spots, you'll end up with a series of lines marking the painted area.

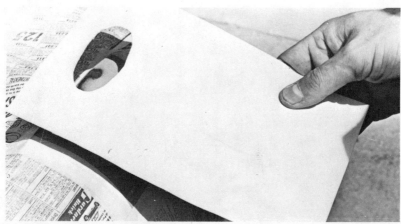

7. You can avoid a lot of excess overspray by cutting a hole in a piece of cardboard that approximately matches the area you are going to paint. Hold the cardboard steady over the area as you spray the primer on. If you haven't painted before, it's a good idea to practice on something before you try painting your car. Don't hold the paint can in one spot. Keep it moving and you'll avoid runs and sags.

8. The primered area should look like this when you have finished. It's better to spray several light coats than one heavy coat. Let the primer dry for several minutes between coats. Make sure you've covered all the bare metal.

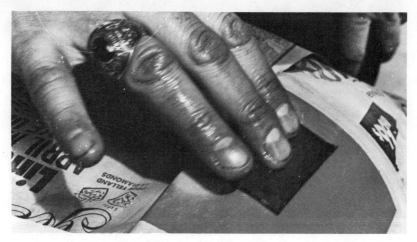

9. After the primer has dried, sand the area with wet 400 paper, wash it off and let it dry. Your final coat goes on next, so make sure the area is clean and dry.

10. Spray the touch-up paint on using the cardboard again. Make the first coat a very light coat (known as a fog coat). Remember to keep the paint can moving smoothly at about 8–12 inches from the surface.

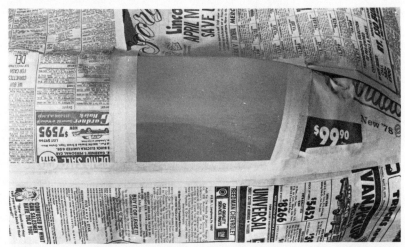

11. Once you've finished painting, let the paint dry for about 15 minutes before you remove the masking tape and newspaper.

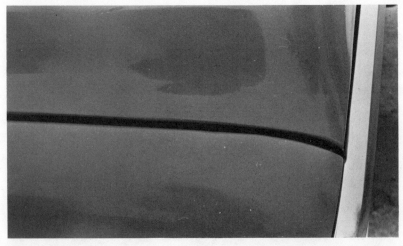

12. Let the paint dry for several days before you rub it out lightly with rubbing compound, and the finished job should be indistinguishable from the rest of the car. Don't rub hard or you'll cut through the paint.

Repairing Rust Holes With Fiberglass

1. The job we've picked here isn't an easy one mainly because of the location. The compound curves make the work trickier than if the surface were flat.

2. You'll need a drill and a wire brush for the first step, which is the removal of all the paint and rust from the rusted-out area.

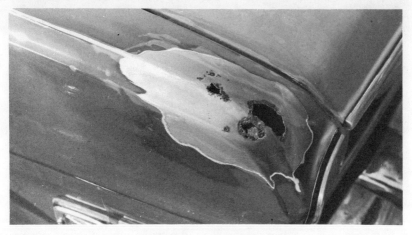

3. When you've finished grinding, the area to be repaired should look like this. Grind the paint back several inches in each direction to ensure that the patch will adhere to the metal. Remove all the damaged metal or the rust will return.

4. Tap the edges of the holes inward with a ballpeen hammer to allow for the thickness of the fiberglass material. Tap lightly so that you don't destroy any contours.

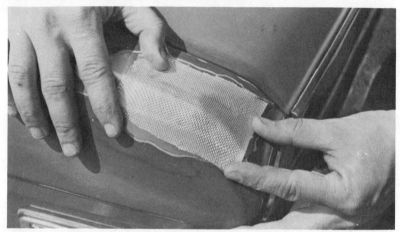

5. Follow the directions of the kit you purchase carefully. With fiberglass repair kits, the first step is generally to cut one or two pieces of fiberglass to cover the hole. Quite often, the procedure is to cut one patch the size of the prepared area and one patch the size of the hole.

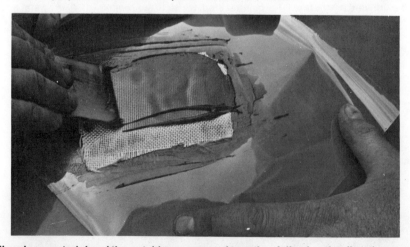

6. Mix the fiberglass material and the patching compound together following the directions supplied with the kit. With this particular kit, a layer type process is used, with the entire mixture being prepared on a piece of plastic film known as a release sheet. Keep in mind that not all kits work this way. Be careful when you mix the catalyst with the resin, as too much catalyst will harden the mixture before you can apply it.

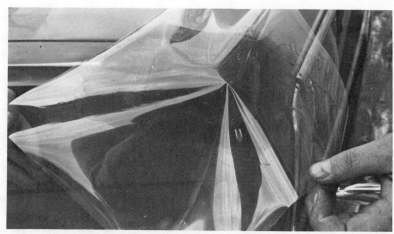

7. Spread the material on the damaged area using the release sheet. This process is essentially meant for smooth flat areas, and as a result, the release sheet would not adhere to the surface properly on our test car. If this happens to you, you'll probably have to remove the release sheet and spread the fiberglass compound out with your fingers or a small spreader.

8. This is what the fiberglass mixture looked like on our car after it had hardened. Because of the contours, we found it nearly impossible to smooth the mixture with a spreader, so we used our fingers. Unfortunately, it makes for a messy job that requires a lot of sanding. If you're working on a flat surface, you won't have this problem.

9. After the patch has hardened, sand it down to a smooth surface. You'll probably have to start with about grade 100 sandpaper and work your way up to 400 wet paper. If you have a particularly rough surface, you could start with a half-round plastic file.

10. This is what the finished product should look like before you apply paint. Many of the kits come with glazing compound to fill in small imperfections left after the initial sanding. You'll probably need some. We did. The entire sanding operation took about an hour. Feather the edges of the repaired area into the surrounding paint carefully. As in any other body job, your hand is the best indicator of what's smooth and what isn't. It doesn't matter if it looks smooth. It's got to feel smooth. Take your time with this step and it will come out right.

11. Once you've smoothed out the repair, mask the entire area carefully, and spray the repair with primer. Keep the spray can moving in steady even strokes, overlap every stroke, and keep the spray can about 8–12 inches from the surface. Apply several coats of primer, letting the primer dry between coats.

12. The finished product (in primer) looks like this. If you were going to just spot paint this area, the next step would be to spray the correct color on the repaired area. This particular car is waiting for a complete paint job.

Appendix

General Conversion Table

Multiply by	To convert	To	
2.54	Inches	Centimeters	.3937
30.48	Feet	Centimeters	.0328
.914	Yards	Meters	1.094
1.609	Miles	Kilometers	.621
.645	Square inches	Square cm.	.155
.836	Square yards	Square meters	1.196
16.39	Cubic inches	Cubic cm.	.061
28.3	Cubic feet	Liters	.0353
.4536	Pounds	Kilograms	2.2045
4.226	Gallons	Liters	.264
.068	Lbs./sq. in. (psi)	Atmospheres	14.7
.138	Foot pounds	Kg. m.	7.23
1.014	H.P. (DIN)	H.P. (SAE)	.9861
—	To obtain	From	Multiply by

Note: 1 cm. equals 10 mm.; 1 mm. equals .0394″.

Conversion—Common Fractions to Decimals and Millimeters

Common Fractions	Decimal Fractions	Millimeters (approx.)	Common Fractions	Decimal Fractions	Millimeters (approx.)	Common Fractions	Decimal Fractions	Millimeters (approx.)
1/128	.008	0.20	11/32	.344	8.73	43/64	.672	17.07
1/64	.016	0.40	23/64	.359	9.13	11/16	.688	17.46
1/32	.031	0.79	3/8	.375	9.53	45/64	.703	17.86
3/64	.047	1.19	25/64	.391	9.92	23/32	.719	18.26
1/16	.063	1.59	13/32	.406	10.32	47/64	.734	18.65
5/64	.078	1.98	27/64	.422	10.72	3/4	.750	19.05
3/32	.094	2.38	7/16	.438	11.11	49/64	.766	19.45
7/64	.109	2.78	29/64	.453	11.51	25/32	.781	19.84
1/8	.125	3.18	15/32	.469	11.91	51/64	.797	20.24
9/64	.141	3.57	31/64	.484	12.30	13/16	.813	20.64
5/32	.156	3.97	1/2	.500	12.70	53/64	.828	21.03
11/64	.172	4.37	33/64	.516	13.10	27/32	.844	21.43
3/16	.188	4.76	17/32	.531	13.49	55/64	.859	21.83
13/64	.203	5.16	35/64	.547	13.89	7/8	.875	22.23
7/32	.219	5.56	9/16	.563	14.29	57/64	.891	22.62
15/64	.234	5.95	37/64	.578	14.68	29/32	.906	23.02
1/4	.250	6.35	19/32	.594	15.08	59/64	.922	23.42
17/64	.266	6.75	39/64	.609	15.48	15/16	.938	23.81
9/32	.281	7.14	5/8	.625	15.88	61/64	.953	24.21
19/64	.297	7.54	41/64	.641	16.27	31/32	.969	24.61
5/16	.313	7.94	21/32	.656	16.67	63/64	.984	25.00
21/64	.328	8.33						

Conversion—Millimeters to Decimal Inches

mm	inches	mm	inches	mm	inches	mm	inches	mm	inches
1	.039 370	31	1.220 470	61	2.401 570	91	3.582 670	210	8.267 700
2	.078 740	32	1.259 840	62	2.440 940	92	3.622 040	220	8.661 400
3	.118 110	33	1.299 210	63	2.480 310	93	3.661 410	230	9.055 100
4	.157 480	34	1.338 580	64	2.519 680	94	3.700 780	240	9.448 800
5	.196 850	35	1.377 949	65	2.559 050	95	3.740 150	250	9.842 500
6	.236 220	36	1.417 319	66	2.598 420	96	3.779 520	260	10.236 200
7	.275 590	37	1.456 689	67	2.637 790	97	3.818 890	270	10.629 900
8	.314 960	38	1.496 050	68	2.677 160	98	3.858 260	280	11.032 600
9	.354 330	39	1.535 430	69	2.716 530	99	3.897 630	290	11.417 300
10	.393 700	40	1.574 800	70	2.755 900	100	3.937 000	300	11.811 000
11	.433 070	41	1.614 170	71	2.795 270	105	4.133 848	310	12.204 700
12	.472 440	42	1.653 540	72	2.834 640	110	4.330 700	320	12.598 400
13	.511 810	43	1.692 910	73	2.874 010	115	4.527 550	330	12.992 100
14	.551 180	44	1.732 280	74	2.913 380	120	4.724 400	340	13.385 800
15	.590 550	45	1.771 650	75	2.952 750	125	4.921 250	350	13.779 500
16	.629 920	46	1.811 020	76	2.992 120	130	5.118 100	360	14.173 200
17	.669 290	47	1.850 390	77	3.031 490	135	5.314 950	370	14.566 900
18	.708 660	48	1.889 760	78	3.070 860	140	5.511 800	380	14.960 600
19	.748 030	49	1.929 130	79	3.110 230	145	5.708 650	390	15.354 300
20	.787 400	50	1.968 500	80	3.149 600	150	5.905 500	400	15.748 000
21	.826 770	51	2.007 870	81	3.188 970	155	6.102 350	500	19.685 000
22	.866 140	52	2.047 240	82	3.228 340	160	6.299 200	600	23.622 000
23	.905 510	53	2.086 610	83	3.267 710	165	6.496 050	700	27.559 000
24	.944 880	54	2.125 980	84	3.307 080	170	6.692 900	800	31.496 000
25	.984 250	55	2.165 350	85	3.346 450	175	6.889 750	900	35.433 000
26	1.023 620	56	2.204 720	86	3.385 820	180	7.086 600	1000	39.370 000
27	1.062 990	57	2.244 090	87	3.425 190	185	7.283 450	2000	78.740 000
28	1.102 360	58	2.283 460	88	3.464 560	190	7.480 300	3000	118.110 000
29	1.141 730	59	2.322 830	89	3.503 903	195	7.677 150	4000	157.480 000
30	1.181 100	60	2.362 200	90	3.543 300	200	7.874 000	5000	196.850 000

To change decimal millimeters to decimal inches, position the decimal point where desired on either side of the millimeter measurement shown and reset the inches decimal by the same number of digits in the same direction. For example, to convert 0.001 mm to decimal inches, reset the decimal behind the 1 mm (shown on the chart) to 0.001; change the decimal inch equivalent (0.039″ shown) to 0.000039″.

Tap Drill Sizes

Screw & Tap Size	National Fine or S.A.E. Threads Per Inch	Use Drill Number
No. 5	44	37
No. 6	40	33
No. 8	36	29
No. 10	32	21
No. 12	28	15
1/4	28	3
5/16	24	1
3/8	24	Q
7/16	20	W
1/2	20	29/64
9/16	18	33/64
5/8	18	37/64
3/4	16	11/16
7/8	14	13/16
1 1/8	12	1 3/64
1 1/4	12	1 11/64
1 1/2	12	1 27/64

Tap Drill Sizes

Screw & Tap Size	National Coarse or U.S.S. Threads Per Inch	Use Drill Number
No. 5	40	39
No. 6	32	36
No. 8	32	29
No. 10	24	25
No. 12	24	17
1/4	20	8
5/16	18	F
3/8	16	5/16
7/16	14	U
1/2	13	27/64
9/16	12	31/64
5/8	11	17/32
3/4	10	21/32
7/8	9	49/64
1	8	7/8
1 1/8	7	63/64
1 1/4	7	1 7/64
1 1/2	6	1 11/32

Decimal Equivalent Size of the Number Drills

Drill No.	Decimal Equivalent	Drill No.	Decimal Equivalent	Drill No.	Decimal Equivalent
80	.0135	53	.0595	26	.1470
79	.0145	52	.0635	25	.1495
78	.0160	51	.0670	24	.1520
77	.0180	50	.0700	23	.1540
76	.0200	49	.0730	22	.1570
75	.0210	48	.0760	21	.1590
74	.0225	47	.0785	20	.1610
73	.0240	46	.0810	19	.1660
72	.0250	45	.0820	18	.1695
71	.0260	44	.0860	17	.1730
70	.0280	43	.0890	16	.1770
69	.0292	42	.0935	15	.1800
68	.0310	41	.0960	14	.1820
67	.0320	40	.0980	13	.1850
66	.0330	39	.0995	12	.1890
65	.0350	38	.1015	11	.1910
64	.0360	37	.1040	10	.1935
63	.0370	36	.1065	9	.1960
62	.0380	35	.1100	8	.1990
61	.0390	34	.1110	7	.2010
60	.0400	33	.1130	6	.2040
59	.0410	32	.1160	5	.2055
58	.0420	31	.1200	4	.2090
57	.0430	30	.1285	3	.2130
56	.0465	29	.1360	2	.2210
55	.0520	28	.1405	1	.2280
54	.0550	27	.1440		

Decimal Equivalent Size of the Letter Drills

Letter Drill	Decimal Equivalent	Letter Drill	Decimal Equivalent	Letter Drill	Decimal Equivalent
A	.234	J	.277	S	.348
B	.238	K	.281	T	.358
C	.242	L	.290	U	.368
D	.246	M	.295	V	.377
E	.250	N	.302	W	.386
F	.257	O	.316	X	.397
G	.261	P	.323	Y	.404
H	.266	Q	.332	Z	.413
I	.272	R	.339		

Anti-Freeze Chart

Temperatures Shown in Degrees Fahrenheit +32 is Freezing

Cooling System Capacity Quarts	Quarts of ETHYLENE GLYCOL Needed for Protection to Temperatures Shown Below													
	1	2	3	4	5	6	7	8	9	10	11	12	13	14
10	+24°	+16°	+ 4°	−12°	−34°	−62°								
11	+25	+18	+ 8	− 6	−23	−47								
12	+26	+19	+10	0	−15	−34	−57°							
13	+27	+21	+13	+ 3	− 9	−25	−45							
14			+15	+ 6	− 5	−18	−34							
15			+16	+ 8	0	−12	−26							
16			+17	+10	+ 2	− 8	−19	−34	−52°					
17			+18	+12	+ 5	− 4	−14	−27	−42					
18			+19	+14	+ 7	0	−10	−21	−34	−50°				
19			+20	+15	+ 9	+ 2	− 7	−16	−28	−42				
20				+16	+10	+ 4	− 3	−12	−22	−34	−48°			
21				+17	+12	+ 6	0	− 9	−17	−28	−41			
22				+18	+13	+ 8	+ 2	− 6	−14	−23	−34	−47°		
23				+19	+14	+ 9	+ 4	− 3	−10	−19	−29	−40		
24				+19	+15	+10	+ 5	0	− 8	−15	−23	−34	−46°	
25				+20	+16	+12	+ 7	+ 1	− 5	−12	−20	−29	−40	−50°
26					+17	+13	+ 8	+ 3	− 3	− 9	−16	−25	−34	−44
27					+18	+14	+ 9	+ 5	− 1	− 7	−13	−21	−29	−39
28					+18	+15	+10	+ 6	+ 1	− 5	−11	−18	−25	−34
29					+19	+16	+12	+ 7	+ 2	− 3	− 8	−15	−22	−29
30					+20	+17	+13	+ 8	+ 4	− 1	− 6	−12	−18	−25

For capacities over 30 quarts divide true capacity by 3. Find quarts Anti-Freeze for the ⅓ and multiply by 3 for quarts to add.

For capacities under 10 quarts multiply true capacity by 3. Find quarts Anti-Freeze for the tripled volume and divide by 3 for quarts to add.

To Increase the Freezing Protection of Anti-Freeze Solutions Already Installed

Cooling System Capacity Quarts	Number of Quarts of ETHYLENE GLYCOL Anti-Freeze Required to Increase Protection													
	From +20° F. to					From +10° F. to					From 0° F. to			
	0°	−10°	−20°	−30°	−40°	0°	−10°	−20°	−30°	−40°	−10°	−20°	−30°	−40°
10	1¾	2¼	3	3½	3¾	¾	1½	2¼	2¾	3¼	¾	1½	2	2½
12	2	2¾	3½	4	4½	1	1¾	2½	3¼	3¾	1	1¾	2½	3¼
14	2¼	3¼	4	4¾	5½	1¼	2	3	3¾	4½	1	2	3	3½
16	2½	3½	4½	5¼	6	1¼	2½	3½	4¼	5¼	1¼	2¼	3¼	4
18	3	4	5	6	7	1½	2¾	4	5	5¾	1½	2½	3¾	4¾
20	3¼	4½	5¾	6¾	7½	1¾	3	4¼	5½	6½	1½	2¾	4¼	5¼
22	3½	5	6¼	7¼	8¼	1¾	3¼	4¾	6	7¼	1¾	3¼	4½	5½
24	4	5½	7	8	9	2	3½	5	6½	7½	1¾	3½	5	6
26	4¼	6	7½	8¾	10	2	4	5½	7	8¼	2	3¾	5½	6¾
28	4½	6¼	8	9½	10½	2¼	4¼	6	7½	9	2	4	5¾	7¼
30	5	6¾	8½	10	11½	2½	4½	6½	8	9½	2¼	4¼	6¼	7¾

Test radiator solution with proper hydrometer. Determine from the table the number of quarts of solution to be drawn off from a full cooling system and replace with undiluted anti-freeze, to give the desired increased protection. For example, to increase protection of a 22-quart cooling system containing Ethylene Glycol (permanent type) anti-freeze, from +20° F. to −20° F. will require the replacement of 6¼ quarts of solution with undiluted anti-freeze.

Index

25 Ways

TO BETTER GAS MILEAGE

The Federal government's goal is to cut gasoline consumption 10% by 1985. In addition to intelligent purchase of a new vehicle and efficient driving habits, there are other ways to increase gas mileage with your present car or truck.

Tests have shown that almost ¾ of all vehicles on the road need maintenance in areas that directly affect fuel economy. Using this book for regular maintenance and tune-ups can increase fuel economy as much as 10%, depending on your vehicle.

1. **Replace spark plugs regularly.** New plugs alone can increase fuel economy by 3%.

2. **Be sure the plugs are the correct type and properly gapped.**

3. **Set the ignition timing to specifications.**

4. If your vehicle does not have electronic ignition, **check the points, rotor and cap as specified.**

5. **Replace the air filter regularly.** A dirty air filter richens the air/fuel mixture and can increase fuel consumption as much as 10%. Tests show ⅓ of all vehicles have air filters in need of replacement.

6. **Replace the fuel filter** at least as often as recommended.

7. **Be sure the idle speed and carburetor fuel mixture are set to specifications.**

8. **Check the automatic choke.** A sticking or malfunctioning choke wastes gas.

9. **Change the oil and filter as recommended.** Dirty oil is thick and causes extra friction between the moving parts, cutting efficiency and increasing wear.

10. **Replace the PCV valve** at regular intervals.

11. **Service the cooling system** at regular recommended intervals.

12. **Be sure the thermostat is operating properly.** A thermostat that is stuck open delays engine warm-up, and a cold engine uses twice as much fuel as a warm engine.

13. **Be sure the tires are properly inflated.** Under-inflated tires can cost as much as 1 mpg. Better mileage can be achieved by over-inflating the tires (never exceed the maximum inflation pressure on the side of the tire), but the tires will wear faster.

14. **Be sure the drive belts (especially the fan belt) are in good condition** and properly adjusted.

15. **Be sure the battery is fully charged for fast starts.**

16. **Use the recommended viscosity motor oil to reduce friction.**

17. **Use the recommended viscosity fluids in the rear axle and transmission.**

18. **Be sure the wheels are properly balanced.**

19. **Be sure the front end is correctly aligned.** A misaligned front end actually has wheels going in different directions, creating additional drag.

20. **Correctly adjust the wheel bearing.** Wheel bearings adjusted too tight increase rolling resistance.

21. **Be sure the brakes are properly adjusted and not dragging.**

22. **If possible, install radial tires.** Radial tires deliver as much as ½ mpg more than bias belted tires.

23. **Install a flex-type fan** if you don't have a clutch fan. Flex fans push more air at low speeds when more cooling is needed. At high speeds the blades flatten out for less resistance.

24. **Check the radiator cap for a cracked or worn gasket.** If the cap doesn't seal properly, the cooling system will not function properly.

25. **Check the spark plug wires for bad cracks, burned or broken insulation.** Cracked wires decrease fuel efficiency by failing to deliver full voltage to the spark plugs.